Annual Predictive Techniques
of the Greek, Arabic and Indian Astrologers

Martin Gansten

The Wessex Astrologer

Published in 2020 by
The Wessex Astrologer Ltd
PO Box 9307
Swanage
BH19 9BF

For a full list of our titles go to www.wessexastrologer.com

© Martin Gansten 2020
Martin Gansten asserts his moral right to be recognised as
the author of this work

Cover illustration: Rete of Indo-Persian astrolabe crafted by Muḥammad
Muqīm of Lahore in 1643/4, now in the History of Science Museum,
Oxford.

Cover design by Jonathan Taylor
Author photo by Anna Gansten

A catalogue record for this book is available at The British Library

ISBN 9781910531419

No part of this book may be reproduced or used in any form or by any
means without the written permission of the publisher.
A reviewer may quote brief passages.

जीवान् भ्रामयते सर्वान् यन्त्रारूढान् स्वमायया।
ज्ञानात्मने ह्यास्याय निर्भ्रमाय नमोऽस्तु ते ॥

Preface

THIS BOOK IS the fruit not only of study and practice, but also of stimulating and instructive discussions with a number of people over the course of years and, in some cases, decades. Special thanks are due to Konrad Klawikowski, Jeffrey Kotyk, Tommy Larsen and Ola Wikander, both for extended conversations and for reading the present work (wholly or partly) in manuscript. The chart illustrations were produced with João Ventura's Flatangle application, and I am most grateful to João for going out of his way to accommodate my special requirements. I likewise extend my heartfelt thanks to all who gave permission for their nativities and life events to be shared as learning exercises. Finally and most importantly, no words can express my gratitude to my wonderful wife Anna, whose unfailing love and encouragement sustain me in all things, including the writing of this book.

The cover shows a detail (the rete or rotating part) of an astrolabe. Few objects so encapsulate the transmission of astronomy-astrology across cultures as this device. Its Greek name, meaning 'star-taker', made its way first into Arabic and from there into Sanskrit; but the Jain monk Mahendrasūri – composing the first Indian work on the subject in the fourteenth century, shortly before Chaucer wrote his *Treatise on the Astrolabe* – called it simply *yantrarāja*: 'the king of instruments'. The astrolabe greatly facilitated the casting of accurate horoscopes and the calculation of directions, two procedures fundamental to the topic of this book. It thus stands as a reminder both of the interconnectedness of the horoscopic astrology practised in different epochs and regions of the world and of the vital significance of attentively applied techniques to the astrologer's art.

Symbols used in this book

Planets		**Zodiacal signs**		**Aspects**	
☉	Sun	♈	Aries	☌	Conjunction
☽	Moon	♉	Taurus	✱	Sextile
☿	Mercury	♊	Gemini	☐	Square
♀	Venus	♋	Cancer	△	Trine
♂	Mars	♌	Leo	☍	Opposition
♃	Jupiter	♍	Virgo		
♄	Saturn	♎	Libra		
		♏	Scorpio		
		♐	Sagittarius		
		♑	Capricorn		
		♒	Aquarius		
		♓	Pisces		

Contents

Preface	v
Symbols used in this book	vi
1. An Introduction	1
PART I: BACKGROUND	5
2. The Myth of Western Astrology	7
3. Some Technical Basics	13
4. Ptolemy's Predictive Package	23
5. The Annual Revolution (Solar Return)	46
PART II: PRACTICE	65
6. Primary Directions in Annual Prediction	67
7. Annual Profections and the Ruler of the Year	84
8. Judging the Revolution Figure (Solar Return Chart)	102
9. Critical Times and Periods within a Year	161
Appendix I: Zodiacal Dignities and Aspect Orbs	195
Appendix II: Primary Directions Formulae	197
Appendix III: Software Settings for Traditional Directions	205
Appendix IV: Example Chart Data	212

Glossary	213
Bibliography	226
Index	233

1
An Introduction

THIS IS A book on practical astrology, a guide to concrete prediction written for astrologers by an astrologer. I state this at the outset because I have also published extensively on the history of astrology in my capacity as an academic. The present book, while informed by academic scholarship (others' as well as my own), is not a neutral historical study: it affirms that accurate astrological prediction is possible – indeed, is a learnable skill – and, by implication, that any world view that does not allow for such a thing is necessarily flawed. But I state this on the authority of my personal experience rather than that of academic degrees or affiliations.

As the title says, the book deals particularly with astrological predictions made for each year of life. It is intended for intermediate students of astrology and presupposes a basic knowledge of the elements that go into astrological interpretation: planets, signs, houses and aspects. If you are already familiar with some form of what is loosely called 'traditional' (roughly, pre-nineteenth-century) astrology – Hellenistic, medieval, Renaissance, or Indian – then so much the better; if not, an open and curious mind will do.

Annual predictions are what David Pingree (1933–2005), the late historian of astrology and related subjects, called 'continuous astrology', distinguishing this from 'the basic natal reading' and quipping that it was 'designed to guarantee the astrologer constant patronage'.[1] Pingree and other scholars later extended the concept of continuous astrology to serve as a blanket designation for any sort of predictive technique. But although a theoretical distinction can be made between static delineation and dynamic prediction, in practice they are necessarily interdependent, as will be clear from a moment's consideration. Astrology has always been concerned with the twin questions of *what* and *when*, and it is almost inconceivable that astrological clients of any era would have been content with wholly undated predictions such as 'You will marry' or 'You will fall ill' (to say nothing of 'You will die'). The continuous unfolding of the potential inherent in a nativity is an integral part of astrological interpretation, and as we shall see in the following chapters, year-by-year predictions have been in use since the earliest times of horoscopic astrology.

As also indicated by the title, I draw chiefly on source texts in Greek, Arabic and Sanskrit, applying the methods taught in them to a number of contemporary example charts. Contrary to what would-be purists might think, this is not an exercise in modern syncretism or an untraditional 'pick-and-mix' approach. Rather, a secondary purpose of the book is to draw attention to the close historical links that already exist between regional variants of the single knowledge system that we know as horoscopic astrology, some of which I have explored in my academic work.[2] Chapter 2 will address this topic in greater detail. I should also point out that the book by no means covers *all* predictive techniques found in ancient and medieval sources: an exhaustive account, if at all possible, would also be exhausting to author and reader alike. Instead, I present a conservative selection of core techniques that I have found to work reliably and that form an organic whole: primary directions, profections, revolutions and transits.

By what may look like design but is actually a happy coincidence (or perhaps part of a greater causality), this book follows fairly closely in time on Benjamin Dykes's annotated translation of Abū Ma'shar's (787–886) Arabic work on annual predictions – a work that did attempt to be, for its time, exhaustive.[3] While I am grateful to have been able to refer in several places to that translation, it should probably be mentioned that the present work was well under way before the former came to my attention. In fact, my personal interest in annual techniques and my academic work on the history of the Indian Tājika school (which is particularly associated with such techniques) have developed side by side over the better part of a decade. Tājika astrology is a Sanskritized version of medieval Perso-Arabic astrology, and the works of Abū Maʿshar appear to have been among its major sources, along with those of Sahl ibn Bishr and some others.

I have divided this book into two parts. The former, shorter part introduces the basic concepts and techniques of annual prediction and provides some historical background. The latter part is practical in nature and consists largely of examples taken from real life, using contemporary nativities to illustrate these techniques. Although the different layers of prediction demonstrated in this part are ultimately meant to be integrated, they have first been presented in separate chapters for pedagogical reasons, each chapter building on the preceding ones. A particular event connected with an example nativity may thus be discussed in several of the last four chapters of the book, in order to demonstrate how to synthesize increasingly complex information.

In selecting example charts, my ambition has been to provide accurately timed nativities of 'ordinary' people whose lives are known to me or whom I have been able to interview personally, rather than relying on the second-hand event reports, and sometimes dubious or contested birth times, of so-called celebrity charts. Although this policy has admittedly led to a certain overrepresentation of academics, I do not believe the selection to be more skewed than the usual fare of actors, politicians and rock stars found in most astrology books. All nativities discussed have birth times that are both well-documented and credible, meaning that I have avoided charts with times that seem suspiciously neat, even if those times are found in black on white in birth records and thus technically merit an AA rating by Rodden criteria. Data for all charts are given in Appendix IV; the non-celebrity charts have been anonymized and are used, for natives still alive, with permission. Where possible, I have preferred to include multiple events for a single nativity rather than increasing the number of nativities used. This is because a single 'hit' in any one nativity is more likely to be coincidental, and I wish to demonstrate that the techniques discussed in this book do work consistently not just across horoscopes, but over a lifetime within the same nativity.

When citing or quoting earlier authors, or when I want to refer the reader to a more detailed discussion of some particular topic, I have given references in the form of endnotes for each chapter. The endnotes also state the source of any translations given from the Greek, Latin, Sanskrit, Arabic or Hebrew; but they contain no additional facts or arguments, and may be safely ignored unless you actually want to look up a reference (full publication details of works cited are found in the bibliography). Translations that are not my own have sometimes been modified in order to assist the reader by keeping technical vocabulary – such as 'direction' for the Greek *aphesis*, or 'division' for the Arabic *qisma* – consistent throughout the book (and to correct the occasional misprint). All such modifications have been duly noted.

Endnotes
1. See Pingree 1973: 120 f.
2. See especially Gansten 2019; Gansten 2020 (both available online under Open Access).
3. Dykes 2019b.

Part I
Background

2
The Myth of Western Astrology

In fact, what is wrong about Abū Ma'shar's history is that it is too simple, representing the transmission as being linear when in fact the celestial sciences were constantly being transmitted in appropriate circles, revolving back and forth between the peoples whom he mentions.

— David Pingree[1]

IN THE MINDS of many practising astrologers in the western world today, and underlying many otherwise useful historical overviews, is an idea — not always fully conscious or articulated — of the development of horoscopic astrology along these lines:

Western astrology	**Eastern astrology**
Ancient Mesopotamia	India (not included)
Ancient Egypt	
The Graeco-Roman world	
Sassanian Persia	
The Arabic-speaking world	
Medieval and Renaissance Europe	
Modern western culture	

There is something wrong with this picture — in fact, several things. For one, not all the cultures listed in the left-hand column are normally designated as 'western' in other contexts; some of them are actually routinely contrasted with western culture. To be sure, they are all west of India; but the vantage point of the people making these lists is rarely Indian. For another, as stated by David Pingree in the quotation above, the transmission of astrology did not take place in the linear fashion suggested by such a list, but rather moved 'in appropriate circles'. And for a third, that repeating spiral of transmission certainly included India.

It must be admitted that Indian astrologers, too, and even western practitioners of Indian-style astrology (known in Sanskrit as *jyotiṣa* or *jyotiḥśāstra*), often perpetuate a historically incorrect view of their system as being essentially separate and different from 'western' astrology. Several factors seem to contribute to this misconception. Prominent among them are the choice of zodiacal framework (discussed in Chapter 3); the cultural and religious contexts in which astrology has been practised in South Asia; Indian nationalism, rooted in the colonial-era independence movement; and a mysticizing of the Sanskrit language, with technical vocabulary that is sometimes claimed to be untranslatable.

The truth of the last matter is that while translation is always an approximation, particularly across great distances in time or space, Sanskrit is no less (or more) translatable than Greek or Arabic or any other language with a long and complex history. With regard to religious context, astrology, like virtually all traditional knowledge systems in India, is described in many texts as having been revealed by gods or semi-divine sages and transmitted through a succession of venerable teachers (the same, incidentally, is true of many works from the Hellenistic world). In none of them, however, is *jyotiṣa* referred to as 'Vedic' astrology, a misnomer that seems to have originated in North America in or around the 1980s. In fact, 'Vedic' in some circles has become a fuzzy term of approval applied to almost any aspect of precolonial Indian culture, so that we hear of 'Vedic mathematics', 'Vedic music', and even 'Vedic cuisine'. But in that same culture, Vedic (*vaidika*) was a well-understood technical term applied only to things or people directly connected with the body of ancient texts known as the Vedas. In that text corpus there is no horoscopic astrology at all, although lunar phases and asterisms are used to determine the proper times of some Vedic rituals.

Far from being the discovery of a single civilization, reverently passed down through the ages, astrology has thrived most in times and areas of cultural amalgamation. The Hellenistic era, in which people and ideas travelled swiftly along routes opened up by the conquests of Alexander and cultures connected through the Greek language, was one such period. The spread of Islam resulted in several more, the first of which came about through the conquest of Persia in the seventh century and subsequent close contacts with Byzantine civilization. Continued Muslim expansion during the medieval period, first westwards across northern Africa into southern Europe and then eastwards into India, brought Latin and Sanskrit traditions of learning, respectively, into contact with Arabic-language knowledge systems; and the fall of Constantinople in the fifteenth century caused a surge of Greek scholars and texts into the Latin west. In more recent times, European colonialism and world wars, followed by modern information technology, have led to massively increased globalization. It goes without saying that all these historical periods and processes are problematic in many respects; but without in any way condoning military, religious or political expansionism, it must still be admitted that they have each contributed to a flowering of astrology as cultures have clashed and mingled.

While there has thus never been a culturally 'pure' tradition of horoscopic astrology, it is certainly possible to distinguish regional variants. 'Western astrology' might do as a general term for the youngest of these, present in western Europe for the past millennium or so. We may then speak of the Indian variants as eastern, and perhaps designate the Byzantine, Persian and Arabic traditions as 'central astrology'. Most importantly, however, we need to acknowledge that these variant traditions have influenced each other in multiple ways.

India: the missing piece of the jigsaw

Let us focus briefly on India, which is the area typically left out of the history books for the mundane reason that western historians, even when fluent in Greek, Latin and/or Arabic, rarely know any Sanskrit (a fact with historical causes of its own). Horoscopic astrology reached the Indian subcontinent from the Greek-speaking world some time in the early centuries CE, as evinced by a large number of Greek technical loanwords. It absorbed indigenous astral lore centred on the twenty-seven or twenty-eight asterisms (*nakṣatra*) and adapted seamlessly to the prevailing tenet of *karma*: actions in one lifetime shaping one's (astrologically discernible) fate in the next, thereby creating a framework within which new action is performed, and so on.[2] Astrological doctrines apparently developed in India, such as the ubiquitous ninth-parts of a sign (*navāṃśa*), later made their way into Persia, and during the great eighth-century Arabic project of translating and synthesizing astrological works from different regions, Indian astrologers were present in Baghdad, bringing their Sanskrit texts with them. Medieval Muslim, Jewish and Christian authors such as Abū Maʿshar, Abraham ibn Ezra and Guido Bonatti all refer to Indian teachings, apparently without any qualms about compromising the purity of their supposedly 'western' tradition or about 'pick-and-mixing'.

The amalgamated Arabic-language astrology, based largely on Persian and Byzantine sources but with Syrian and Indian influences, spread not only to Latin Europe, but also back to India some time in the early second millennium CE. This new style of astrology, apparently transmitted by people of Persian ethnicity, differed enough from the pre-Islamic Indian style to form a separate school known as Tājika ('Persian'). Tājika astrology, still practised in India today, was soon associated above all with annual predictions or *varṣaphala* 'results [literally, fruits] of the year'. It seems fair to observe that these Perso-Arabic astrological teachings were misunderstood or reinterpreted to a greater degree in India than in medieval Europe. This is almost certainly due at least in part to the fact that India already had a well-established tradition of horoscopic astrology which acted to some extent as a distorting lens, with new ideas being interpreted in terms of preexisting astrological categories. On the other hand, Tājika is perhaps the longest-surviving continuous tradition of annual astrology anywhere in the world, and the practical experience accumulated by Indian practitioners over many centuries certainly merits attention. Sanskrit sources also occasionally preserve Perso-Arabic doctrines that were lost in the Latin translations.

In Mughal times, both classical (pre-Islamic-style) Indian astrology and Tājika were typically practised by members of hereditary communities who preserved these knowledge systems as their intellectual property. From the late nineteenth century, under the influence of western Theosophists, astrology in India began to be popularized and to some extent reformed, typically by practitioners belonging to the professional middle class, more fluent in English than in Sanskrit, and doing astrology as a hobby. Modern practitioners often combine the two styles according to their own understanding and predilections, with the result that Tājika has now been subsumed under the recently invented category of 'Vedic astrology'. In present-day India, the historical origins of Tājika are thus often largely forgotten, ignored, or even denied.

The far east and west

Some readers may wonder why I insist on including India in the global history of astrology but say nothing of Chinese astrology, Mayan astrology, and so on. The answer is that I use 'astrology' as a shorthand for *horoscopic* astrology in the full technical sense: astrology that uses the ascendant (Greek: *hōroskopos*) and other houses, along with the twelve zodiacal signs, seven visible planets, and the aspect system. This is the tradition that reached India twice – from the Hellenistic and the Perso-Arabic world – and continued to develop there. Other cultures, including those of East Asia and the Americas, have had their own systems of astral and/or calendric divination, but those are independent of and unrelated to the methods discussed in this book. Horoscopic astrology did actually reach China and its surrounding areas in the medieval period, as demonstrated by the recent research of scholars such as Jeffrey Kotyk and Bill Mak, but it never replaced or merged with the indigenous systems the way it did in India, and did not form part of the 'spiral of transmission' mentioned above. What is typically called 'Chinese astrology' in English today is a wholly separate knowledge tradition.

By now I hope it is clear that there is no sharp divide between east and west in the history and practice of horoscopic astrology – just a continuum of ideas and practices with Latin Europe at one far end and India at the other. If we are in search of contrast, history will serve us better than geography: the most fundamental differences in outlook are those between 'modern astrology' – the brainchild of Alan Leo (1860–1917) and his fellow Theosophists a little more than a century ago, subsequently transformed under the influence of depth psychology – and the astrological tradition of the preceding two millennia, which by comparison is strikingly homogeneous. It is from that greater tradition that the techniques presented in this book are drawn.

Endnotes
1. Pingree 1989: 227.
2. For the concept of *karma* in traditional Indian versus modern western astrology, see Gansten 2010.

3
Some Technical Basics

THE METHODS PRESENTED in the following chapters rest not only on textual sources from several interrelated astrological traditions, but also on my own practical work with traditional astrology generally over thirty years, and with primary directions and annual prognostication for more than a decade. Below I present the technical parameters that I have found to work best and that will be used throughout the book. Readers will naturally not want to take my choices as the final word, nor should they; but if these parameters differ from what you typically use, I suggest that you at least make a few experiments of your own with them. You may be surprised by what you find.

Zodiac

The greatest stumbling block for many readers (though not for those already doing 'Vedic' or Indian-style astrology) will no doubt be my use of a sidereal zodiac. Contrary to what some may think, however, there is nothing inherently Indian or alien to 'western' tradition about a decision to anchor the zodiac, when used for astrological purposes, to the fixed stars rather than the changing seasons. The zodiac – complete with the planetary terms that will play a major role in chapters to come – originated in Mesopotamia, where it was defined with reference to the stars, that is, sidereally.[1] Babylonian astronomer-astrologers did employ a division of the zodiac into twelve equal parts beginning with the vernal equinox, which is useful for its constant relation to the seasonal rhythms and the symmetrical rising times of its twelfth-parts; but they explicitly defined that equinox as being offset from the beginning of Aries by a certain number of degrees.

The tropical division of the zodiac, beginning with the equinox, was for several centuries confined to calendric and astronomical procedures. This was true even after Hellenistic astronomers began equating the equinox point with 0° Aries. The first author of any surviving work to suggest that the tropical definition be adopted for the purpose of astrological interpretation was Claudius Ptolemy.[2] By contrast, his contemporary Vettius Valens, also writing in Alexandria in the second century CE, makes it clear at the beginning of his work that he uses a zodiac offset from the equinox by some degrees:

> Aries is by nature watery, with thunder and hail. *From its first degree to the equinox*, it is stormy, full of hail, windy, destructive. The middle degrees up to 15° are mild [and fruitful; the following degrees are hot and cause plagues] of animals. This sign has 19 bright stars. On the belt are 14 bright stars, 27 dim, 28 somewhat bright, and 48 faint.[3]

Ptolemy's opinion became widely popular only centuries after his death, and the Persians and Indians, who had adopted horoscopic astrology from the Hellenistic world at an earlier period, preserved the sidereal framework. (The tropical definition of the zodiac was still used for astronomical and calendric purposes, a point that has confused some modern proponents of 'tropical Vedic' astrology.) Early Arabic-language astrologers such as Māshā'allāh and Sahl ibn Bishr, who relied largely on Persian sources, likewise used sidereal parameters.[4] This specifically means that the lore of annual revolutions or solar returns, the subject matter of this book, developed in a sidereal setting – a fact rarely acknowledged by modern western practitioners of traditional astrology, who tend simply to transpose the methods described by these authors to the tropical zodiac which they consider to be the norm.

This is not a book on the history of the zodiac, so suffice it to say that knowledge of precession was by no means universal among astrologers in Hellenistic times and Late Antiquity, and that many blithely continued in their writings to relate the zodiacal signs *both* to the fixed stars *and* to the seasons. This was also a time when the difference between tropical and sidereal positions amounted only to a few degrees and was often within the error margin of the formulae used to calculate planetary positions in the first place. (Some astrologers believed in the theory of trepidation, a back-and-forth movement which meant that the difference would never be greater than 8° either way.) Today, however, we must choose: the difference between the two zodiacs is now some 24°–25° and increasing.

The exact precessional value (or *ayanāṃśa*, to use the Sanskrit term, frequently employed even outside Indian contexts) is a matter of some contention among astrologers, just like other variables such as house division or aspect orbs; but the difference between the most commonly used values is no more than a degree or two – a very modest figure compared to the discrepancy between house systems! I have experimented with several values over the years but keep returning for reasons of predictive accuracy to the Krishnamurti *ayanāṃśa*, which has been used for all charts in the book. (Readers who attempt to recreate charts with their preferred software may still find a small difference in the longitude of the Moon, which has been corrected for parallax throughout as discussed in Chapter 6.)

Houses

All charts have also been calculated using the quadrant house system known today as Alcabitius, which was the method most commonly used by medieval Arabic and European astrologers; the earliest preserved description of it, found in the work of Rhetorius, probably dates from the fifth or sixth century.[5] Alcabitius cusps are quite close to the so-called Porphyry system which was used in Hellenistic times and is described by Vettius Valens, who attributes it to an earlier author named Orion.[6] (In India, the Porphyry system is named after the eleventh-century author Śrīpati, who used its cusps as midpoints of the houses – as did the third-century Hellenistic astrologer Pancharius, though whether a historical link exists between the two is not known.) Very occasionally I refer to equal houses, which are simply thirty-degree segments of the zodiac counted off from the ascendant degree. The cusps of the equal houses thus all correspond to that of the first house and need not be separately marked. Ptolemy, Valens and the fourth-century Roman astrologer Firmicus Maternus all describe this system.[7]

Because they use the astronomical midheaven or meridian, quadrant house systems relate to the daily rhythms of rising, culminating and setting (the equatorial coordinate system). Equal houses, on the other hand, relate to the aspectual relationships of the signs (the ecliptical coordinate system). These are both valid astrological considerations, and both seem to have contributed to the traditional significations of the houses. It is therefore not surprising if both systems should be able to offer useful insights in the practical work of chart interpretation. The challenge lies in teasing out the symbolic logic of any particular signification: does the fifth house relate to children because it follows the lower midheaven (*imum caeli*, IC) or because it is configured with the ascendant by a trine aspect – or perhaps both?

Whole-sign houses – which simply equate the rising sign with the first house, the next sign with the second house, and so forth, irrespective of degrees – have become increasingly popular among present-day astrologers interested in traditional techniques. Although I do not doubt that this approach was often used in antiquity (as it still is in India), it is never, to my knowledge, actually prescribed by any ancient author. It is, however, criticized by several, and I believe that it was always more in the nature of a convenient approximation than a system. Furthermore, it may not have been *quite* as common as its modern proponents like to think: statements and example charts claimed as evidence of whole-sign houses in fact often agree just as well with an equal-house system, so that it might be best to keep an open mind on the intentions of the ancient authors. Even the concept of 'a sign' is not always clear-cut: like 'degree', it was sometimes used by ancient authors in a discrete sense (the signs being Aries, Taurus, etc.) and sometimes as a unit of measurement – in this case, consisting of thirty consecutive degrees. Astrologers still use the word 'sign' in this way today, as when we say that a planet at 7° Taurus is exactly one sign ahead of a planet at 7° Aries. We see an example of the same usage in Firmicus Maternus' treatment of the houses:

> The second place from the ascendant is located in the second sign and takes its beginning from the 30th degree from the ascendant degree and extends its powers through 30 remaining degrees. [...] The third place is that which is placed in the third sign from the ascendant, which takes its beginning from the 60th degree from the ascendant degree and leaves off at the 90th degree. [...][8]

Translator James Holden suggests in a footnote that Firmicus meant to say that the second house *begins* in the second sign and so forth; but once we grasp that 'sign' can also be a unit of measurement, there is no need for such exegesis. Rather, Firmicus' phrasing is a reminder that the meaning of words – not least technical concepts – very much depends on context.

Most importantly from my personal point of view, I have not found whole-sign houses to work consistently in practice, although I used them for the first few years of my astrological studies. That is not to say, for instance, that a planet above the horizon in the east cannot belong to the first house: Ptolemy mentions a five-degree offset from the cusp for precisely that reason, and one early commentator states that 'the Egyptians' used offsets as large as fifteen degrees.[9] My own experience confirms that a planet closely conjunct the ascendant or another cusp acts as belonging to that house, although I am not prepared to define 'closely' to the exact number of degrees: my sense is that this may depend at least partly on other factors, such as the cusp falling within the planet's orb of aspect and/or in the same terms.

A vital point to note with regard to the choice of both zodiac definition and house system – and to any other technical matter on which astrologers disagree – is that because the number of astrological symbols is limited, different parameters will sometimes yield similar results. For instance, charts cast for the same nativity in a tropical and a sidereal zodiac, or with whole-sign and quadrant houses, may indicate the same planet and/or house being activated in a symbolically meaningful manner at the time of an event. Such statistically unavoidable occurrences do *not* prove that all astrological methods are equally valid (nor, as critics would have it, that they are all equally arbitrary and meaningless). They are simply not useful for determining which methods are most consistently correct. The most helpful examples for that purpose will necessarily be the ones that differ most starkly between systems. For instance, is Venus in its fall in Virgo or in its domicile in Libra? Angular in the first house or cadent in the twelfth? – and so on.

Planets, rulerships and dignities

The charts used in this book contain only the seven traditional, visible planets: the Sun and Moon, Mercury, Venus, Mars, Jupiter and Saturn. In my discussion of these charts I likewise use the traditional rulership scheme, where the two luminaries rule Leo and Cancer, respectively, and the other five planets rule the signs fanning out in either direction from there. Thus, Mercury rules Virgo and Gemini; Venus rules Libra and Taurus; Mars rules Scorpio and Aries; Jupiter rules Sagittarius and Pisces; and Saturn rules Capricorn and Aquarius. This symmetrical arrangement means that the domiciles of the two benefics form benefic aspects with that of the nearest luminary – sextiles in the case of Venus, trines for Jupiter – while the domiciles of malefic Mars similarly form squares, and those of malefic Saturn oppose the signs of the luminaries. The lunar nodes (known in Indian astrology as Rāhu and Ketu) and the lots or so-called Arabic parts (called *sahamas* in Tājika) are not part of my basic interpretative approach and have not been included in the charts – not because I reject them on principle, but because I have not (yet) found them consistently to add enough detail or clarity to outweigh the confusion of a cluttered chart. Although data for all nativities are given in Appendix IV, enabling readers to recalculate charts and include whatever elements they prefer, I do encourage you to explore the interpretative power of these seven fundamental symbols.

In addition to domiciles, I occasionally refer to the traditional dignities of exaltation (with its corollary debility of fall) and triplicity, and very frequently to the terms. These are set out in Appendix I. Although decans or faces form part of the Arabic, Latin and Indian traditions (pre-Islamic as well as Tājika) and are included in the chart design used for this book, they do not play as prominent a role in the Greek sources, and I personally do not use them in interpretation. Triplicities and terms both exist in more than one version, and several of the Graeco-Arabic dignities were further misunderstood or reinterpreted by the Indian Tājika tradition, where the triplicities are known as *trirāśi*, the terms as *haddā* (from Arabic *ḥadd*) or sometimes as *trimśāṃśa* 'thirtieth-parts'.[10] (The latter name, reflecting the fact that the terms in Greek are often simply called *moirai* 'degrees', more usually denotes a different system of terms found only in pre-Islamic Indian astrology.) I use what may be described as the standard set of terms, often called Egyptian or Dorothean and followed by both Arabic and Tājika traditions; a table of these is given in Appendix I. I typically do not consider the twelfth-parts (dodecatemories, or *dvādaśāṃśa* in Sanskrit), nor the many other subdivisions of zodiacal signs found in Indian astrology (pre-Islamic and Tājika), the most prominent of which is the ninth-part or *navāṃśa*.

It may be noted here that some modern translators have invented new names for certain dignities, as well as for other technical concepts. For instance, terms are called 'bounds' or 'confines', angles are called 'pivots' or 'stakes', and so forth. Although I sympathize with the intention of bringing out the underlying ideas of the original Greek and/or Arabic vocabulary more clearly, I strongly suspect that to most readers, the new terminology actually conveys little more than the old; and in the process, astrological works written in English from the seventeenth to the nineteenth century become increasingly unintelligible to new generations of readers as their technical language is lost in a babel of competing translations. For these reasons, I have endeavoured as far as possible to use well-established, traditional terminology.

Aspects

The classical aspects mentioned above – sextile, square, trine and opposition, in addition to the conjunction – are the ones recognized by the Greek, Arabic and Tājika traditions and used in all examples. The variant aspect system found in pre-Islamic Indian astrology on the one hand, and the so-called minor aspects that have existed in western astrology for the past four centuries on the other, are not included. When an aspect is within one degree (60 minutes of arc) of perfecting its ideal angle, such as 120° for the trine, it is called partile; when it is in the process of perfecting but not yet partile, applying; and when in the process of moving away from that angle, separating. The orbs of light of the planets, that is, the margins within which they are considered to form their aspects, are listed in Appendix I.

A distinction is made between the two sextiles, squares or trines that each planet casts forward and backward in the zodiac: they are known as dexter and sinister, or right and left, respectively. This terminology can be slightly confusing, as an aspect usually exists between two planets, both of which 'behold' the other (the literal meaning of *aspect*). If the Moon in Pisces is applying to Venus in Taurus, then the Moon is casting a left-hand sextile to Venus while Venus is casting a right-hand sextile to the Moon – meaning that the Moon is at the right-hand or dexter *end* of the aspect. The planet at the dexter end – that is, the one sending its aspect forward in the order of the signs, in this case from Pisces through Aries into Taurus – is usually considered to have the upper hand in the aspect configuration and is said to cast a *superior* aspect. The superior square has been regarded since ancient times as a particularly powerful, dominating aspect.

Endnotes

1. For the Mesopotamian origins of the terms, see Jones and Steele 2011.
2. See Ptol. *Tetr*. I 10, transl. Robbins 1940: 59–61.
3. Vett. Val. I 2,3, transl. Riley 2010: 2. Emphasis added.
4. For Māshāʾallāh, see Chapter 5 below (note 8). For Sahl's use

of the Sassanian sidereal zodiac, see Dykes 2019a: 7 (note 13).
5. See the translation and comment in Holden 2009: 211–214. For the dating of Rhetorius, see Gramaglia and Dykes 2017: 25–29.
6. See Vett. Val. III 2, transl. Riley 2010: 59.
7. See Ptol. *Tetr.* III 11,3, transl. Robbins 1940: 273; Vett. Val. IX 3,21–25, transl. Riley 2010: 154; Firm. Mat. II 19, transl. Holden 2011: 65–68.
8. Firm. Mat. II 19,3–4, transl. Holden 2011: 65 (translation slightly modified).
9. See Anon. *Quad.* 1559: 109.
10. See Gansten 2018 for details.

4
Ptolemy's Predictive Package

A SUBSTANTIAL PART of the predictive techniques discussed by astrological authors of Late Antiquity, the Islamic Golden Age and the European High Medieval period can be traced back to a single, surprisingly short text. To an even greater extent, the same is true of the techniques used from the Renaissance, when the Latin west began its rediscovery of Greek language and literature, up to the nineteenth century. (For reasons not yet fully known, but probably related at least in part to an early break in transmission, the Indian Tājika tradition preserved only parts of the Graeco-Arabic heritage.) The source text in question is the final chapter of Ptolemy's *Apotelesmatics*, better known as the *Tetrabiblos*.

In that brief chapter, Ptolemy outlines the techniques known today as primary directions, profections and transits against the backdrop of a division of life into seven ages assigned to the planets, and discusses how they relate to each other. Partly similar descriptions of these techniques are given by other authors – notably Dorotheus, who lived a century before Ptolemy and was a major source for Perso-Arabic astrology generally, although it is sometimes difficult to say with certainty whether a particular doctrine derives from him: with the exception of a few fragments, the Greek text of Dorotheus' verse work has been lost, and only an interpolated second-hand translation in Arabic (via Persian) survives. Occasionally, later Greek authors paraphrase Dorotheus in prose, but in doing so they often mix his teachings with those of others, including Ptolemy.

Not because I regard Ptolemy as uniquely authoritative, but rather because his concise account has been so influential, the present chapter will be structured around it, adding technical and historical details as needed. The next chapter will then introduce the annual revolution or solar return chart, which is not mentioned by Ptolemy but was soon added as another layer to his hierarchy of prediction. Finally, the second part of the book will demonstrate the practical use of these techniques in order, each chapter building on the preceding one and using numerous examples drawn from real life.

The universal division of life into seven ages did not play as important a part in later tradition as did the other techniques, and it will not be used in the examples. Briefly stated, the rulerships of the ages are assigned to the planets in order of apparent velocity so that the Moon rules the first four years of life, Mercury the next ten up to age 14, Venus the eight up to 22, the Sun the nineteen up to 41, Mars the fifteen up to 56, Jupiter the twelve up to 68, and Saturn the remainder of life. In Persian tradition this system appears at some point to have been replaced or at least complemented by another arrangement of planetary periods and subperiods similar to the *daśā* systems of Indian astrology and known as *fardār* or *firdār* (a word of uncertain meaning, though some believe it to be of Greek origin and related to *period*). Below, however, we shall restrict ourselves to the combined use of directions, profections, revolutions and transits, which form a well-integrated whole and a solid foundation for annual predictions.

Primary directions

The individualized part of Ptolemy's predictive system begins with the *aphesis* ('sending out, releasing') or direction of the most important significators, which he takes to be the two chief angles (the ascendant and midheaven), the two luminaries (the Sun and Moon), and the Lot of Fortune (always calculated according to the formula which other authors use chiefly for daytime nativities: measure the distance from the Sun to the Moon in the order of the signs and add the same distance to the ascendant). Ptolemy relates the ascendant especially to the body and journeys; the midheaven to actions, friendship, and having children; the Sun to dignities and glory; the Moon to mental states and marriage; and the Lot of Fortune to property. While some of these assignations are open to debate, Ptolemy's main point is well taken: life is typically a mixture of good and bad, and no single direction can be expected to reveal the quality of all facets of life at any given point in time.

> One may, for example, lose a relative and receive an inheritance, or at once be prostrated by illness and gain some dignity and promotion, or in the midst of misfortune become the father of children, or have other experiences of this sort which are apt to occur.[1]

On the rare occasions when all of life seems either glorious or gruelling, says Ptolemy, all or most of the significators will be found to be simultaneously under the influence of the benefics or the malefics, respectively. We should note, however, that Arabic-language authors place particular emphasis on the directions of the *hīlāj* or hyleg (the chief significator of life, determined according to complex rules that differ somewhat from author to author) and of the ascendant. ʿAlī ibn Abī r-Rijāl wrote in the eleventh century:

> Indeed, one should perform the *athazir* [*at-tasyīr*, direction] of the degree of the ascendant whether it be the *hylech* [*hīlāj*] or not, because from it the condition of the native is known with respect to his body, and to his

health or infirmity: for it is the significator of life and the soul.[2]

What does it mean for a significator to be under the influence of a planet? As the significator moves symbolically through the nativity, it will meet in turn with different planets or with their points of aspect, and it will always be in the terms belonging to some planet or other. Ptolemy views the succession of conjunctions and aspects as a sort of relay race: once a significator has made contact with a planet, the influence of that planet remains in force until the significator makes another contact, 'and the planets which govern the terms are to be

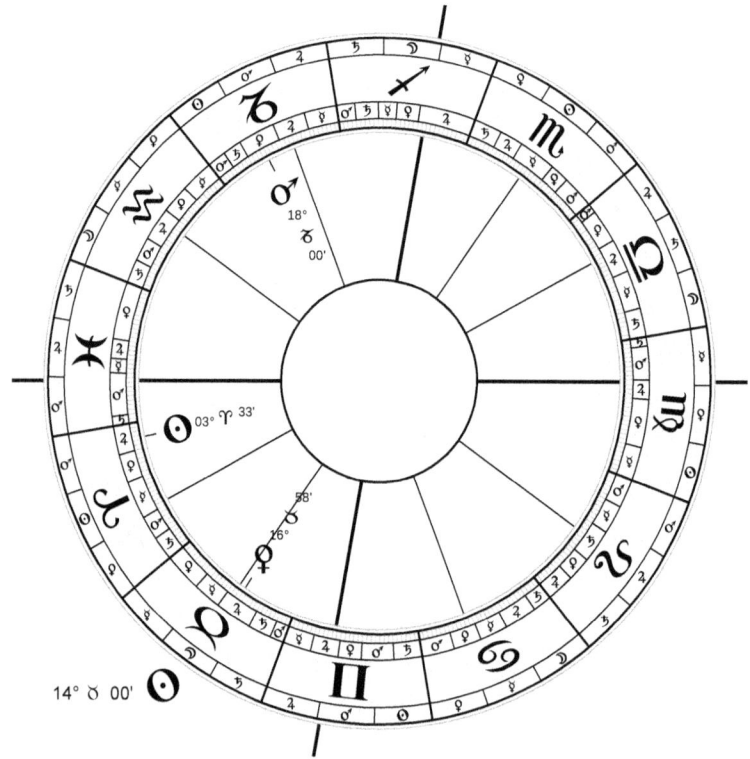

Figure 1: The Sun in the natal first house as significator directed through the terms of Jupiter in Taurus.

given a part of the rulership'. By this model, a significator is constantly subject to the influence *both* of the planet it was last in aspect or conjunction with *and* of the ruler of the terms it is passing through, and the former is the more important one, even if the aspect occurred ten or twenty years ago. Occasionally, of course, the latest aspect and the terms may belong to the same planet.

To illustrate, let us take a hypothetical nativity with the Sun in the first house in Aries (figure 1). Putting the matter of actual calculation to one side for the moment, we can see that the Sun at birth was in the first terms (0°–6°) in Aries, ruled by Jupiter. As the native aged, the Sun would be gradually directed through the terms of Venus, Mercury, Mars and Saturn in turn, before moving into the terms of Venus at the beginning of Taurus. Each of these planets in turn would thus become the term ruler of the Sun. As the Sun reached the terms of Jupiter (14°–22°) in Taurus, it would also encounter the body of Venus, closely followed by the trine aspect of Mars, and these two planets would therefore influence matters signified by the Sun, alongside its term ruler Jupiter.

A fact not remarked on by Ptolemy, but worth keeping in mind, is that the terms (and sign) occupied by a significator at a given time will vary with the sidereal or tropical zodiac used, whereas directions to the bodies and aspects of the planets, being based on relative distances, are zodiac-independent. If Ptolemy actually practised astrology – which we do not know, as he gives no examples – he would have used tropical terms; but Dorotheus, Valens and the Persian astrologers used sidereal terms, as seen from their example charts.

Although most medieval Arabic authors favoured Ptolemy's mathematically consistent method of directing over earlier, cruder methods, they differ to some extent from his approach to interpretation, probably taking their cue from other authorities such as Dorotheus. They give priority to the terms currently occupied by the significator, which they call the *division* (Arabic *qisma*) – not necessarily in the sense that the ruler of the terms (the *divisor*, Arabic *qāsim*) has the final say, but in that major importance is attached to planets whose bodies or aspect points *fall in* the division (or, according to some authors, closely precede it).[3] This means that the influence of a planet may begin before its direction perfects, provided that it (or its aspect point) is in the terms being activated.

Some of the Persian and Arabic authors do seem to consider the divisor as more important than the aspecting planet – and also to imply that when no planet is present in or aspecting the division, the significator will be under the sole influence of the divisor – while others, leaning more towards Ptolemy, say the opposite. What is most interesting, however, is not the relative proportions of influence of the two planets (which in any case may vary depending on other factors, discussed below), but the ways in which those influences *combine* to produce an event, or a series of events. In real life, house positions, rulerships, aspects and so on will all affect the outcome, but the generalized descriptions given by these authors are based chiefly on the natures and universal significations of the planets – and, of course, expressed in terms of medieval life and society. Take, for instance, the combinations of Venus and Saturn as described by two different authors:

> [Saturn as divisor, al-Andarzaghar:]
> Then judge for the aspect of Venus that he will marry and will have a child and perhaps obtain wealth from that woman. Because it is from the division of Saturn, his child will die and intense grief will come upon him, and he will lament for his child and hate his wife.[4]

[Saturn as divisor, Abū Maʿshar:]
And if Venus was the one partnering with him in the management of the division, they indicate that he will marry, and a child will be born to him, and distresses and detestable things will afflict him, and one of his children or his women will die, so long as she is the manager in these terms.[5]

[Venus as divisor, al-Andarzaghar:]
And if Saturn aspects Venus herself then he will marry a woman at least for a few days, and because of the aspect of Saturn death will separate them and will bequeath to him long-lasting sadness.[6]

[Venus as divisor, Abū Maʿshar:]
And if the division belonged to Venus and Saturn partnered with her in the management, they indicate trouble in the affairs he is devoted to, and abstention in the matter of women, and distresses because of them, and the illness of some of them (or their death), and something detestable and different quarrels will affect him. Now if, along with his management in the terms of Venus, Saturn was aspecting her and making her unfortunate, it indicates that he will find little joy in women and because of them, and then [the women] will certainly be ruined, and he will have many distresses [...].[7]

We can see from these examples how the combination of same two planets is often interpreted quite similarly irrespective of which is the divisor and which the promissor (participating by aspect or conjunction). In the present case, the suggested interpretations either way have the themes of love, marriage and children (Venus) commingling with those of discord, death and grief (Saturn).

How long do the effects of directions last?
These particular interpretations also highlight an important point concerning timing: the *duration* of the effects of a direction may depend partly on astrological factors, but quite often it is inherent in the type of event itself. The death of a loved one is permanent, no matter how many benefic directions follow it (though there may be other loves). Certain injuries and illnesses are incurable, even if they may be alleviated. On a more positive note, once a child is born, or professional status attained, they will typically continue to exist even after the benefic direction comes to an end – unless the nativity indicates their loss and that indication is activated by malefic directions.

Purely astrological factors that affect the duration and stability of the results of a direction include, first of all, the direction progressing from one set of terms to another, so that the divisors change – although it should be noted that Saturn and Mars each have two sets of terms placed back to back (across the junctions of Libra with Virgo and Scorpio, respectively). Abū Ma'shar considered the nature of the sign occupied by a divisor or promissor to be important, movable signs indicating more transitory results, fixed signs more stable ones, and double-bodied signs results that come and go.[8] Others, such as Renaissance astrologer Johann Schöner (1477–1547), emphasized the nature of the planets themselves, saying that Mars acts quickly while Saturn tends to signify more long-lasting effects.[9]

With the exception of those cases where the results of a direction are *by nature* long-lasting, I cannot say that I have found Ptolemy's notion of the influence of a promissor necessarily enduring until the next promissor takes over to hold good. In my experience, the influence of a promissor may be felt in a general way for several years but often peaks in the year when the directed aspect or conjunction perfects and then wanes – sometimes quite soon after perfecting, though this will depend partly on other factors. If the nature of the promissor (benefic or malefic) is similar to that of the ruler of the terms and of planets activated by profection, its influence may be felt for a longer time than if they are of opposite natures.

Some technical vocabulary
At this point it may be as well to go over some basic terminology that you will encounter in coming chapters and that also recurs in many earlier works on primary directions. We have already met with the *significator*, which is simply a point in the chart that signifies any matter in life. This may sometimes be a non-luminary planet; but Ptolemy, as noted above, typically restricts himself to the angles, luminaries, and Lot of Fortune. (The one exception he mentions occurs in the context of determining the length of life.)

We also encountered the *division*, the terms that a directed significator is currently passing through (or the period of time corresponding to that motion), and the *divisor*, the ruler of those terms. The planet or aspect encountered by a significator is called the *promissor* (or sometimes *promittor*) because it promises something for the matter signified – even if the 'promise' can sometimes be more in the nature of a threat! As seen from the quotations above, the promissor is sometimes said to 'partner with' or participate in the action of the divisor, and some authors use the poetic phrase 'lord of the rays' for a planet participating by aspect, conceived of as a ray of light.

Benjamin Dykes, who has published a number of valuable translations of medieval texts from both Arabic and Latin, prefers to render *qisma* and *qāsim* (or the corresponding *divisio* and *divisor*) as 'distribution' and 'distributor', respectively; but although these are possible meanings, I am not convinced that they are the intended ones. The terms and their corresponding periods do, after all, *divide* a sign and a life in a very concrete sense, and although planets may be said to distribute other things, such as fortune and misfortune, a planet 'dividing the times' makes more sense to me than one 'distributing the times'. I have therefore kept the terminology *division* and *divisor*, used in English at least since the seventeenth century.[10]

Historically, *qāsim* very likely began as a translation of the Persian *bakhtār*, which is found in the compound *jārbakhtār* or *jānbakhtār* (Latinized, with the Arabic article *al-*, as *algebuthar*, with variants). This Persian word may have been misunderstood even before it entered Arabic: the older word *jār-*, meaning 'time', was confused with the better-known *jān-*, meaning 'soul' or 'life'. In my earlier book on primary directions I mistakenly followed scholars like Bouché-Leclercq in accepting the latter variant and relating it to the Greek *biodotēr* 'giver of life', which does exist but is used in a different context. The Greek term that *jārbakhtār* was actually meant to translate was almost certainly *chronokratōr* 'ruler of time' (or 'time lord'), a word that can be applied to any planet influencing a given period of life and which will recur frequently below with the Latinized spelling chronocrator. *Bakhtār* has connotations of lordship or rulership but literally means 'divider', and this literal meaning seems to have been in the mind of the Arabic translators who coined the term *qāsim*.

How are directions calculated?

Above I mentioned a significator 'moving symbolically through the nativity', without detailing how that motion is calculated or conceptualized. The truth is that while the conceptual part is fairly straightforward, the calculations – involving spherical trigonometry – are more cumbersome. For readers who wish to try their hand at them, armed with patience and a scientific calculator, the necessary formulae are given in Appendix II. Fortunately, reliable and even free software now exists that will do the same job in a matter of seconds. Most software still requires a bit of tweaking to make it produce entirely traditional directions, however, and Appendix III describes how to achieve this.

Conceptually, primary directions are based on the primary (apparent) motion of the celestial sphere – or, put differently, on the daily rotation of the earth on its axis. Just as we can see the Sun rise in the east every morning, culminate at midday, and set in the west in the evening, so every planet and every zodiacal degree has its own unique daily cycle. This rotation is measured along the celestial equator, with each degree rising or culminating in approximately four minutes of clock time and corresponding to one year of life, so that six hours after birth produce directions for a full 90 years.

As Ptolemy explains, the ascendant, or a planet exactly on the ascendant, is directed by rising times or oblique ascensions. If you were born exactly at sunrise with Jupiter in the second house, and if, two hours later, Jupiter should be exactly on the eastern horizon, then at age 30 (corresponding to 30° of oblique ascensions or two hours of time) both the ascendant *and* the Sun would be said to be directed to the body of Jupiter, and to whatever part of the zodiac Jupiter occupied. This is despite the fact that the Sun by its *secondary* motion (that is, by transit) would hardly have changed its position in the zodiac at all in those two hours. So the significator's symbolic motion through the zodiac is actually accomplished by the zodiac being moved across the natal significator, which is kept fixed.

The same principle applies when directing the midheaven or a planet on the midheaven, except that we use culminating times, or right ascensions, instead of rising times. This is because the same part of the zodiac will take different amounts of time to rise, set or culminate. A sign that rises slowly, such as Libra in the northern hemisphere, will be opposite in the zodiac from one that rises quickly, such as Aries; but naturally Aries must also be slow to set, and Libra quick to set, or else they could not oppose each other on the eastern and western horizon at the same time. The time they each take to culminate will be somewhere in between, and very nearly the same for both signs.

The most complex scenario is when the significator is a point (such as the Sun in figure 1 above) placed neither on the horizon nor on the meridian. The principle is still the same: we want to move the zodiac *across* the natal significator, symbolically equating this with the significator moving *through* the zodiac. The problem is that while the horizon and the meridian are great circles, which every planet or zodiacal degree is bound to cross at some time, a planetary significator is just a body or point in space, and its apparent trajectory will almost never intersect with that of the promissor. Ptolemy's solution is to say that when a planet or zodiacal degree reaches the *same proportional relationship* to both horizon and meridian as the significator had in the nativity – that is, having completed the same proportion of its journey from rising to culminating, or from culminating to setting, etc. – they are considered to be conjunct. This is known as the proportional semi-arc method or mixed ascensions. Again, calculations are given in Appendix II; for a fuller exploration of the concepts involved, I refer to my earlier book on primary directions.

A slightly different solution, suggested by some of the Arabic-language astrologers (such as Muḥammad ibn Muʿādh al-Jayyānī, 989–1079) and popularized in Europe by Regiomontanus (actual name Johann Müller, 1436–1476), is to *make* every significator into a circle by constructing an artificial horizon or 'circle of position' running through the body of the planet in question. The directions of that significator will then be measured by oblique ascensions to its quasi-horizon, eliminating the need for mixed ascensions altogether. Two centuries later, Placido de Titi or Placidus (1603–1668) advocated a return to Ptolemy's semi-arc system but also created his own position-circle method, meant as a simplified version of that system and yielding arcs of direction considerably closer to it than those of Regiomontanus. That method is generally known as Placidean directions under the pole of the significator.

As a historical aside, so-called secondary progressions or the progressed horoscope – perhaps the most popular predictive technique in western astrology apart from transits during the past century or so – are a hybrid method made up of the primary direction of the angles and a simplified, streamlined version of Placidus' secondary *directions*. (Directions, not progressions: Placidus also invented a third technique that he did call progressions, but which moved on a different time scale altogether.) This hybrid was created by Alan Leo, who never fully mastered primary directions and was criticized for it by some of his contemporaries. There is thus nothing 'secondary' about the motion of the angles in 'secondary progressions', nor could there be: secondary motion refers to the proper motion of a planet through the zodiac – a motion that the angles, being points of intersection between great circles, do not possess.

Direct and converse

So far we have assumed that the significator is being directed forward in the zodiac (by letting the zodiac pass over its natal position by primary motion, or daily rotation). This is the standard mode of directing, commonly known as *direct motion*. But it is also possible to direct a significator symbolically backwards through the zodiac, against the order of the signs, by conceiving of the *zodiac* as being fixed in its natal position and moving the significator itself with the primary motion. This is known as *converse motion*, and Ptolemy mentions it as being suitable for determining the length of life in some cases. Later astrologers made wider use of converse directions, although they were typically regarded as somewhat less powerful than directions in direct motion.

The two salient points to note here are, first, that *all* traditional directions – whether they are called direct or converse – are made *with* the clockwise primary motion; and second, that the mode of directing does not change the fact that the significator is the point *signifying* a given area of life, while the promissor is the point *promising* some change in that area. Both these conceptual pairs have been increasingly misunderstood since the nineteenth century, following the modern break in European astrological tradition. Today the misunderstandings have become the norm, so that 'converse' directions are typically calculated *against* the primary motion (that is, backwards in time, into the prenatal period), while 'significator' and 'promissor' are taken simply to mean the fixed and the moving point, respectively. Without rectifying these misunderstandings, it will not be possible to grasp the intentions of earlier authors writing on directions. This is also a major reason not to trust astrological software implicitly (see Appendix III), as software developers overall tend very naturally to know more about calculations and programming than about the history of astrology.

Related to the above is the traditional way of designating a direction: irrespective of whether it is direct or converse – that is, no matter which point is kept fixed and which is moved with the primary motion – it is always the significator that is said to be directed *to* the promissor, not the other way round. In my earlier book I myself did not adhere consistently to this convention (which had begun to break down by the seventeenth century), but it will be used throughout the following chapters.

A final point to note concerns the relationship between primary directions and house systems: there isn't one. Contrary to what some modern writers claim, using semi-arc ('Placidus') directions in no way obliges you also to use Placidus houses, nor do those who direct by circles of position (the 'Regiomontanus' way) have to use Regiomontanus houses. The semi-arc system of direction comes to us from Ptolemy, who mentions no other system of house division than equal houses; and al-Qabīṣī himself, whose instructions for house division have given name to the Alcabitius system, directed by Ptolemaic or 'Placidean' semi-arcs. The notion of a separate system of direction to go with every house system is purely a twentieth-century invention and may be safely disregarded.

Directions and Indian astrology
Despite their importance in the Hellenistic tradition, primary directions (and related concepts such as the hyleg doctrine) seem not to have made it to India in the first wave of transmission, which occurred in the early centuries of the Common Era. With the second wave, from the Perso-Arabic cultural area, directions did briefly enter India but were not properly understood, and soon disappeared again. The only surviving Tājika work dealing with natal astrology in full, as opposed to just annual revolutions, is Samarasiṃha's *Karmaprakāśa* or *Light on Actions*, also known as *Manuṣyajātaka* or *Human Nativities*. This work includes the following brief passage on timing using the terms (known as *hadda* or *haddā*, from Arabic *ḥadd*):

> In all signs of the nativity, the number of years for each *haddā* is that of the extension of the *haddā*. The native will have the nature of that [planet] which rules the terms or whose light is here, and of the places of those [planets].
> Suppose there were four degrees in the [first] *hadda* of Gemini ascendant, with forty minutes added:

corresponding to that, four years and eight months had elapsed; the ruler of the period (*daśā*) was Mercury. By its nature, the child would be quick to speak; even in infancy, its tongue would be swift and strong. The light of Mars falls after two degrees: from that time, the results of its nature [would manifest].[11]

This is meant to be a summary of an example found in Abū Bakr al-Ḥasan ibn Khaṣīb's ninth-century work on nativities, but misses the point of Abū Bakr's mathematical explanation. In the original example, 1° Gemini is on the ascendant, with 5° of Mercury's terms *remaining* (not elapsed). These zodiacal or ecliptical degrees are then converted to 4°40′ of oblique ascension, which in turn are equated with four years and eight months.[12] In a later chapter, Samarasiṃha again touches on the same example, calling the directional periods *kisimā* (from Arabic *qisma*, division), but then confusing them with the *fardār* periods.

Later Tājika works include garbled versions of directional procedures, such as the use of mixed ascensions, and some methods used for timing *within* a year are called *tāsīra* (from Arabic *tasyīr*, which generally refers to directions but is sometimes used for profections as well). But the use of directions as a higher-level timing technique is missing from the Sanskrit sources, and Tājika astrologers who want a bird's-eye view of the native's life tend to fall back on the *daśā* systems of classical Indian astrology.

Profections

The promissors and divisors are what Ptolemy calls *general* or *universal* chronocrators: they provide the most fundamental layer of interpretation, and their influence can last for many years. The next layer in his predictive hierarchy comprises the *annual* chronocrators, which are found by the much simpler technique known since early modern times as annual profections: a significator is simply moved forward in the zodiac by one sign per year, thus completing a round of the zodiac every twelve years, at ages 12, 24, 36 and so on. The ruler of the sign of the year in question is the ruler of that significator in that year. The Persian and Arabic astrologers especially emphasized the profections of the ascendant, just as they did its directions, and called its domicile ruler 'the ruler (or lord) of the year'.

The word *profection* looks as if it had been derived from the Latin verb *proficio* 'to advance' or *proficiscor* 'to set out', and modern-day astrologers typically accept this etymology when they think about it at all.[13] The Greek phrase used by Ptolemy, however, is *tou sunteleioumenou zōdiou* 'of the sign being reached at the end', which exactly matches the meaning of the standard Arabic terms *burj al-muntahā* and *burj al-intihā'* found in works that were later translated into Latin.[14] (In the Tājika tradition, the same Arabic designations were Sanskritized as *munthahā* or *munthā* and *inthihā* or *inthā*, respectively.) Giuseppe Bezza's hypothesis that the original Latin translation from the Arabic was *perfectio*, in the sense of a motion being concluded or completed, and that *profectio* is the result of a misreading (the scribal abbreviation p̄ for *per-* being interpreted as ꝑ for *pro-*), is therefore almost certainly correct.[15] Despite this, the conventional term 'profection' will be used throughout this book to avoid confusion.

Whereas Ptolemy's treatment of profections is limited to a few sentences, his contemporary Vettius Valens describes his own approach to the system (which he calls *paradosis* 'transmission, handing over') in great detail over three of his nine books. Valens accepts many significators, including the non-luminary planets, although the angles, luminaries and chief lots are the most important. A major difference between his view and Ptolemy's is that Valens regards any planet *in* the sign of the profection – natally or, if there is none, by transit at the revolution of the year – as more significant than its ruler. This approach means that any planet can follow any other as annual chronocrator of a given significator, without the restrictions imposed by the scheme of domicile rulerships – where, for instance, Mars can only be followed by Venus or Jupiter, because Aries is followed by Taurus and Scorpio is followed by Sagittarius. Valens places great importance on noting which planet 'hands over' to which, giving interpretations for each such combination.[16] If the two planets involved are configured by aspect or conjunction in the nativity, that configuration will be activated at the time of the transmission.

Valens also addresses the fact that the same profections to the nativity repeat every twelve years, and suggests that similar events do tend to occur as a result of this – similar, but not identical, because the higher-order chronocrators, the transits, and the 'recasting of the nativity' (discussed in our next chapter) will be different. The more the planets at the revolution of the year mirror their configurations in the nativity, either by transits to natal positions or by transiting planets repeating the same aspects between themselves, the more certain the expected results. Similar points are made in the extant Arabic version of Dorotheus and by medieval Arabic authors, who emphasize the importance of repetition for a planet in the sign of the profection to manifest its results in the year. If, for instance, the annual profection reaches the sign where Mars was in the nativity, and Mars by transit at that time had either returned to the same sign or was aspecting it, the results expected from Mars would be more likely to occur, particularly if the nature of the aspect agreed with the nature of the expected event. We shall return to this principle below; for now, we may just note that the transits of some planets at the revolution of the year will vary more than others. The Sun by definition always returns to its natal sign and degree; Mercury may move as far away from its original position as a sextile by sign (though not by degree); and Venus may achieve a square at most.

Transits

The final layer of Ptolemy's hierarchy is transits, sometimes called ingresses, which he says 'play no small part in the prediction of the times of events'. Transits are, of course, the first (sometimes the only) predictive technique encountered by students of modern astrology, but they were used rather differently in earlier forms of the art, where they depended largely on other methods of prediction.

Ptolemy particularly relates the transits of Saturn to the 'general places of the times', that is, the places of directed significators; Jupiter to the 'places of the years' or annual profections; the Moon to the daily profections; and the remaining planets to the monthly profections. Ptolemy's idea is clearly to connect the slowest-moving transits with the slowest-changing chronocrators and so forth; but we may be justified in asking whether the transit of malefic Saturn is really the best tool for timing the result of a favourable direction, or that of benefic Jupiter for timing an unfavourable profection. Moreover, as Jupiter transits the zodiac in just under twelve years, it practically moves in tandem with the profections: if Jupiter was in the third sign from the ascendant of your nativity, its transit will be in or near the third sign from your profected ascendant throughout your life.

Ptolemy also states that the natal configurations of a planet with a significator will affect the results of its transit relative to the same place. If they were in harmonious aspect in the nativity, a harmonious transiting aspect will give favourable results, but a transiting opposition will be unfavourable. If they were not harmoniously related in the nativity, and are also of opposite sect, then a transiting square or opposition will be unfavourable, but not the other aspects. This seems slightly slanted towards the negative.

More useful advice on transits, in my opinion, is found in other ancient and medieval authors, who give particular importance to two principles: paying attention to the chronocrators – that is, the planets already activated by direction and profection – and noting the transits at the revolution of the year, when rulership of the profection is handed over from one planet to another. In the context of summarizing Dorotheus' teaching on transits, an excerpt attributed to Stephanus the Philosopher (eighth century?) states:

> It is not necessary to examine the transits of all the stars, but only those of the chronocrators, or those of the encountering [star] and of the ruler of the terms. For Ptolemy says that whenever the same [stars] should rule both the times and the transits, the outcome is unmixed. And we, persevering in constant trials, find that the same transits contribute greatly to the outcomes of the periods, not only when the stars arrive in the places having authority over the fixing, but also in the place of the times found from the circumambulation. For we also find the great Ptolemy assuring us of this in the 2nd and 3rd and 4th book of the *Apotelesmatics* [that is, *Tetrabiblos*].[17]

In this context, 'stars' means the moving stars, that is, the planets; circumambulation (*peripatos*, literally 'going around') is a synonym of directions; and the encountering star is the promissor that a significator encounters as it makes its way around the nativity. The 'fixing' (*pēxis*) seems, from a comparison with other Greek sources, to mean the nativity itself (corresponding broadly to the Latin term *radix* or 'root' chart). Transits of the chronocrators and to the places of the directed significators form a cornerstone of the method propounded in this book and will be illustrated by detailed examples in its second part. The use of transits as a timing technique *within* a single year of life is discussed in Chapter 9.

How the techniques fit together

Ptolemy sums up his approach by saying that the directions have the greatest authority in determining events, while the profections assist or obstruct them, and the transits strengthen or weaken their results. In other words, the full effect of a direction to a promissor may not necessarily be felt in the month or even the year when it perfects: if the direction is favourable but the profection and transits are unfavourable, or vice versa, the results of the direction may only be fully experienced once those obstructions have passed. This is an important principle to bear in mind, both in prediction and when attempting to rectify an uncertain birth time using primary directions.

Ptolemy also reminds us (and I agree) that the rulerships of the planets in the nativity remain in effect throughout life, and that their good or evil effects depend not only on their combined natures, but also on their natal relationships with the places that they now govern as chronocrators – that is, with the significators of which they are currently divisor or promissor by direction, or whose profected position they rule. If, in addition, the chronocrator of a particular significator also ruled or had some authority over that significator in the nativity, its effects for good or bad will be very pronounced.

To illustrate this with a positive example, the midheaven being directed through the terms of Jupiter or to its body or aspect is generally a good sign for matters related to work and honours. If Jupiter in the nativity is well configured with the midheaven, perhaps by a trine aspect, the good effects are more certain, and even more so if Jupiter itself ruled the natal midheaven – as if, to make our example as favourable as possible, the midheaven were in Pisces and Jupiter trined it from its exaltation in Cancer in the first house. The triumphs that we might expect from such a direction would be most likely to occur in a year when Jupiter itself ruled the midheaven or the ascendant by profection and was in a favourable place by transit, or at least when the malefics did not rule and influence. The further away we get from this sort of idealized situation – if, for instance, our chronocrator (Jupiter) should not be configured with the significator (the midheaven) in the nativity, or not by a good aspect, or should lack authority over it – the more mixed and ambiguous results we may expect.

In addition to the aspects of transiting planets, Ptolemy states that the aspect relationships between the sign of an annual or monthly profection on the one hand, and the 'place of the cause' on the other, will help determine the time of an event. Unfortunately he does not explain what this last phrase means in the present context. If we were to take it as the natal place of the significator itself – for instance, if we profected the Sun as a significator of honours and noted the aspect relationship between that profection and the Sun in the nativity – then it would be true for everyone, at all times, that ages 3, 6 and 9, and all ages derived by adding multiples of 12 to them (such as 27, 30 and 33), would correspond to squares or oppositions by annual profections. Similarly, ages derived by adding multiples of 12 to 2, 4, 8 and 10 would correspond to sextiles or trines. The predictive value of such a technique seems doubtful, but perhaps Ptolemy had something entirely different in mind, such as the place of a *directed* significator (as directions were said to 'determine' events). His terse style makes it difficult to say with certainty.

Although Ptolemy's work became very influential with time, it is too brief to be used as a complete guide to prediction. As seen from the quotation from Stephanus the Philosopher above, however, later generations of astrologers complemented Ptolemy's hierarchy of prediction with material from other Hellenistic authors, taking it in new and fruitful directions. These developments are the topic of the following chapter.

Endnotes

1. Ptol. *Tetr*. IV 10,15, transl. Robbins 1940: 449.
2. Abenragel 1551: 157. My translation via the Latin.
3. For the latter amendment, see al-Qabīṣī IV 12, transl. Burnett et al. 2004: 127.
4. Transl. Burnett and al-Hamdi 1991/92: 321–322.
5. Transl. Dykes 2019b: 318 (translation modified).
6. Transl. Burnett and al-Hamdi 1991/92: 331.
7. Transl. Dykes 2019b: 325 (translation modified).
8. See Dykes 2019b: 332 ff.
9. See *Opusculum* IV 10, transl. Hand 1994: 89 f.
10. See, for instance, Lilly 1647: 784 (where the terminology is used in a secondary sense, with reference to profections rather than directions).
11. *Karmaprakāśa* 13.1–3. My translation from the Sanskrit.
12. See Albubather 14, transl. Dykes 2010: 136 f.
13. See, for instance, Dykes 2019b: 37.
14. Ptol. *Tetr*. IV 10,20, transl. Robbins 1940: 453.
15. See Bezza 1996.
16. See Vett. Val. IV 17–25, transl. Riley 2010: 84–90.
17. See CCAG 2: 198. My translation from the Greek.

5
The Annual Revolution (Solar Return)

THE USE OF annual profections, in which the rulership of a significator such as the ascendant was handed over from one planet to the next once a year, and the attention given to planetary positions by transit at the time of this handover – the revolution of the year – eventually gave rise to the practice of casting an entire new chart for each year of life. The historical details of this development are still largely unknown. The extant Arabic version of Dorotheus (the lost Greek original of which dates from the first century CE) does not mention a separate revolution chart but states that a new year of life begins 'when the Sun enters the beginning of the minute in which he was on the day the native was born'.[1] Vettius Valens in the second century CE speaks of a 'recasting of the nativity' (*antigenesis*) which clearly is a separate chart, but one with a symbolic rather than an astronomically true ascendant degree:

> We consider the recasting of horoscopes to be essential because the recasting contributes greatly to the temporal interchange of the chronocrators. Sometimes the recasting increases the strength of the results, sometimes it is indicative of delays in the results. After we calculate precisely the positions of the stars on the birth date in the current year, we will find the Ascendant as follows: while the Sun is still in the natal sign, we examine where

the Moon was then and when the Moon will come to the exact same degree where it was at the nativity, and we call that point the Ascendant.[2]

Although Valens' instructions are not exactly unambiguous, it is clear that his curious method differs from what we know as a 'solar return' today. Its invention was presumably due to the difficulty of determining the exact time, and thus the true ascendant, of the revolution. Persian astrologers later tried to solve this problem by defining the duration of the solar year with great precision. That duration in days and fractions would then be used as a constant, and finding the exact time of a revolution would be a simple matter of multiplying the constant by the number of years elapsed from birth. In reality, things are a little more complex, as the true length of the solar year (as opposed to its mean or average length) varies slightly from one year to the next. This is chiefly due to the phenomenon of perturbation caused by the gravitational attraction of other bodies on the orbit of the earth, which was not generally understood before Newton, and so the use of an annual constant to calculate revolutions remained standard procedure for many centuries.

We find such a constant in the so-called *Book of Aristotle*, attributed by Burnett and Pingree to Māshā'allāh ibn Atharī (ca. 740–815) but recently convincingly demonstrated by Dykes to have been authored by the Persian astrologer Zādānfarrūkh al-Andarzaghar, probably in the seventh century.[3] This may be the earliest preserved work to speak explicitly both of the calculated ascendant of the revolution figure and of houses reckoned from it, although the text as we have it is not as clear or detailed on the latter subject as the voluminous treatment by Abū Maʿshar some two hundred years later.[4] Abū Maʿshar's work became very popular, was translated in part into both Greek and Latin, and also seems partly to underlie the Sanskrit (Tājika) literature on revolutions. It has already been referenced above, and we shall have reason to return to it repeatedly below.

Sidereal versus tropical year: precision through precession

The value given by al-Andarzaghar for the duration of the year (365.25833 days) raises a major technical consideration peculiar to annual revolutions. The continuous drifting of the equinoctial points with reference to the fixed stars, known as the precession of the equinox, means that the *sidereal* solar year is some twenty minutes longer than the *tropical* solar year. Simply put, when the Sun returns to the exact place it occupied a year earlier *relative to the equinox* – the point where the ecliptic intersects the equator, and day and night are equal in length – the equinox itself will have moved very slightly (in the opposite direction) with respect to the fixed stars, so that the Sun still has another twenty minutes to go before it returns to its original place *relative to the stars*. The duration of the year used by al-Andarzaghar is a sidereal value (based on the stars), just half a minute different from that used by Indian Tājika astrologers a millennium later (365.25875 days), and within three minutes of the modern average value for the sidereal year (365.256363 days).[5]

Some Tājika authors noted that the observable return of the Sun to its position in the nativity did not always agree exactly with the time calculated by the use of an annual constant. This would have been partly due to perturbation as mentioned above, but probably chiefly to the slight imprecision in the annual constant itself. Other, less empirically inclined astrologers criticized this notion on theoretical grounds.[6]

The peripatetic Jewish scholar and astrologer Abraham ibn Ezra (ca. 1089–1167, originally from Spain) lists various opinions about the length of the year, which he ascribes to Indian, Persian, Syrian, Arabic and Greek authorities. The figures associated with Ptolemy and with some of the Arabic authors (including al-Battānī and Yaḥyā ibn Abī

Manṣūr) correspond approximately to the modern average value for the tropical year (365.2421875 days), whereas the other values are sidereal. Ibn Ezra does not use this terminology, however, but only states vaguely that 'most of [the values] are correct, although they require a long explanation'.[7] The value he ascribes to the Indians, mentioned first, is in fact that used by al-Andarzaghar, while the figure he associates with the Persians is very close to it. Another medieval text, probably also authored by ibn Ezra, states that Māshā'allāh and Abū Maʿshar used this same sidereal Persian value for the length of the year.[8] Māshā'allāh's work on the revolutions of nativities no longer survives, but the extant text of Abū Maʿshar's in fact twice endorses Ptolemy's tropical value, whereas in other places he does use a sidereal year, as well as chart examples with sidereal longitudes.[9] This could be interpreted simply as technical ineptitude or inconsistency on the part of Abū Maʿshar – a charge levelled at him even during his lifetime[10] – but could also conceivably suggest that the text as we have it was interpolated (if so, presumably quite early in its transmission history) by some Arabic author who favoured Ptolemy.

Although the later European tradition of astrology was almost exclusively tropical, exceptions have existed. The Italian astrologer and theologian Francesco Giuntini (1523–1590) shows an unusual awareness of sidereal parameters precisely in the context of annual revolutions, and the relevant passage from his *Speculum Astrologiae* or *Mirror of Astrology* deserves to be quoted in full:

> Moreover, there are some astrologers who, in order rightly to adopt Ptolemy's precepts in astrological predictions, prepare the figures of the heavens and the places of the planets according to the motion of the eighth sphere, and indeed by this method: the true place of the Sun is to be sought, which on the day of completion [of the year] is

taken from the ephemerides; next, the apparent precession of the vernal equinox is to be subtracted from that [place]. Thus remains the true place of the Sun reckoned from the first star of Aries, and not from the intersection [of the ecliptic] with the vernal point, which place of the Sun the ephemerides verily do not display by the common [mode of] calculation.

All remaining [places] are completed by the customary method for fashioning a figure of the houses. The places of the planets having been calculated from the ephemerides in this way, the true precession is likewise to be subtracted from the same, at the time duly fixed, and what results constitutes the true place of the planet according to the fixed stars or asterisms, not according to the twelfth-parts [of the tropical zodiac] which we commonly use. This method in judgements, moreover, which agrees in the highest degree with experience, we have defined in our treatise on the judgements of nativities.[11]

The Indian Tājika texts offer indirect evidence from the opposite side, as it were: although the tradition as a whole is explicitly sidereal, some practitioners were aware of the existence of tropical practices. One of the more well-informed authors seems to have been Yādavasūri, who may have lived in the early 1600s and who occasionally criticized his fellow Brahmans for 'not understanding Yavana [i.e., Muslim] tradition'.[12] In his *Tājikayogasudhānidhi* or *Nectar Ocean of Tājika Configurations* he wrote concerning the profection (*inthihā*):

When precession has been added to the ascendant of the nativity, the ruler [of the sign] where the *inthihā* [falls] is the ruler of the year. If it is a benefic, one should declare the result to be good; if a malefic planet, it is not auspicious. That [method] is approved by Romaka.[13]

The use of tropical longitudes, derived here by adding precession or *ayanāṃśa* to the default sidereal figures, is thus associated particularly with 'Romaka' – a word meaning 'the Roman' or possibly 'the Romans'. In the medieval period, this appellation would have referred to astrologers of Byzantine ethnicity, whose use of Ptolemaic tropical tables did indeed contrast with sidereal Persian and Indian practice. I am aware of only a single Indian work in Sanskrit actually advocating the use of tropical values as being more correct than sidereal ones. This is the late *Sāyanābdaphalodgama* or *Manifestation of Results of the Tropical Year*, authored by an otherwise unknown Raṅganātha around 1650, which again opens with a reference to 'Romaka'.[14]

Twenty minutes in a year may not seem much, but the difference is cumulative: already at the age of three, a native's sidereal and tropical revolutions will be about an hour apart, and by one's mid-thirties the difference will amount to twelve hours. This means that the difference between a sidereal and a tropical revolution is far greater than that between the corresponding natal charts. In a sidereal and a tropical *nativity* cast for the same set of data, planets will occupy the same houses and form the same aspect angles by degree, even if most sign placements differ. In a sidereal and a tropical *revolution* cast for the same year of a native's life, the planets will occupy not only different signs, but different houses as well, and the faster-moving planets – especially the Moon – may be involved in different aspect configurations. In short, these will be two completely unrelated horoscopes.

Some astrologers who experiment with sidereal revolution charts and find the house placements they produce more reliable, but who still (for whatever reason) do not wish to let go of the tropical zodiac, favour a hybrid approach of 'precessed tropical' revolutions – in other words, using the tropical zodiac but the sidereal duration of the year. As this means that the zodiacal position of the Sun in the revolution will *not* in fact be identical to that of the nativity but will shift by more than a degree over an average human lifespan, I personally find such an approach inconsistent – especially if the technique is referred to as a 'solar return'.

Location and the proper use of the revolution figure
Another question peculiar to revolution charts is for which location to cast them. So far I have not come across any ancient or medieval author addressing this question; the earliest discussion I have been able to find on the matter is that by Jean-Baptiste Morin de Villefranche (1583–1656), who favoured casting the chart for the location where the native happened to be at the exact time of the revolution.[15] Some present-day astrologers similarly advocate relocating the solar return chart, and a few even give advice on where to spend your birthday in a given year so as to ensure the most favourable chart. As such discussions are absent from the writings of earlier astrologers, it seems reasonable to assume that those astrologers simply cast the revolution chart for the place of birth, which is the practice I recommend and have followed in this book.

Once the revolution figure is cast, the next question is what to do with it. Contrary to the claims of many books and Internet resources, the 'solar return' is *not* an independent horoscope to be interpreted just like a nativity, albeit valid for only one year. Whether your annual chart is cast in a sidereal zodiac or the tropical one, precessed or non-precessed, relocated or not, regarding it as an independent entity will inevitably result in hit-and-miss predictions (unless those predictions are too vague to be falsifiable in the first place). This, in fact, is what for many years made me doubt the validity of the technique.

Having said that, the annual chart actually is of great predictive value because it provides us with details in the form of the positions of the planets in the houses at the time of the revolution, as well as their mutual configurations – as long as we know which planets to pay attention to. There are two basic ways of doing this, although they ultimately come down to the same considerations. The first approach is the open-ended question: 'What is going to happen in this year of life?' To find out, we examine the planets that are activated as chronocrators in that year – promissors, divisors, the ruler of the year – and any planets configured with them, taking note of their natures, dignities, rulerships and so on.

The other approach starts with a question on a specific topic: Will I have a child this year? What will my finances be like? Will I change jobs? In order to answer such questions, we need to find the planet or planets signifying the matter under consideration in the nativity and determine whether they are active as chronocrators, or configured with the chronocrators, in the year – and, if so, whether they are well or ill disposed. Similarly, we can examine any planets occupying the relevant house in the revolution to see if they are configured with the chronocrators or perhaps casting an aspect into the division of a major significator (that is, the terms through which it is currently directed). The more ways a signification is activated by the chronocrators, the more certain and prominent it will be in the year. If a given area of life is not activated at all, this indicates a lack of change in that area during the year in question.

House positions in the revolution are also important for assessing the *impact* of a chronocrator in a given year. A planet activated by direction or profection but placed in a cadent house in the revolution figure will typically have little power to manifest its significations, whereas one occupying an angle, particularly the ascendant or midheaven, will do so easily – though always within the boundaries defined by the nativity. If, for example, the ascendant is directed in a year to the trine of Jupiter, ruler of the second house, and Jupiter is unafflicted in the first house of the revolution (or some other powerful and appropriate house, such as the eleventh house of gain, where it rejoices), then we can safely predict that the native's finances will improve in that year – the condition of Jupiter (and of the significators of wealth generally) in the nativity determining the upper limit of that improvement. But if Jupiter should occupy the sixth or twelfth house of the revolution, it is unlikely to effect any major improvement on its own in the current year.

Naturally, the best-case scenario is for an activated significator to be well-placed both in the nativity and in the revolution, whereas a significator badly placed in both times would give the worst results. When the indications of the two charts differ, one principle mentioned by Abū Ma'shar and repeated by Tājika authors is that a planet being better placed in the revolution than in the nativity shows a (temporary) improvement; if the situation is the reverse, a (temporary) deterioration.[16] The Tājikas tend to interpret this as the first six months of the year being bad and the last six months good or vice versa, but things are rarely as clear-cut as that: as discussed in Chapter 9, timing within a year depends on a number of factors.

The revolution ascendant and other houses

Abū Ma'shar, whose motto seems to have been 'Include everything', repeatedly uses three different sets of houses to assess the placement of a single planet (or the configuration of two or more planets) at the time of the revolution: the houses of the nativity, the profection, and the revolution. This is fairly useless advice, as three sets of houses will typically place a single planet in three wholly different positions at once (quite often simultaneously angular, succedent *and* cadent), making judgement impossible. My own recommendation, based on experience, is to judge planets at the time of the revolution by their house positions in the revolution figure, just as we use natal house positions to assess planets in the nativity.

With regard to house *rulerships*, which will partly determine the matters signified by a planet, Abū Maʿshar again vacillates between his three sets of houses, although he considers natal rulerships to be the strongest. The Indian Tājika works more clearly (if not universally) favour natal rulerships, and this agrees with my experience: the houses of the nativity stamp a planet with significations retained throughout life. Thus, if two planets are configured in the revolution, at least one of them being a chronocrator, their impact and/or the circumstances in which they manifest their significations will be shown by their house placements in the revolution, but the significations themselves are mostly carried over from the nativity. For example, imagine that, for a person with Aries rising in the nativity, the ascendant is directed through the terms of Mercury; and that Mercury itself is conjunct Venus, ruler of the natal second and seventh houses, in the eleventh house of the revolution. As a result of this configuration we might predict marriage or a romantic relationship (Venus and the seventh house), perhaps after meeting through friends (eleventh house), and/or financial gains (Mercury and the eleventh house), possibly from good investments (second house).

Abū Maʿshar followed earlier authors like al-Andarzaghar in attaching particular importance to the ascendant of the revolution and planets in it – both at the time of the revolution itself and in the nativity (as if 10° Taurus were rising in the revolution and natal Mars were at 15° Taurus). He considered it to be almost, though not quite, on a level with the profected ascendant, and regarded the ruler of the revolution ascendant as a chronocrator in its own right; and in this he was followed by the Indian Tājika authors. Having put his opinion to the test (examining both tropical and sidereal revolutions for the sake of thoroughness), I believe that Abū Maʿshar seriously exaggerated the importance of the revolution ascendant, although I am prepared to agree that ruling or occupying it may reinforce the importance of a planet that is *already* a major chronocrator, such as the divisor or the ruler of the year, or configured with one. Some examples will be discussed in Chapter 8.

Varieties of configuration and the Tājika *yogas*

An important point to consider whenever a chronocrator is configured with one or more planets is the precise nature of that configuration. Is the aspect or conjunction in question partile (occurring within a degree), or is it in the process of applying or separating? Be sure to note whether that process will actually be completed, as results are sometimes reversed by a planet turning retrograde (or, if already retrograde, turning direct) or changing signs. A separating aspect can indicate a few different things depending on the context: it may signify an actual separation (between friends, spouses, and so on), an expected event (good or bad) falling through, or a situation that is wholly or partly in the past – either recently completed or continuing from a previous year.

Other not uncommon scenarios include the translation or collection of light. In a translation of light, two planets – such as a chronocrator and a significator of some matter under consideration – are not themselves connected, but a third planet makes a connection between them by separating from one and next applying to the other. In a collection of light, the two unconnected planets both apply to a third planet, which creates the connection. Similarly, when an applying planet occupies a place where the planet applied to has dignity (chiefly by domicile or exaltation), such as Mercury in Aries applying to Mars or the Sun, the latter is said to 'receive' the former, which typically means that it will behave more graciously – although sometimes reception may play out more in terms of dependence or power balance between people, the receiving or 'host' planet having the upper hand. When the planet applied to has no dignity in the sign of the applying planet, and perhaps would even be in debility there (as if Mercury in Aries applied to Saturn), the situation is the opposite and is called non-reception. All these types of configuration may have a bearing on events during a year, and some of them are illustrated by the example charts discussed in the second part of the book.

One of the most well-known overviews of varieties of planetary configuration is that of Sahl ibn Bishr in the early ninth century.[17] Sahl's list of sixteen categories is also the origin of the sixteen so-called Tājika *yogas*, although the last few items on the list were split up the wrong way by the Tājika translators, and some of the definitions were misunderstood. Table 1 shows Sahl's original list with English translations and the Sanskritized names used in Tājika works (sometimes with variant spellings).[18] In addition to the categories discussed above, this list includes such items as house position (an angular or succedent planet is 'advancing', while a cadent one is 'retreating'); strength and weakness based on zodiacal placement and other considerations; and more detailed analyses of aspect configuration. Prohibition is an applying aspect being interrupted by the intrusion of a malefic, while being 'void of course' (or, in a more modern idiom, 'on an empty path' – that is, meeting no-one) means a lack of application. A strong planet may commit its strength to another by applying to it, while a planet applying to its ruler (that is, being received) commits its disposition and nature to that ruler; and return of light means that the planet applied to hands back whatever is committed to it, because it is unable to take on the responsibility. Some of these latter categories are both rather complex and insufficiently explained by Sahl and others, but the basic principles involved are nevertheless very useful in interpreting aspect configurations.

Repetition and nativity-revolution contacts

A major factor in interpreting a revolution figure correctly is *repetition*, which can take different forms. House connection is one such form: if a chronocrator, or a planet configured with a chronocrator, is connected with a house in the nativity by ruling or occupying it, and then occupies the same house in the revolution, the signification of the planet in that house is likely to manifest strongly in that year. For example, if Venus, being activated by direction or profection, rules the natal fifth house and also occupies the fifth in the revolution figure, the native may have a child in that year (if his/her time of life agrees), or some particularly fortunate event relating to children may take place – more surely so if Venus is dignified and well-aspected at both times. Conversely, if Saturn should occupy the fifth house at both times, misfortune is likely to befall the children (or the native with respect to children), particularly if Saturn is in debility and/or afflicted both in the nativity and in the revolution.

Repetition may also take the form of a planet returning to its own natal position by sign, terms, or degree, each subtype being stronger than the preceding. (The astronomical chances of a planetary return roughly coinciding with the solar return differ from planet to planet depending on the complexity of their cycles relative to the Sun, the eight-year cycle of Venus being perhaps the one most easily observed.) Such a return can strongly reactivate the significations of the planet in the nativity – again, given that it is a chronocrator or configured with a chronocrator. However, if its house placement in the revolution does not agree – if, for instance, a planet were powerfully placed in the tenth house of the nativity and returned to the same terms in the revolution, but with those terms now falling in the twelfth house – then the results would be less certain and stable.

Arabic name	English meaning	Sanskritized name
1. *iqbāl*	1. Advance	1. *ikkavāla*
2. *idbār*	2. Retreat	2. *induvāra*
3. *ittiṣāl*	3. Application	3. *itthaśāla*
4. *inṣirāf*	4. Separation	4. *īsarāpha*
5. *naql*	5. Translation	5. *nakta*
6. *jāmiʿa*	6. Collection	6. *yamayā*
7. *manʿa*	7. Prohibition	7. *manau*
8. *qabūl*	8. Reception	8. *kambūla*
9. *ghayr al-qabūl*	9. Non-reception	9. *gairikambūla*
10. *khalāʾ as-sayr*	10. Being void of course	10. *khallāsara*
11. *radd*	11. Return	11. *radda*
12. *dufʿa l-quwwa*	12. Committing strength	12. *duḫphālikuttha*
13. *dufʿa t-tadbīr ...*	13. Committing disposition ...	13. *dutthotthadabīra*
... *wa-ṭ-ṭabīʿa*	... and nature	14. *tambīra*
14. *quwwa*	14. Strength	15. *kuttha*
15. *ḍuf*	15. Weakness	16. *duruḫpha*
16. *aḥwāl al-qamar*	16. Conditions of the Moon	– –

Table 1. Sahl ibn Bishr's sixteen categories and the Tājika *yogas.*

A scenario that deserves particular mention is when a promissor that has already given rise to a major event in recent years returns to the same terms in the revolution, resulting in a repetition of the event. For example, imagine a nativity with late Scorpio rising and the ascendant currently being directed through the terms of Mars in Sagittarius, with Venus as ruler of the seventh house present in those terms in the nativity. One possible outcome of such a direction would be the native marrying in the year when the conjunction with Venus perfects – say at age 29 – only to divorce a year later (the divorce being signified by Mars, and subject to such indications in the nativity). But if Venus in a subsequent revolution were to return to the same terms (which could happen at age 32, given Venus' eight-year transit cycle), while the directed ascendant is still present there, Venus would renew its natal promise and indicate remarriage.

The annual profection reaching a sign in which a planet is making a return is a similar, if not equally powerful, indication of that planet renewing its significations. In fact, as mentioned in the previous chapter, some texts – including the Arabic version of Dorotheus – suggest that a planet natally present in the sign of the annual profection will be fully able to give its expected results *only* if also present in or aspecting that sign in the revolution.[19]

A third form of repetition occurs when a chronocrator is configured with another planet in the nativity, and the same two planets are again configured in the revolution. For instance, if Mercury forms a natal trine with Jupiter, and then, at a time when either of them is ruler of the year (or divisor, or promissor), Mercury and Jupiter are conjunct in the revolution, the signification of the natal aspect will be activated. This is obviously a more complex situation with many possible variations. The type of aspect in the revolution may be the same as in the nativity (such as a trine at both times), or of a similar type (such as a trine at one time and a sextile or conjunction at the other), or dissimilar (such as a trine and a square). Likewise, the dignities, house positions, and so on of the two planets may be similar or dissimilar. The greater the similarity between the figures, the more pronounced the results indicated in the nativity will be, for better or worse. Abū Ma'shar states that a repeating configuration indicates an event caused by something in the native's past, whereas a configuration present only in the revolution suggests a more recent cause.[20]

There are also meaningful contacts between the revolution and the nativity that do not involve repetition. Perhaps the most important of these is when a planet in the revolution casts an aspect into the division (that is, terms) of a directed significator: this scenario will be discussed with many chart examples starting in the next chapter. With regard to planet-to-planet contacts, a chronocrator in the revolution may be placed in or near the natal degree of another planet or vice versa. When a revolution planet conjoins a natal chronocrator, it will affect the chronocrator's results for better or worse according to its own nature and condition, and may also add details relating to the circumstances in which those results manifest. The chronocrator itself conjoining the natal position of another planet may similarly activate the significations of that planet. As always, multiple connections make for more stable and certain results: if Saturn is a chronocrator and exalted in Libra in the nativity, in a good house and a diurnal chart, and Jupiter in the revolution is in or near that same degree, then Saturn can be expected to give good results conforming to the nature and rulership of Jupiter in that year; but if, in addition, *revolution* Saturn is in Aquarius (where it has the dignity of domicile) around the same degree, trining the conjunction in Libra, then the good is even further enhanced. If, on the other hand, revolution Mars should be in its fall in Cancer, squaring the conjunction in Libra, it will detract from the good and introduce conflict and unpleasantness.

Now that we have got an overview of some of the most important techniques used for making annual predictions by astrologers writing in Greek, Arabic, and Sanskrit, it is time to see how those techniques perform when applied to real, contemporary nativities. The two following chapters will focus on directions and profections, respectively, in both cases combining them with transits at the time of the revolution. In the final two chapters, we shall integrate these considerations with the figure of the annual revolution and with more fine-grained timing techniques.

Endnotes

1. *Carm. astr.* IV 1,1, transl. Dykes 2017: 197.
2. Vett. Val. V 3,3–6, transl. Riley 2010: 97 (translation slightly modified).
3. See Burnett and Pingree 1997: 1–9; Dykes 2019a: 27–32.
4. For an example, see *Lib. Arist.* IV 15, transl. Dykes 2009: 210.
5. See *Lib. Arist.* IV 1,2, transl. Dykes 2009: 185; Burnett and Pingree 1997: 196 f.; *Hāyanaratna* 1.6, transl. Gansten 2020: 111–117.
6. See *Hāyanaratna* 1.6, transl. Gansten 2020: 119–123, discussing *Tājikasāra* 41 and *Tājikabhūṣaṇa* 1.8–9.
7. *Sefer ha-Moladot* IV 1, transl. Sela 2014: 183 f.
8. *Liber de rationibus tabularum*; see Sela 2014: 341.
9. See Dykes 2019b: 5 f., 74 f., 157 f., 632.
10. See Dykes 2019b: 3 ff.
11. Junctinus 1581: 1012. My translation from the Latin.
12. For Yādavasūri, see Gansten 2017: 125–128 (correcting some mistakes of Pingree's).

13. *Tājikayogasudhānidhi* 8.29. My translation from the Sanskrit (manuscript sources; no known editions).
14. No known editions. I have seen only the incomplete manuscript Chandra Shum Shere d. 805 of the Bodleian Library.
15. See *Astr. Gall.* XXIII 4, transl. Holden 2002: 7 ff.
16. See Dykes 2019b: 187 f.
17. See Dykes 2019a: 52–71. Note that Dykes's translations of several technical terms differ from those employed here.
18. First discussed by Gansten and Wikander (2011); see also Gansten 2020: 23–26.
19. See *Carm. astr.* IV 1,22–34, transl. Dykes 2017: 200 f.
20. See Dykes 2019b: 424 f.

Part II
Practice

6
Primary Directions in Annual Prediction

[Astrologers] know future events on the basis of their craft; ⟨this is so because⟩ they are knowledgeable about ⟨how to cast⟩ natal horoscopes, ⟨about how to⟩ direct the degrees along the terms and along the aspects of the planets and the two luminaries, and ⟨about how to cast the horoscope at⟩ the revolution of the year, month, week, and day.

– Abraham ibn Ezra[1]

WITH THIS CHAPTER we begin to look at practical chart examples, focusing first on directions. (We can dispense with the modifier 'primary', introduced by Placidus in the seventeenth century, as we are not going to use any other kind of direction.) The basic terminology of this technique – such as significator, promissor and divisor – was explained in Chapter 4; but before we delve into the examples, a few technical variables relating specifically to directions need to be addressed. For readers interested in exploring these issues in greater depth, I refer to my earlier book on directions. Here I simply describe the parameters which I have since found to work best, and which are therefore used in all real-life examples given below. (Appendix III explains how to set up software to match these parameters.) I encourage you to go over each example slowly and methodically, preferably several times. Unless otherwise stated, all directions described in this book are made in direct motion, meaning that the significator moves symbolically forward along the zodiac.

Aspects and latitude

Like all astrologers up to the early modern period, I use only aspects in the zodiac for directions – that is, the ordinary kind of aspects that we consider when reading a natal chart. If Venus is at 10° Taurus in the nativity, then directing the ascendant to a trine of Venus means rotating the chart with the primary motion (clockwise) until 10° Virgo or 10° Capricorn is on the ascendant, and so on. The so-called mundane aspects introduced by Placidus, which are not points in the zodiac at all but rather proportions of semi-arcs (the time it takes a planet to go from rising to culminating, from culminating to setting, etc.), will not be used here.

A related question is whether directions involving the Moon and the non-luminary planets should consider their latitude, that is, make use of their actual bodies some distance away from the ecliptic – and, if so, whether latitude should also be somehow assigned to their points of aspect. (The question does not arise for the Sun, which by definition is always on the ecliptic.) When the Moon or any non-luminary planet is a significator, I always direct its actual body (that is, the planet *with* latitude considered) rather than its projected position on the ecliptic. Aspect points, on the other hand, are not bodies but merely sensitive points on the ecliptic, and I do not assign any latitude to them.

However, there are two exceptions: experience has taught me that conjunctions and oppositions with latitude give correct and often striking results. Why should this be? My best guess is that such conjunctions and oppositions are not aspects in the usual sense, but rather relate to the concept of paranatellonta or co-risings. When a significator is directed to the conjunction or opposition of a promissor with latitude, the two are, as it were, located on the same horizon, either on the same side or on opposite sides. (This means that the opposition of a planet also has the opposite kind of latitude: if the planet itself is 2° *north* of the ecliptic, its opposition point will be 2° *south* of the ecliptic.) When the significator is the ascendant, this is literally the case; and as discussed in Chapter 4, some astrologers have devised methods of direction based on artificial horizons or circles of position which mean that the promissor is always brought to the 'horizon' of the significator (or vice versa in the case of a converse direction). Although I do not use such methods in this book, I still consider co-risings a valid metaphor for understanding conjunctions and oppositions with latitude.

These zodiacal conjunctions and oppositions with latitude (*cum latitudine* in Latin) will always be identical with the corresponding 'mundane' (*in mundo*) conjunctions and oppositions advocated by Placidus, but it is important to understand that this does not apply to other types of aspect. A direction involving a trine, square or sextile in the zodiac, whether with or without latitude, is wholly different from a Placidean so-called mundane trine, square or sextile – which, as already mentioned, are not based on geometrical relationships between the signs or planets but rather on their cycles of rising, culminating and so forth. Imagine, for instance, a chart where the midheaven is directed to the body of Mercury, located at 20° Sagittarius with little or no latitude, while the directed ascendant is simultaneously at 20° Aries. In the traditional sense, the latter would be a direction of the ascendant to the (zodiacal) *trine* of Mercury, but Placidus – who did not accept zodiacal directions as valid for the angles – would consider the ascendant to be directed to the (mundane) *square* of Mercury. In my earlier book I used the terms 'mundane' and 'with latitude' wholly interchangeably when speaking of conjunctions; but although the two designations do coincide in practice, their conceptual frameworks are different, and in this book I consistently use 'with latitude'.

When a planet has considerable latitude, its conjunctions or oppositions with and without latitude, respectively, may be years apart. In such cases, the promissor *without* latitude may be best conceptualized as an aspect point on the ecliptic and will be as effective as other such points, although the directions *with* latitude (the 'co-rising' directions) are often more notable. When planets have only a little latitude, conjunctions/oppositions with and without latitude may occur within months or even days of each other, and which of them coincides more nearly with important events may depend chiefly on other factors, such as profections, revolutions and transits.

Equation of time or 'key'

Ptolemy and other astrologers of the Hellenistic era and Late Antiquity all equated 1° of primary motion – that is to say, of ascensional degrees, measured along the celestial equator – with one year of life. Medieval and, especially, early modern astrologers came up with many variations on this measurement: some fixed, others variable, but all averaging a value close to 1° per year. The purpose of these modifications, often called 'keys', was to match the time when a direction perfected more closely with the times of major events signified by that direction; but as noted in the seventeenth century by Morin de Villefranche (who was himself a proponent of the fixed Naibod key of 0°59′08″ per year), no matter which measurement is adopted, some effects of directions will always manifest before the time of perfection, others after it.[2] I agree with Morin that this fact of life once again depends on factors separate from the directions themselves. All direction examples in this book are based on the simple measurement of 1° per year or 'key of Ptolemy'.

Parallax and secondary motion

Two additional considerations chiefly concern directions involving the Moon, which is much closer to us than the other heavenly bodies and moves around the zodiac much more quickly. The first consideration is that of lunar parallax: whether the position of the Moon should be calculated as observable from the actual place of birth somewhere on the face of the earth or from an imagined point in the centre of the earth. The former is known as the topocentric position, the latter as the geocentric one. The great distance of other planets from us makes the difference between the two models negligible in their case, so that geocentric positions can be used as a matter of convenience. In the case of the Moon, however, especially when it is near the horizon in the nativity, the difference caused by parallax can amount to approximately 1° of longitude (corresponding on average to a year in directions). My experience has been that the topocentric Moon gives far more accurate results, and that is the position used in all example charts.

Somewhat to my surprise, the second possible consideration – namely, that of secondary motion – has not proved as useful. The theoretical argument in favour of it would be that in, say, the three hours after birth that correspond by direction to the first 45 years of life (each ascensional degree taking approximately four minutes of clock time to rise), the Moon will have moved about a degree and a half along the zodiac, so that its position at that time is perceptibly different from its position at birth. In practice, however, I have had to concede that it is the position at birth that seems to work best astrologically, and I have therefore disregarded secondary motion in the example charts.

Directions as a stand-alone technique

As zodiacal signs differ in their rising times – differences that become more marked the further north or south of the equator a person was born – significators located in them progress through the terms and aspects of the planets at very different rates. For persons born with signs of short ascension just about to rise, especially in high latitudes, the ascendant may come under the influence of a new natal promissor and/or divisor nearly every year. In such cases, there can be so much happening by direction alone that revolutions may appear almost

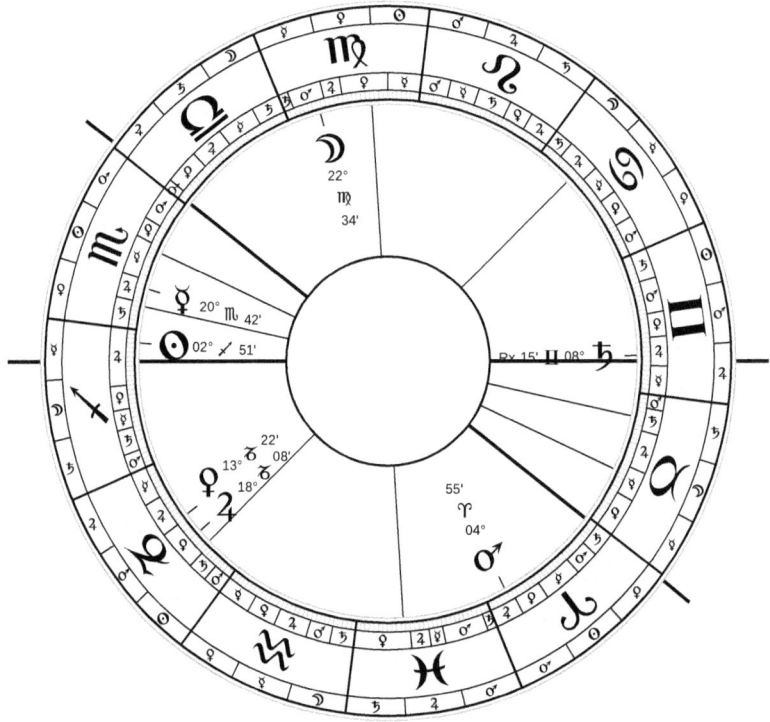

Figure 2: Nativity I.

superfluous. I would nevertheless recommend always including the revolution in your judgements; but to give an idea of the basic method, let us examine one such nativity (figure 2), correlating the major themes and events of the native's adult life as related by himself with the directions of the ascendant and other major significators.

After completing his secondary education at age 18, the native spent a year living in a religious commune before enrolling at university, where he did religious studies. At this time the ascendant was directed through the terms of Mercury (0°–7°) in Capricorn. In addition to being a universal significator of learning, Mercury rules the ninth house of religion and knowledge; it also forms a separating but still close sextile aspect with Jupiter, which has a natural affinity with the same topics. As the native began his university studies, the midheaven – significator of occupation – was exactly directed to this same sextile of Jupiter, at the end of Mercury's terms in Scorpio.

The same two planets continued to exert their influence over the next period in the native's life, with a slight shift in emphasis. As the ascendant entered the terms of Jupiter (7°–14°) in Capricorn at age 22, and the midheaven reached the conjunction of Mercury (which falls in the terms of Jupiter at 19°–24° of Scorpio), the native relocated to a university in a neighbouring country and changed his focus of study to ancient languages for two years. Both planets rule houses related to travel (the third and ninth); the seventh, ruled by Mercury, is also commonly associated with foreign countries. And of course Mercury is a universal significator not only of learning generally but especially of spoken and written language.

Soon after the native had returned home to complete his undergraduate studies at the age of 25, the ascendant reached the conjunction of Venus *without* latitude, followed immediately by the terms of Venus (14°–22°) in Capricorn. Venus is the universal significator of love and marriage but also rules the tenth house of profession. In this period, the native met and married his first wife and embarked on his future career by entering the doctoral programme at his university. Four years later, at age 29, the successful completion of his doctorate brought a rise in status and professional prospects. Although the ascendant at this time was directed through the terms of Saturn (22°–26°) in Capricorn, it was also conjunct both the benefics

(Venus and Jupiter) – *with* latitude, or what I have called 'co-rising' directions – in the same period, largely overshadowing the negative significations of Saturn.

This happy event was followed by a less prosperous period, with lack of employment and strained finances, as the ascendant was directed through the division of Mars (26°–30° Capricorn) at age 29–30. Mars, the malefic contrary to sect, rules the fourth house of parents, and the same period saw the native's mother ill with cancer as the ascendant encountered the opposition of the Moon, universal significator of the mother. (Once more this was a direction *with* latitude, strikingly different from what might be expected just from looking at the two-dimensional chart because the Moon's latitude was unusually great and the place of birth far removed from the equator.) The Moon itself was directed through the terms of Mars, first in Libra and then in Scorpio.

One of the most fortunate periods of the native's life was age 34–35, when the ascendant was directed through the terms of Jupiter (13°–20°) in Aquarius while the Sun (luminary of the sect, and the presumed hyleg) conjoined both the benefics with latitude within a year. Jupiter is a universal significator of children and conjunct Venus, ruler of the fifth house; the native's only child (a daughter) was born in this period. Soon afterwards, the midheaven was directed to the conjunction of the Sun: at this time the native was awarded the academic rank of *docent* and a prestigious, though not permanent, university position.

By contrast, the direction of the ascendant through the terms of Mars (20°–25°) in Aquarius, coinciding with age 36, was described by the native as 'hellish'. In addition to the natural maleficence of Mars, Mercury as ruler of the seventh house of marriage casts a square aspect into these terms. This was the year in which the native's marriage finally broke down despite his many attempts to save it, following a prolonged deterioration in his wife's mental health (the mind being another signification of Mercury). As the ascendant moved into the terms of Saturn (25°–30° of Aquarius) at age 37, a divorce petition was filed and eventually finalized, with the native given sole custody of his daughter. Saturn, which has a little southern latitude, is exactly on the western horizon, the cusp of the seventh house, in the nativity.

A major improvement in the native's situation occurred at the end of the divisional period of Venus (0°–12°) in Pisces, once the ascendant had passed the square of Saturn at age 40. At this time the native entered into a new romantic relationship just as the Moon was directed to the sextile of Venus. The Moon is a universal significator of women, and Ptolemy particularly recommends directing it for predictions relating to marriage. As the ascendant encountered the other sextile of Venus in the terms of Jupiter (12°–16°) in Pisces, the native formally remarried at age 41.

At age 42, the ascendant entered the terms of Mars for the second time in less than six years, now in Pisces (19°–28°) and with a trine rather than a square from Mercury falling in them. At this time the native's parents transferred ownership of a rural property to him, a positive event that agrees with Mercury occupying the eleventh house of acquisition and Mars ruling the fourth house of both home and parents. However, as the ascendant – still in the same terms – approached the conjunction of Mars with latitude the following year, the native's father was diagnosed with an aggressive cancer and died not long afterwards. The Sun as universal significator of the father was simultaneously directed to the opposition of the Moon, ruler of the eighth house, with latitude.

At the native's age of 45, recently concluded at the time of this writing, the ascendant was directed through the terms of Jupiter (0°–6°) in Aries, where it encountered the trine aspect of the Sun. This direction coincided with the attainment of academic tenure.

While it would be foolish to pretend that the above is anything like a complete account of events over a quarter of a century, it should be clear from this example how well the astrological symbolism of directions – including directions through the sidereal terms – can match the objective reality of a person's life. However, it should be stressed that this example is, in astronomical terms, somewhat extreme: in just 45 years of life, the direction of the ascendant has covered some 113° of ecliptical longitude – nearly one third of the zodiac, comprising twenty sets of terms – and formed repeated aspects with each of the seven planets. By contrast, in high-latitude nativities where signs of long ascension are rising, the native may spend a decade or more under the influence of a single divisor. In such cases, other techniques become crucial for making year-by-year predictions.

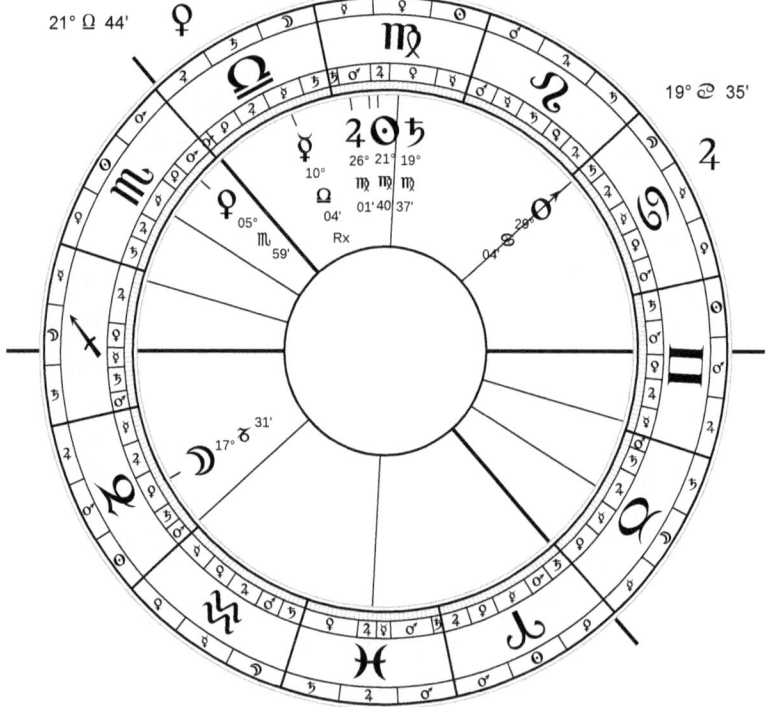

Figure 3: Nativity J with transits at revolution 21.

Recurring patterns: honours and awards

The value of including transits at the annual revolution when judging the effects of directions, even in cases where the major significators do move fairly quickly, is demonstrated by our next example nativity (figure 3). This is another academic, incidentally with the same rising sign as the previous native and with the exact same degree – and the same fixed star (the Northern Claw or Scale, of a Jupiter-Mercury nature) – on the midheaven. In this chart, Venus not only rules that midheaven but occupies the tenth quadrant house (and the eleventh equal house), while the ninth quadrant house (equal tenth) holds its ruler Mercury as well as the Sun, luminary of the sect, flanked by the other two diurnal planets: Saturn and Jupiter, ruler of the ascendant.

Between the ages of 18 and 22, the ascendant was directed through the terms of Venus (14°–22°) in Capricorn, where it encountered the trine aspects first of Saturn and then of the Sun (perfecting at age 21 and 22, respectively). This period marked the start of public recognition for the native by the publication, at age 21, of a widely acclaimed translation of religious texts in an ancient language – an apt expression of Saturn and the Sun in a Mercury sign in the ninth house. But would we have had the confidence to predict such a very positive outcome of the direction from the nativity alone, especially to someone so young?

Looking for confirmation to the transits at the revolution of the year (figure 3), we see that both benefics – Venus being the current divisor and ruling the natal midheaven, Jupiter ruling the ascendant – cast aspects into the terms of the directed ascendant (14°–22° Capricorn). Moreover, they are both in major dignities, Venus occupying its domicile and Jupiter its exaltation, in addition to being in their own terms. These powerful benefic influences clearly support a highly positive interpretation of the direction in this year.

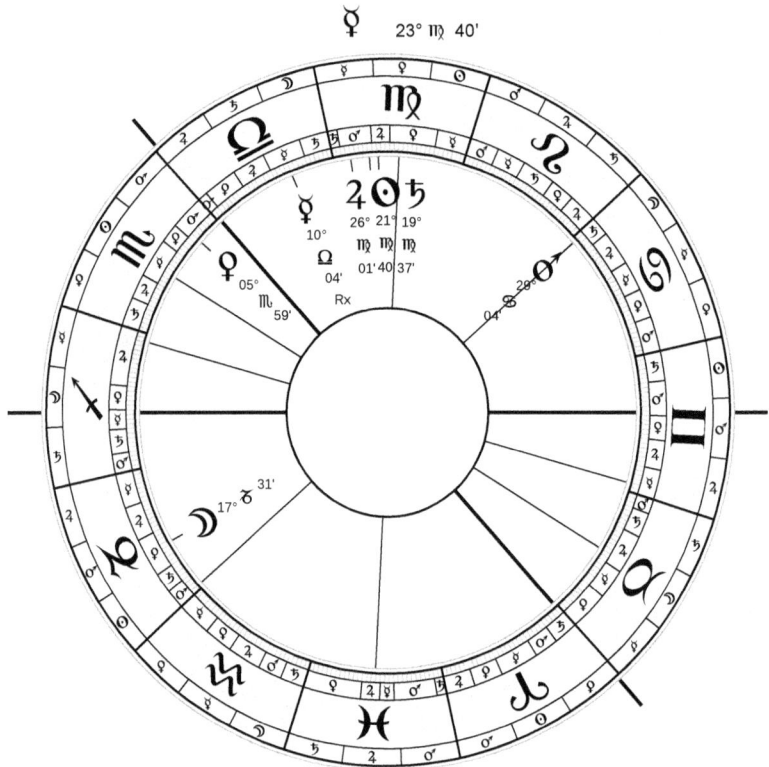

Figure 4: Nativity J with transits at revolution 23.

Even without a direction to a natal promissor, the presence or aspect of a planet in the terms of a directed significator can be highly significant. At age 23, the same native first received a prestigious prize for his first book and, later the same year, published a second one. In that year (figure 4), the midheaven was very appropriately directed to the sextile of the Sun, falling in the terms of Jupiter (19°–24°) in Scorpio; but the ascendant had entered the terms of Saturn (22°–26°) in Capricorn – incidentally signifying some unhappiness in the native's personal life – and was not directed to any promissor. In the revolution of that year, however, Mercury in Virgo cast both a trine aspect into the terms of the directed ascendant and a sextile into the terms of the

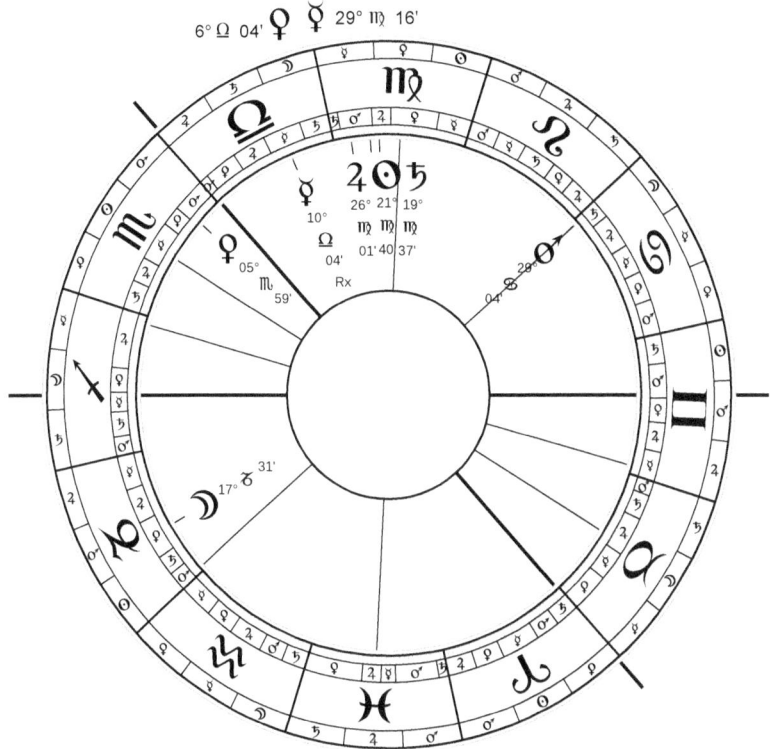

Figure 5: Nativity J with transits at revolution 30.

directed midheaven. Virgo is not only the domicile and exaltation of Mercury but also a double-bodied sign, agreeing with repeated success in the literary field.

Age 30 saw two important directions to the radix perfect, as the Sun (luminary of the sect) conjoined Venus with latitude while the ascendant was directed to the trine of Mercury in the terms of Venus (7°–13°) in Aquarius. Similarly to age 21, when Venus was first divisor of the ascendant, this coincided with a major advancement in the native's career, as he successfully defended his dissertation and obtained his doctoral degree; but the universal significations of Venus manifested as well, in the form of the native's wedding. It is also worth noting that Mercury rules the native's seventh house of marriage (and, incidentally, marks the ascendant in his wife's nativity). At the time of the revolution (figure 5), Venus as divisor and Mercury as promissor were both strong in their domiciles, with Venus just a few degrees shy of Mercury's natal position (and thus of a trine to the directed ascendant).

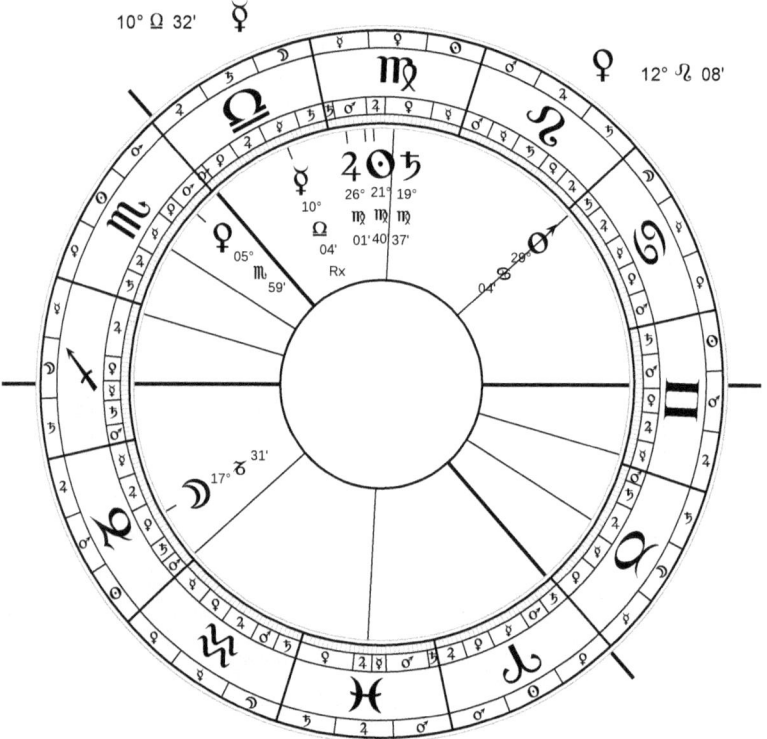

Figure 6: Nativity J with transits at revolution 31.

At age 31 (figure 6), events from eight years before were very nearly repeated as *another* royal academy awarded the native a prize for *another* book. This is an instance of the principle that was mentioned in Chapter 5: although the direction of the ascendant to the (natal) trine of Mercury had already perfected the year before, Mercury returning partially to its natal position in Libra while the ascendant was still in the same terms in Aquarius reactivated the direction, indicating another positive event related to writing and scholarship. Mercury was also made more fortunate by its applying sextile with Venus (divisor of the ascendant and ruler of the midheaven), which likewise cast an aspect into the terms of the directed ascendant.

As a final demonstration from this nativity (for now) of the importance of transiting planets casting aspects into terms activated by direction, let us consider the revolution at age 35 (figure 7), in which the native secured a prestigious research fellowship in a highly competitive setting. The ascendant was directed through the terms of Mars at 20°–25° Aquarius, indicating a number of health problems in

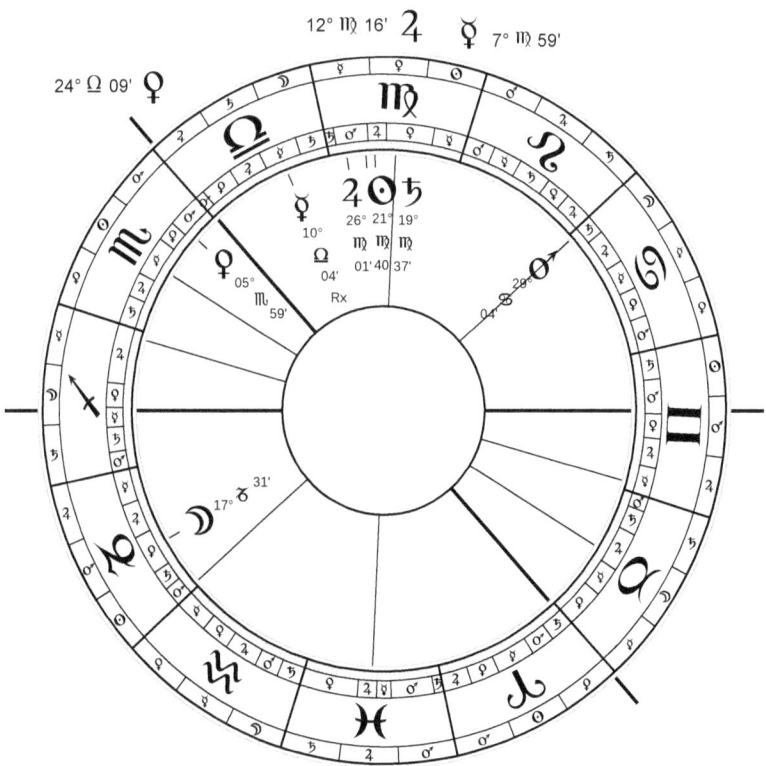

Figure 7: Nativity J with transits at revolution 35.

82   ANNUAL PREDICTIVE TECHNIQUES

this year; but what concerns us here is the trine aspect cast by Venus, ruler of the midheaven, into those terms from a position of dignity in its own domicile and terms. It is also relevant that the midheaven was being directed through the terms of Jupiter (0°–12°) in Sagittarius, and that Jupiter as divisor was not only about to make a heliacal rising, but was also received by Mercury in the latter's domicile/exaltation. Mercury further cast an aspect into the terms of the directed midheaven.

A double accident

As seen from the foregoing examples, planets aspecting the terms of a directed significator at the revolution of the year are important, but so

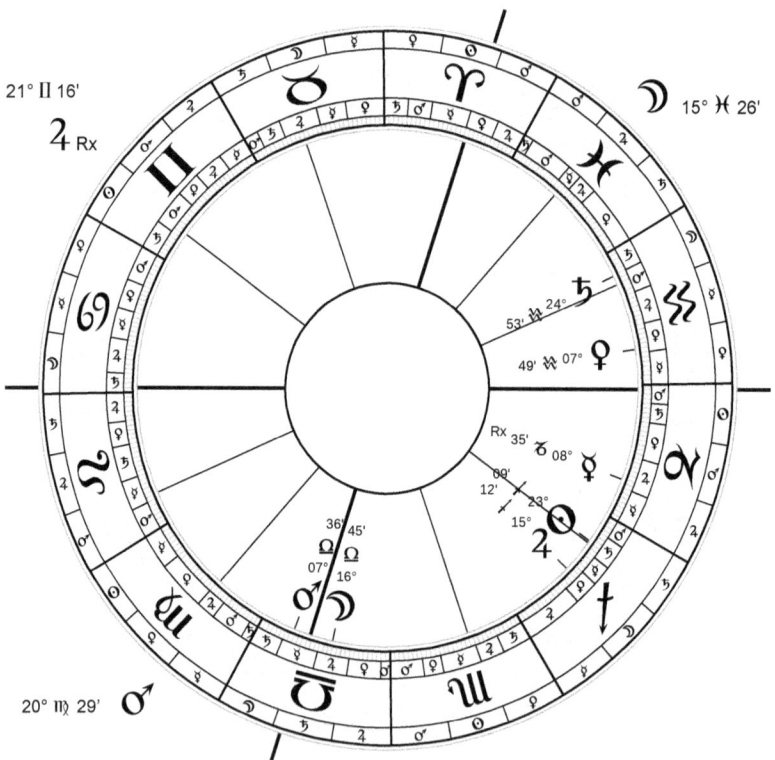

Figure 8: Nativity A with transits at revolution 77.

are the condition and aspect configurations, if any, of the ruler of those terms (the divisor). If both these indications agree, the results are all the more certain.

Figure 8 is the nativity of an elderly man who at age 77 had the misfortune to break first one leg and then, some weeks later, the other. The ascendant in that year was directed through the terms of Jupiter, ruler of the sixth house of illness and injury, at 17°–21° Virgo. It did not meet with any natal promissor, but Mars at the revolution of the year was both transiting those terms partilely on the directed ascendant *and* forming a close, mutually applying square with Jupiter. Moreover, the Moon (ruler of the ascendant and universal significator of the body) was applying to Mars by opposition – a configuration made worse by the facts that the Moon was waxing and the revolution took place by day, both sect factors making Mars more malefic. The divisor (Jupiter) being retrograde and all three planets occupying double-bodied signs indicated a repeated event.

We thus see how transits at the time of the revolution can combine with directions to indicate events during the year ahead with greater detail and certainty. In the next chapter we go on to examine the interactions between transits and another classical predictive technique: annual profections.

Endnotes
1. Commentary on Dan. 2.2, transl. Sela 2014: 6.
2. See *Astr. Gall.* XXII 3,6, transl. Holden 1994: 88 ff.

7
Annual Profections and the Ruler of the Year

HAVING LOOKED AT the interactions between the *universal* chronocrators – that is, the divisors and promissors of directions – and the transits at the time of the revolution, we now turn our attention to the *annual* chronocrators. Readers familiar with the *daśās* of Indian astrology, or with similar systems such as the Hellenistic decennials or the *fardār* periods ('firdaria') of medieval Arabic and European astrology, may find it useful to think of a universal chronocrator as the ruler of a major period (*daśā* or *mahādaśā*), within which each year of life functions as a subperiod (*antardaśā* or *bhukti*).

The ruler of the year: Arabic versus Tājika models
Arabic-language works on annual predictions typically follow Ptolemy in identifying the domicile rulers of the annual profection at the time of the revolution (that is, the birthday) as chronocrators. Specifically, the domicile ruler of the annual profected ascendant is designated *ruler of the year* (with an Arabicized Persian term, *sālkhudā*) – although Abū Ma'shar does occasionally seem to lean towards the view of Vettius Valens, described in Chapter 4 above, that a planet occupying the sign of the profection is more important than its ruler.[1] In fact, Valens includes not only natal placements but also, secondarily, planets transiting that sign at the time of the revolution. Personally, I find that although a *natal* planet in the sign of the profection will often have a say, planets *only* found there in the revolution – and not also ruling the

year or configured with the ruler of the year – have little or no bearing on events during the year in question. I also agree with the majority view that the most consistently relevant indicator of events is the *ruler of the profection sign*.

The Indian Tājika astrologers likewise attach much importance to the ruler of the profected sign (which they call the sign of the *munthahā* or *munthā*, from the Arabic *muntahā* 'arrived at the end, finished'); but they make a distinction between it and the final ruler of the year. This final ruler is selected from among five candidates according to a somewhat complex procedure (similar to the selection of a hyleg or main significator of life), of which Tājika authors give slightly different versions.[2] The five possible candidates are:

1. The domicile ruler of the profected ascendant (*munthahā*)
2. The domicile ruler of the ascendant of the revolution
3. The (primary) triplicity ruler of the ascendant of the revolution
4. The domicile ruler of the luminary of the sect in the revolution
5. The domicile ruler of the ascendant in the nativity

By Tājika rules, the final ruler of the year should be a planet aspecting the rising sign of the revolution, if at all possible. If several candidates aspect the rising sign, preference is given to the planet that is strongest and/or has the greatest number of testimonies, that is, comes up the most times in the list of critera. As this model makes use of triplicities and sect, concepts not present in pre-Islamic Indian astrology, it seems likely to be derived from some as yet unidentified Perso-Arabic source. However, I find the simpler approach – considering the ruler of the profected ascendant as the overall ruler of the year – to work reliably, and that is the approach that will be used below.

Discrete or continuous profections?

Modern practitioners of traditional astrology are sometimes divided over the question of whether to regard profections as a *continuous* motion at the rate of thirty ecliptical degrees a year (corresponding to 2°30′ per month, or 1° in just over twelve days) or as a *discrete* motion, where the ascendant or other profected point makes a quantum leap of one sign once a year, at the time of the revolution. Although the earliest preserved source that *explicitly* describes the continuous nature of profections is the work of ʿUmar ibn al-Farrukhān aṭ-Ṭabarī in the eighth century, in my opinion the two perspectives are actually compatible and may have coexisted from the earliest times of the technique.

The way I regard profections is analogous to tracking the transit of a planet: the motion of a profected point (the most important of which is the ascendant) is continuous, but its 'freeze-frame' position at the time of the revolution still carries special meaning, putting its stamp on the year to come and giving the domicile ruler of that sign authority over the entire year. The continuous profected motion may – again, just like a transit – be used as a timing technique *within* a year, and will be discussed in Chapter 9.

How profections relate to directions

The influence of a divisor and/or promissor is filtered through, or managed by, the ruler (or lord) of the year, which will either reinforce or modify it. The ruler of the year also adds detail to the interpretation, but cannot wholly override the universal chronocrator. Sahl ibn Bishr in the early ninth century cites this simile from his senior contemporary Māshāʾallāh:

> And know that the lord of the division is like a tender [of sheep], and the lord of the year like a hireling; so if the

tender committed himself to his sheep in a powerful way, the hireling would have no power to harm the sheep.³

Having said that, the annual profection can be interpreted in much the same way as the direction of a significator through the terms. The ruler of the year is analogous to a divisor, and any planets occupying the sign of the profection are analogous to promissors. Likewise, the placement of the ruler of the year by transit at the time of the revolution, and its configurations with other planets at that time, are of great importance for determining the results of the coming year.

Naturally, the most striking effects are observed when all levels of the predictive hierarchy – directions, profections and transits – agree. To illustrate, let us make an exception to our general rule and look at a 'celebrity' nativity which may already be familiar to some readers in connection with annual profections, as it has often been used by astrologer Chris Brennan to demonstrate the technique: that of Lisa Marie Presley (figure 9).⁴ Brennan particularly focuses on the fact that Presley came into her inheritance of approximately one hundred million dollars on turning 25 years old. At that time she, like everybody else at age 25, moved into a second-sign profection year; and the second sign from the ascendant in Presley's nativity (sidereally speaking, Leo) contains a well-placed, diurnal Jupiter, signifying wealth. Indeed, by quadrant division, Jupiter is partilely conjunct the second house cusp.

But why did this enormous increase in wealth occur at age 25 and not at 13, 37, or any of the other years in which the profection of the ascendant reached Leo? From the perspective of Ptolemy's predictive hierarchy, the reason is clear: profections only reinforce or modify the effects of directions. And the direction that perfected in Presley's nativity on or around her twenty-fifth birthday was a major one: the Sun – which, in addition to ruling the second house, is both the luminary of the sect (a major significator of the native's fortunes)

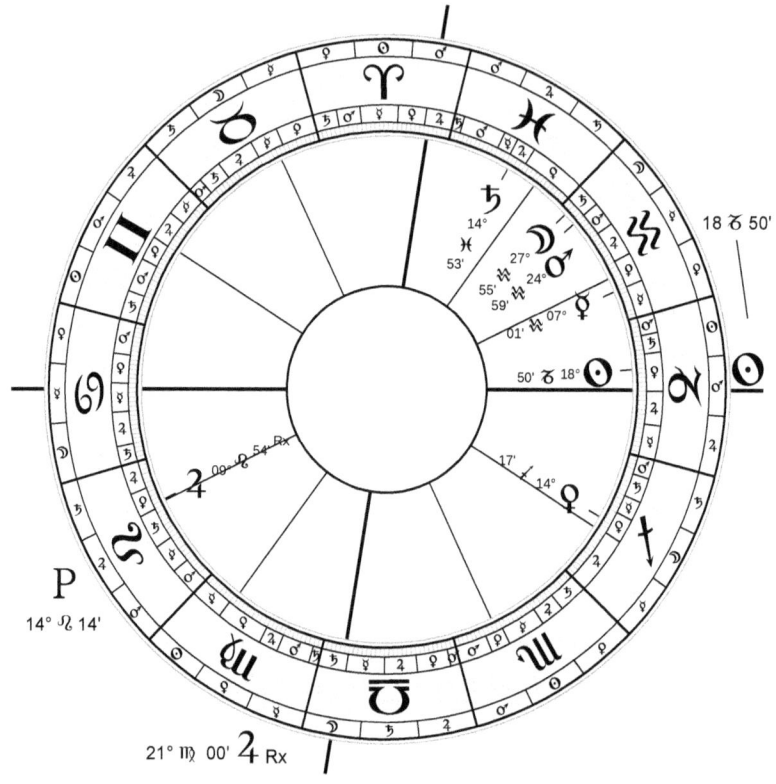

Figure 9: Lisa Marie Presley's nativity with transits at revolution 25 (annual profection of the ascendant marked with P).

and the chief significator of the father in a day birth – was directed to the opposition of Jupiter in that house. Incidentally, this demonstrates what was said in Chapter 6: an opposition with latitude fundamentally means that the significator and promissor are on the same horizon, as it were, and is not necessarily bad. The profection to Leo, ruled by the Sun and occupied by Jupiter, activated the same two planets, thus reinforcing their indication of wealth (Jupiter in the second house) from the father (the Sun). As a final touch, the directed Sun-Jupiter contact was repeated by transit at the time of the revolution, the two planets forming a close and mutually applying trine.

A double accident revisited

For another example of indications being reinforced by the same planets acting as both universal and annual chronocrators, let us revisit the nativity of the elderly man who broke both his legs as discussed in Chapter 6 (p. 82). As he was 77 years old at the time, the profection of the ascendant had completed six rounds of the zodiac already (at age 72) and was now in Sagittarius in the natal sixth house, making Jupiter ruler of the year (figure 10). Because Jupiter was also the divisor of the ascendant (which was directed to 20° Virgo, in the terms of Jupiter), the affliction befalling Jupiter from the applying square with Mars in transit makes its impact felt on both levels, thus confirming the unfortunate event.

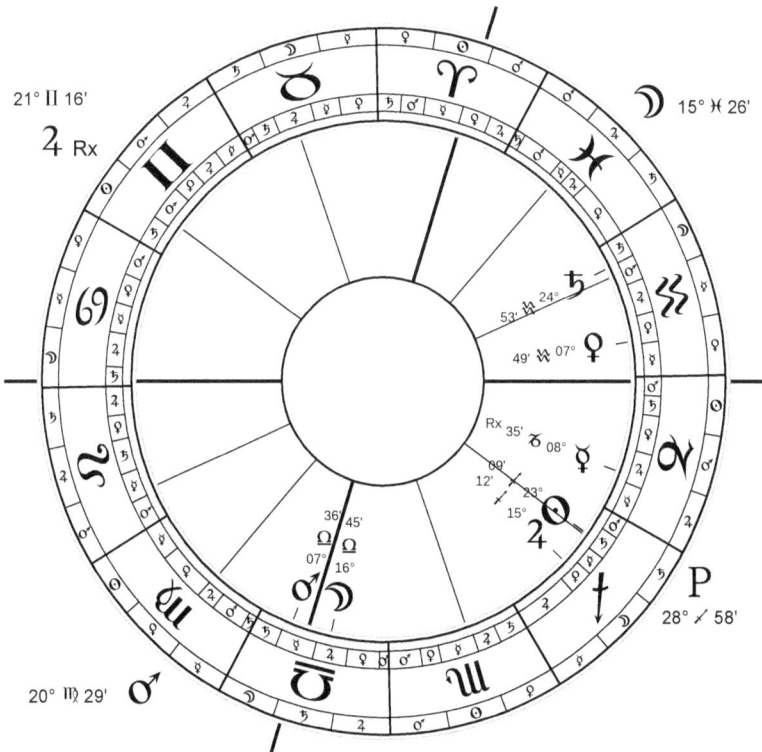

Figure 10: Nativity A with transits at revolution 77.

In both these cases we also see the profection sign itself containing a house with appropriate associations: in Presley's nativity, the second house of finances; in that of the elderly man, the sixth house of illness and injury. Although this is quite a common pattern, from a conceptual point of view such house connections belong, in my opinion, to a second tier of interpretation. The profection to Leo in Presley's chart primarily activates the Sun (ruler of Leo) and Jupiter (occupying Leo). These planets in turn give the results indicated by their natures, house rulerships and positions. Making this distinction is not mere sophistry: a ruler of the year with *two* domiciles (such as Jupiter, which rules both Sagittarius and Pisces) may – depending on other factors, such as directions and the figure of the revolution – act in accordance with the houses falling in *either or both* of those signs. In other words, its action is not limited to the sign in which the annual profection falls.

Having made the point that profections are always subordinate to directions, let us nevertheless focus for the next few examples on the annual profection of the ascendant and the ruler of the year, to see just how much they can tell us about the salient events in a year *without* reference to the directions. The next chapter will then discuss how to integrate both directions and profections with the figure of the revolution, or solar return chart.

Repetitions and permutations

We begin by looking at three different years in a single nativity. The first and second of these include similar themes although the profected sign and ruler of the year differ, whereas the first and third (twelve years apart) share the same profected sign but with different results.

The native experienced two defining life events at age 34 (figure 11). One – the successful completion of his doctorate, setting him

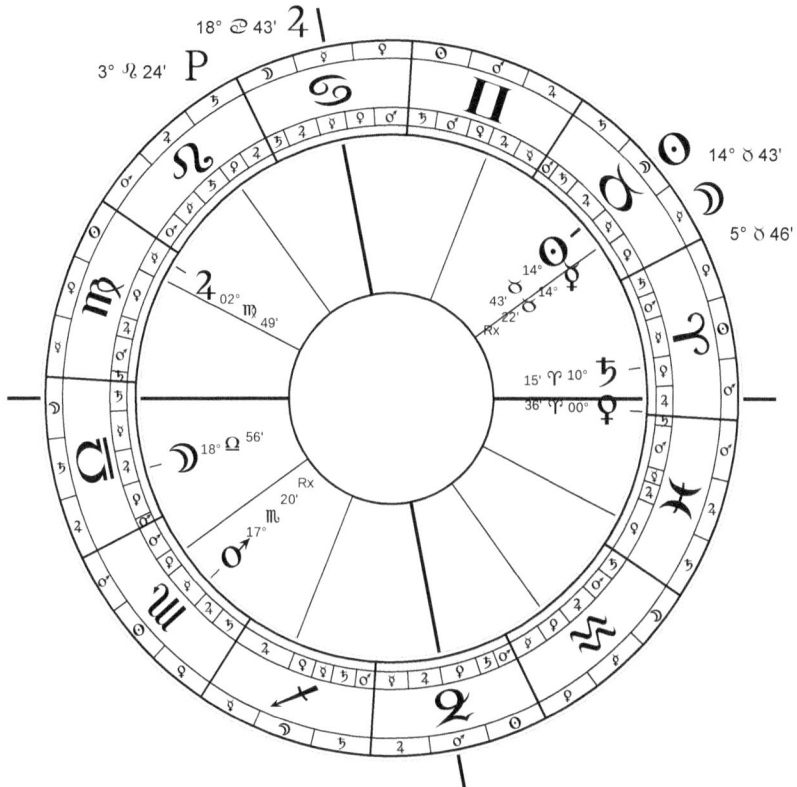

Figure 11: Nativity G with transits at revolution 34.

firmly on the path of his academic career – was positive; the other was negative, as his marriage of ten years broke down and he separated from his wife. The profection of the ascendant had reached Leo, making the Sun ruler of the year; neither the nativity nor the revolution has any planets in Leo. The Sun – which in the revolution had by definition returned to its natal position, reactivating its natal aspects – is in opposition to Mars, ruler of the seventh house of marriage, in the nativity. This clearly agrees with the theme of marital discord and separation, although it is not enough on its own to tell us why that event should take place at age 34 rather than some other Leo profection year (such as age 22 or 46). At the same time, the Moon, ruler of the tenth house of career, was exalted in the revolution, applying to a conjunction with the Sun as ruler of the year, while the Sun itself was applying by sextile to exalted Jupiter. This agrees well with the theme of professional success and honours.

The next year, age 35 (figure 12), the native's career was again furthered by the receipt of a major, three-year research grant. The profection in this year was in Virgo, with the Moon – ruler of the tenth house – in the profection sign in the revolution, closely trining the natal position of Mercury as ruler of the year. Natal Mercury is also partilely conjunct the Sun, ruler of the eleventh house of gain, which once more is returning to and thus reactivating a natal configuration.

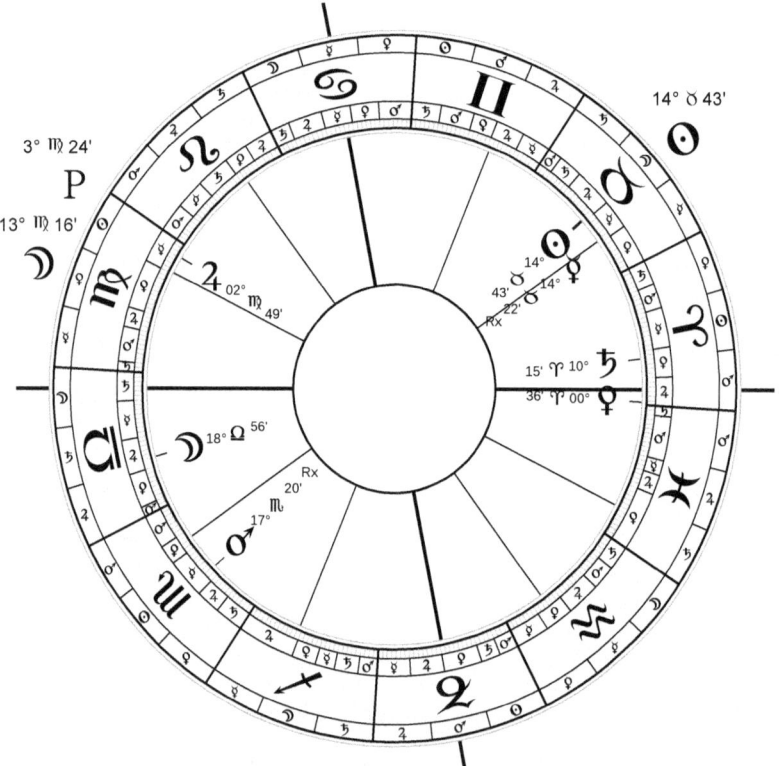

Figure 12: Nativity G with transits at revolution 35.

Although the profection signs differ, we thus see a repetition of the ruler of the tenth being favourably configured with the ruler of the year: in the first case by conjunction, in the second by trine from the sign of the profection itself.

Twelve years after the former revolution, at age 46, the profection again reached Leo (figure 13). No planets were present in that sign. The Sun as ruler of the year naturally returned to its original position opposite natal Mars; even more importantly, Mars itself repeated the configuration by closely conjoining the Sun and opposing its own natal position. In fact, the Sun in the revolution was separating from an opposition to Saturn while applying to the conjunction with Mars,

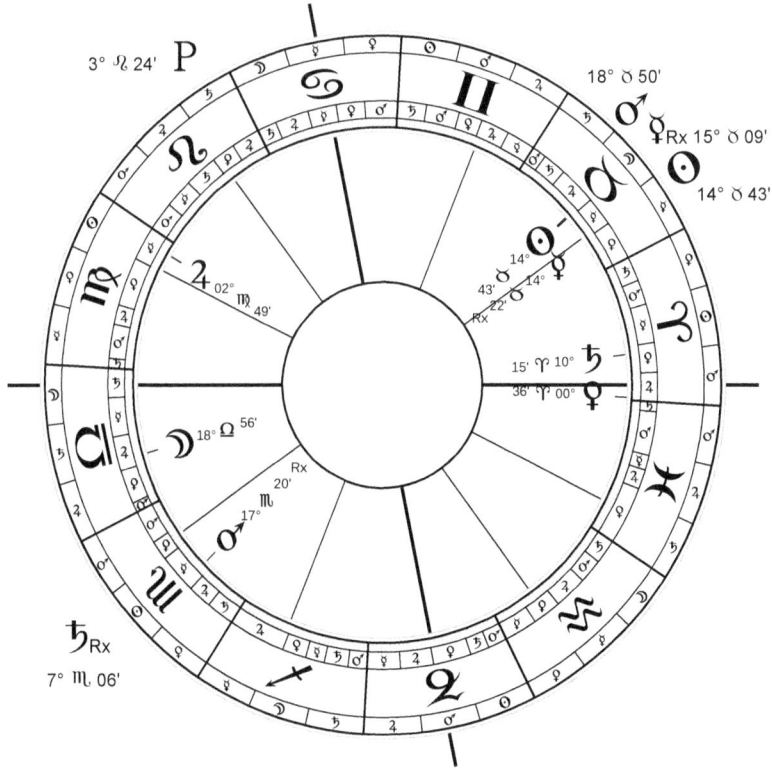

Figure 13: Nativity G with transits at revolution 46.

94   ANNUAL PREDICTIVE TECHNIQUES

a condition known as besiegement. As the Sun is the chief universal significator of the father in a day birth (and also, incidentally, rules the Lot of the Father), it is not surprising that the native lost his father in this year, when his eighth-house Sun was besieged by the malefics.

Comparing the two Leo profection years (figures 11 and 13), we can see that both unfortunate events agree with the Sun-Mars opposition (exacerbated in the second case by the positions of the malefics at the revolution), using simple astrological reasoning: the seventh house relating to marriage, the eighth house to death; the Sun signifying the father; Mars being a malefic, more so in a diurnal nativity; the opposition aspect relating to conflicts. Yet the two events in themselves are very dissimilar. To determine with greater certainty which of the several possibilities will manifest in a given year, we need to include both the higher-level chronocrators – that is, the directions – and the figure of the revolution.

Two deaths

Another double illustration involving death is found in the nativity of figure 14 (discussed in a different context in Chapter 6), where Mars – the malefic contrary to sect – rules the fourth and eleventh quadrant houses and occupies its fall, right on the cusp of the eighth house of death. At age 28, the annual profection of the ascendant had reached Aries, housing the natal IC or lower midheaven (the cusp of the quadrant fourth house, signifying parents). There were no planets in Aries either in the nativity or in the revolution, but Mars as ruler of the year had returned to its sign of fall. In this year the native lost his mother.

The next time Mars ruled the year was at age 35, when the profection reached Scorpio. In that revolution (figure 15), Saturn was present in Scorpio, partially conjunct the degree of the profection

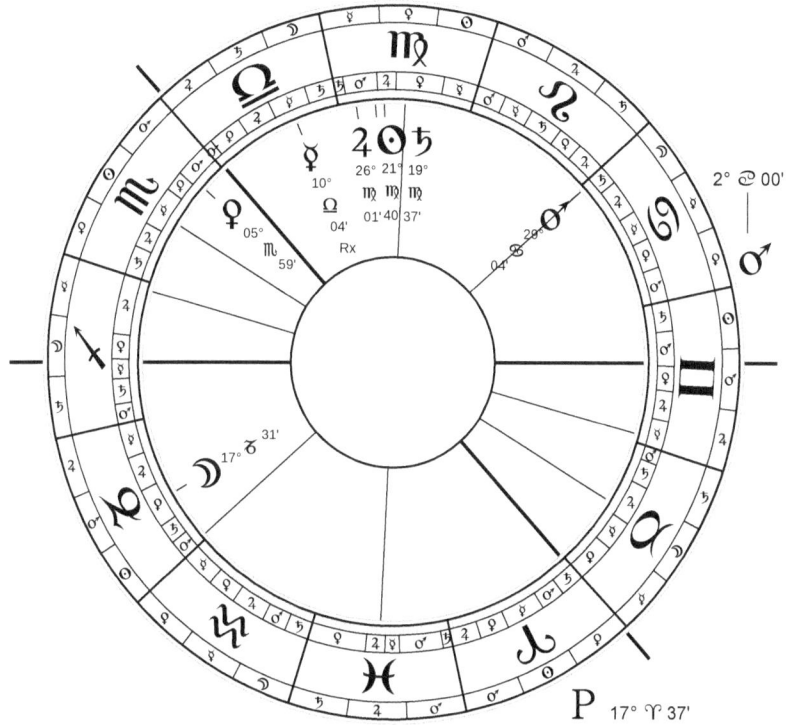

Figure 14: Nativity J with transits at revolution 28.

(which of course is the same degree as that of the natal ascendant), so that both malefics were activated by profection. In this year the native lost a close friend, signified by the eleventh house.

It is important to understand that these indications would not have been enough to predict death with any degree of certainty. The profection and ruler of the year agreeing with an event – or at least not obstructing it, if the event is indicated by chronocrators at a higher level – is a *necessary* but not a *sufficient* condition for that event taking place. Before predicting a major event, particularly of an unpleasant nature (if the ethics of the situation seem to permit predicting it at all), it is best to make sure that it is indicated on every level of the predictive hierarchy: directions, profections and the figure of the revolution.

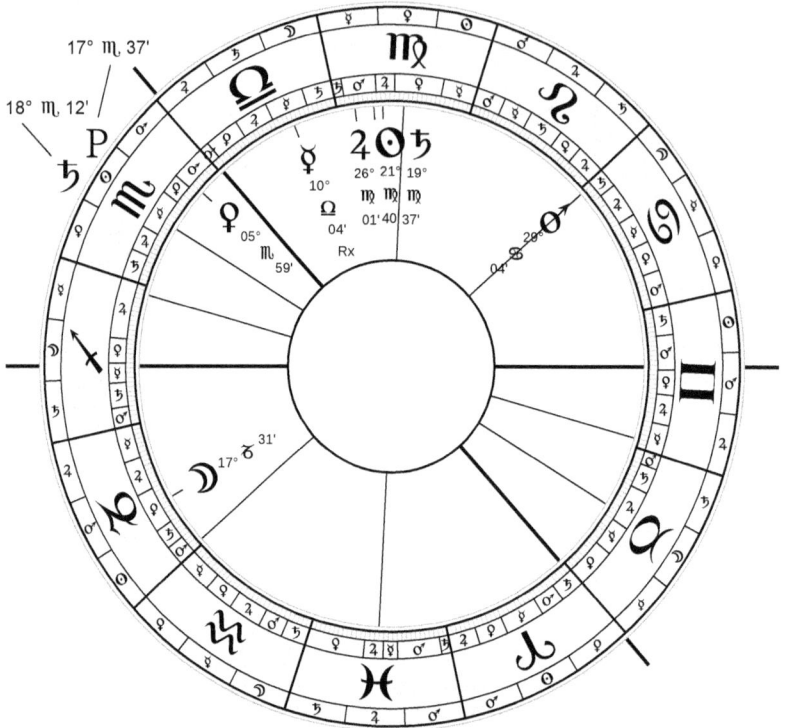

Figure 15: Nativity J with transits at revolution 35.

Rulers and occupants

As noted above, I agree with Ptolemy and most medieval authors in giving more weight to the ruler of the profection sign (that is, the ruler of the year) than to planets located in it. Nevertheless, planets occupying that sign will be activated to a greater or lesser extent, depending on other factors – most importantly, directions and transits at the time of the revolution. When the ruling and occupying planets differ significantly by nature or dignity – for instance, by being benefic and malefic, or in exaltation and fall, respectively – the year can be marked by events of highly varied or even opposite types.

These principles are illustrated by the youthful experiences of the native of figure 16. By way of background, at age 17–19, when the midheaven was first directed to the Sun and the Sun itself as the luminary of the sect was then directed to the body of Mercury, the native had aquired a diploma in computing and gone on to university, but soon lost interest and dropped out. This initial instability was presumably due to Mercury being placed on the cusp of the twelfth house, and possibly to the fallen Sun. (A decade later, the native resumed his studies with excellent results and is now pursuing his doctorate in the field of religious studies.) After the directed midheaven and Sun had both entered the terms of Venus, the native switched to studying music but did not do well, and when the midheaven was directed to the body of Saturn towards the end of age 22, he was forced to give it up as his funding was withdrawn. By this time the ascendant, too, had entered

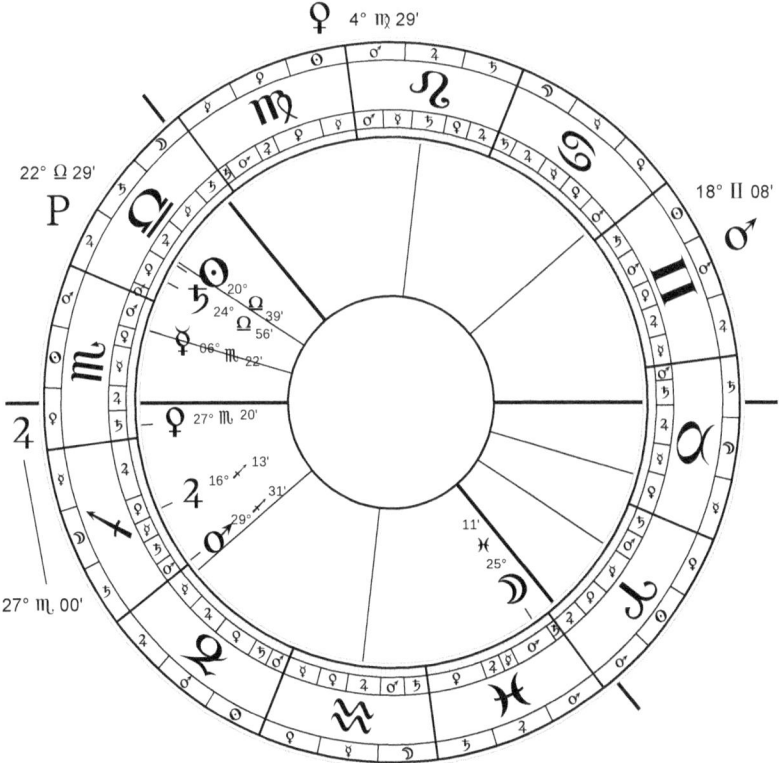

Figure 16: Nativity K with transits at revolution 23.

the terms of Venus, making that planet a highly prominent universal chronocrator.

Our current interest is in the annual profection of the ascendant in Libra at age 23 and in Scorpio at age 24. In the former of these, when Venus ruled the year in addition to being the divisor of both the angles and the sect luminary, Venus themes very naturally dominated. At the time of the revolution (figure 16), transiting Jupiter was partilely conjunct natal Venus, indicating beneficence and prosperity. On the other hand, Venus itself was transiting its sign of fall and approaching a square with Mars, suggesting eventual deterioration. In the nativity, Venus rules the sixth, seventh, tenth and eleventh houses, the last three of which have mainly positive significations, and these largely characterized the year. At its very beginning, the native initiated a romantic relationship (seventh house) which he described as 'semi-serious' and which lasted about a year. Overall, his life was more carefree, in the manner of Venus, and he was reunited with friends (eleventh house) with whom he had lost contact during his time at university.

Perhaps the most interesting feature of the year, however, was the fact that the native significantly increased his earnings by doing what he described as semi-skilled but low-quality jobs on building sites, and particularly that some of this work also involved his friends. Building work is not a signification of Venus but agrees very well with Saturn, which in the nativity rules the second house of finance and occupies the eleventh house of friends in Libra, the sign of the profection, where it is exalted. We have already seen that the midheaven, signifying work, was directed in this year to the body of Saturn. Although this was a malefic direction that coincided at first with the withdrawal of funding for the native's music studies, I have found Morin to be correct in teaching that a dignified malefic produces the good things signified by a house with effort and delays or in an imperfect way.[5] The exalted Saturn in the eleventh as promissor of the midheaven and activated by the annual profection in Libra was thus eventually able to improve the native's finances, in a Saturnian manner and in the company of friends.

In the following year (figure 17), the profection returned to the natal ascendant in Scorpio, making Mars ruler of the year. Because of its eight-year transit cycle, Venus too had returned to within two degrees of its natal position conjunct that ascendant, and was thus doubly activated by profection in addition to continuing to act as a universal chronocrator. We should thus expect both Mars and Venus themes to manifest in this year.

The predominant theme of the year was in fact one that is traditionally very much associated with Mars although it has been largely forgotten in modern astrology – namely, journeys or wandering. The native, whose home was in northern Europe, spent nearly eight months

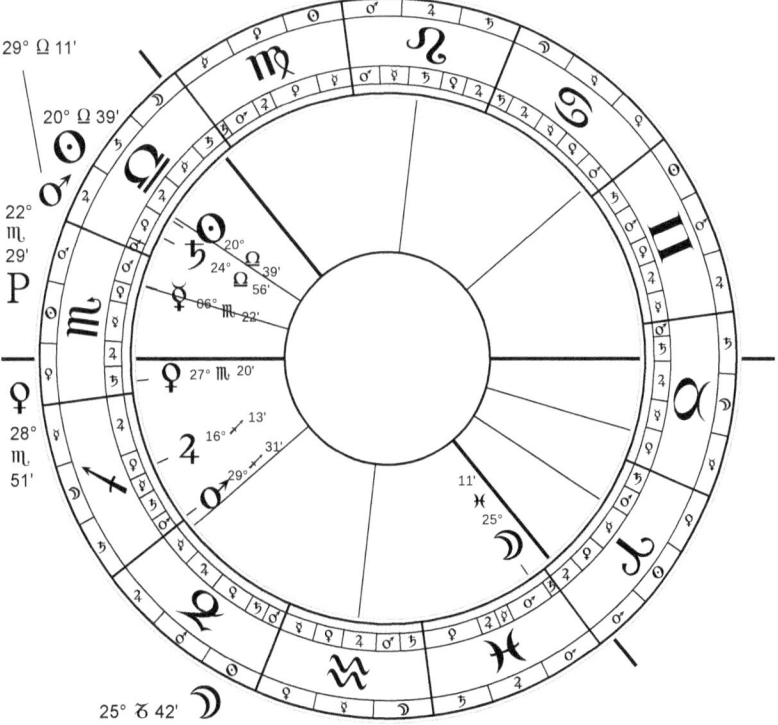

Figure 17: Nativity K with transits at revolution 24.

continuously travelling first in America and then in Australia. This universal signification of Mars is emphasized firstly by its applying conjunction with the Sun, ruler of the ninth house of the nativity (likewise associated with travel), and secondly by the fact that Mars is just about to change signs, a not uncommon indication of change – including changes of residence. But the well-known propensity of Mars for violence and accidents also manifested: some five months into the year, while travelling, the native was attacked and injured. The potential for such events is indicated in the nativity by the applying square between Mars and the waxing Moon (universal significator of the body) in a diurnal figure, and the same configuration is repeated in the revolution.

How, then, did the presence of Venus in the sign of the profection make itself felt? For one thing, like the building work of the preceding year, the travelling was done partly in the company of a friend; but more importantly, during his peregrinations the native began what was to become a six-year romantic relationship with a woman from a different country. Although the circumstances of their meeting – a foreign journey – were dictated by Mars as ruler of the year, the most lasting outcome of the year was therefore signified by Venus, which was activated in three ways: as a universal chronocrator (divisor), as occupying the profection sign in the nativity, and by returning to that natal place by transit at the time of the revolution.

We thus end this chapter as we began, by noting the necessity of combining profections with directions to gain a fuller understanding of their meaning and impact. The next and final step is to integrate both techniques with the figure of the annual revolution, or solar return chart.

Endnotes

1. See Dykes 2019b: 340.
2. For a full discussion of Tājika parameters for selecting the ruler of the year, see *Hāyanaratna* 5.8, transl. Gansten 2020: 457–465. For hyleg procedures, cf. Gansten 2009: 106–128.
3. Transl. Dykes 2019a: 314 (translation modified).
4. See, for instance, Brennan 2017: 539, 544, 550.
5. See *Astr. Gall.* XXI 2,2, transl. Baldwin 1974: 42 ff.

8
Judging the Revolution Figure (Solar Return Chart)

In the last two chapters we have looked at predictions made from the natal chart with its directions and profections. We have included the positions of the planets at the time of the annual revolution and seen how important they can be for accurately gauging the effects of these techniques; but until now we have considered them only as transits relative to the nativity. Now the time has come to include the complete revolution figure – in modern terminology, the solar return chart – in our judgements, employing the principles laid out in Chapter 5.

We begin by re-examining some of the examples discussed in Chapters 6 and 7 to see what additional or confirmatory information the revolution figures have to offer, before moving on to entirely new examples. As a result, this chapter will be the longest in the book. It is also arguably the most important, as it attempts to set out an integrated method of judging the overall results of any year of life. It concludes with an in-depth look at an extended period in the life of a single native, similar to the first example of Chapter 6, but this time employing the full range of techniques discussed rather than directions alone.

Another look at travel and romance

Let us begin with the last example of the preceding chapter, still fresh in our minds, of the native who spent most of age 24 travelling abroad – and, while doing so, initiated a long-term romantic relationship with a woman from another country. The two major chronocrators in that year were Venus, divisor of the ascendant, which had returned to its natal position (in the sign of the annual profection) within a couple of degrees, and Mars, which ruled the year.

With regard to Venus, we may note that it is powerfully angular in the revolution (figure 18), confirming its major impact in this year of life. More particularly, we see that Mars is not only a universal significator of travel and conjunct the Sun as ruler of the ninth house

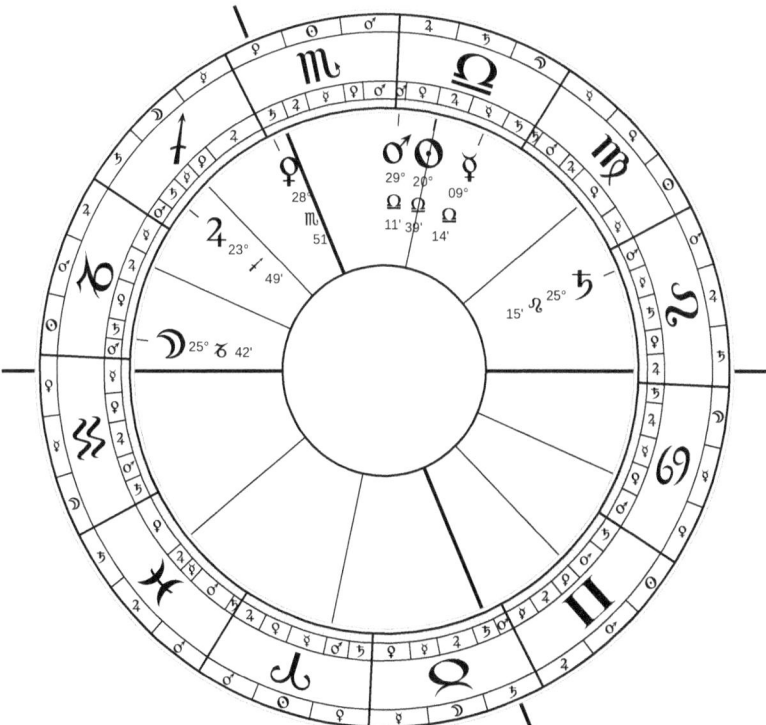

Figure 18: Native K, revolution 24.

of travel in the nativity: both planets also occupy the ninth house of the revolution (the Sun being partilely on the house cusp), strongly reinforcing that signification. This illustrates the principle of the ruler of the year managing or channelling the influence of higher-level chronocrators, as Venus, significator of love and ruler of the seventh house, manifested its results through the foreign journeys indicated by Mars.

Another look at honours and awards

We now return to the series of revolutions coinciding with professional honours in a single nativity discussed in Chapter 6 (pp. 77–82). The native (figure 19) made a name for himself with the publication of his

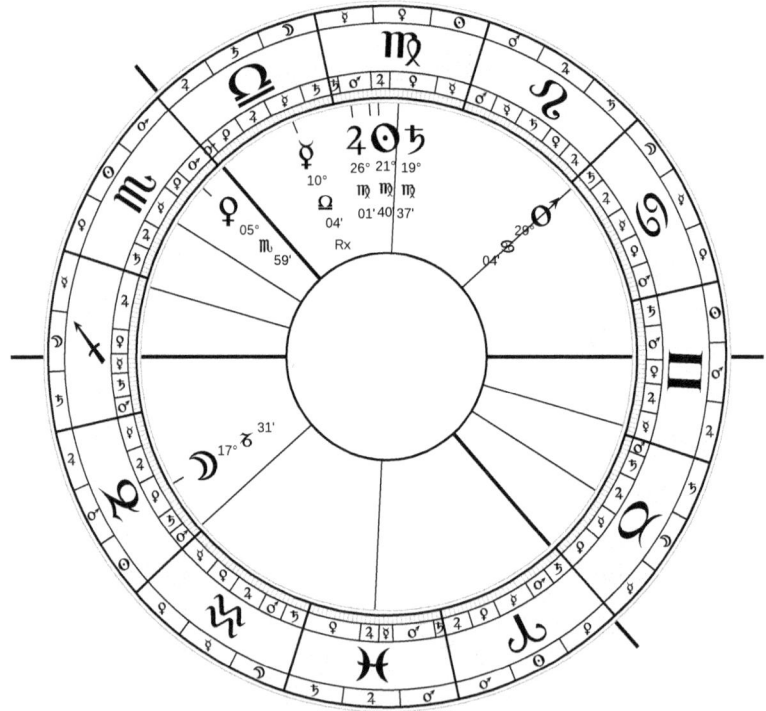

Figure 19: Nativity J.

first scholarly work at the age of 21, and we noted that this coincided not only with the direction of the ascendant through the terms of Venus (ruler of the midheaven in the tenth quadrant house), encountering the trine aspects of Saturn and the Sun, but also with both benefics – Jupiter and Venus – casting their aspects into those terms (14°–22° Capricorn) at the time of the revolution. To this we may add the fact that the annual profection had reached Virgo, making Mercury ruler of the year, which agrees well with the benefic influences manifesting through writing.

In the chart of the revolution (figure 20), we now see that Jupiter and Venus are not only highly dignified by exaltation and domicile, respectively, in addition to occupying their own terms, but are also angular: Jupiter in the first house, Venus in the fourth. This confirms

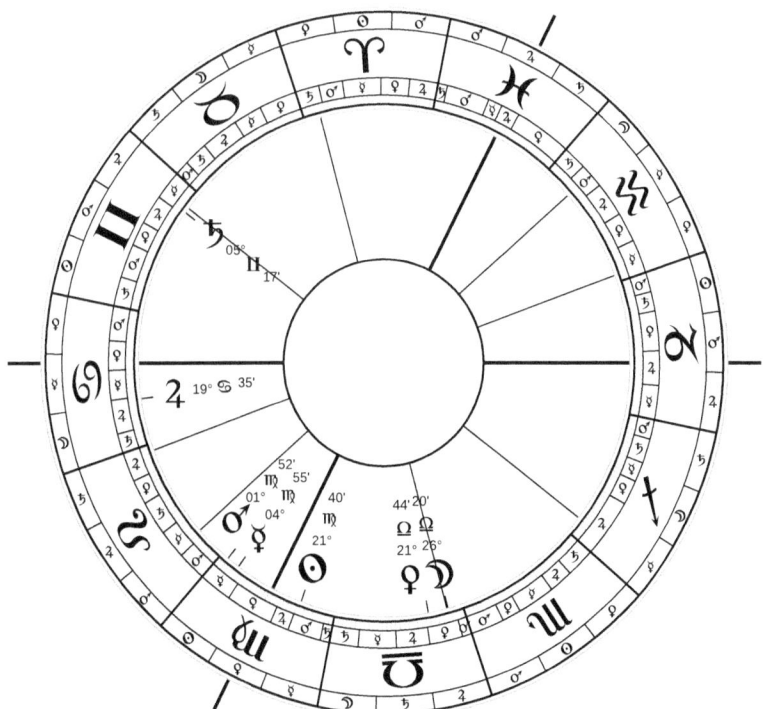

Figure 20: Native J, revolution 21.

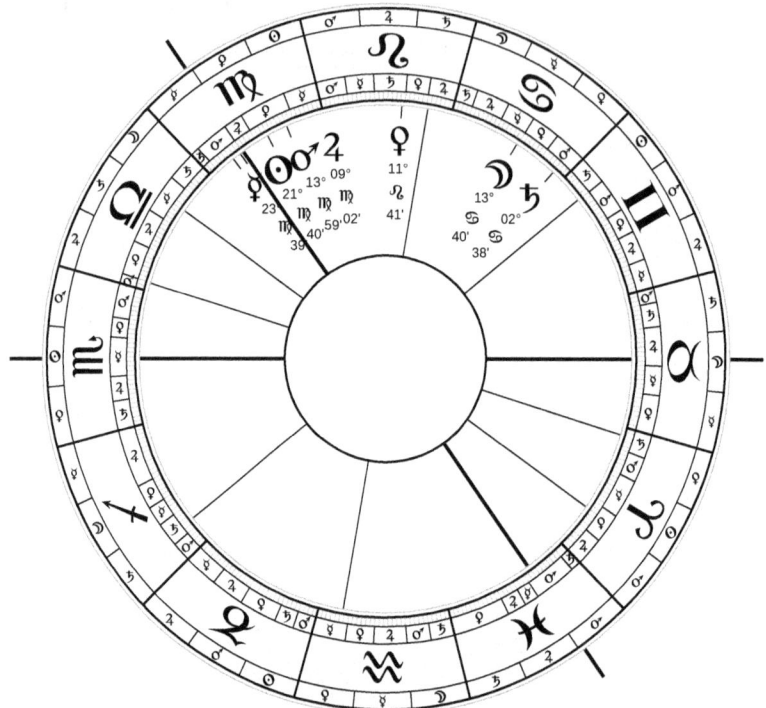

Figure 21: Native J, revolution 23.

their ability to act, that is, to manifest the fortunate potential indicated by their natures and dignities. The Sun as promissor had by definition returned to its natal position – thus repeating its trine aspect to the directed ascendant – and was similarly angular in the fourth house.

We next noted that the native received a royal academy award for his book at age 23, when the midheaven was directed to the sextile of the Sun in the terms of Jupiter (19°–24°) in Scorpio. In the revolution for that year (figure 21), the Sun as promissor is partilely conjunct the midheaven – as classical a configuration for 'honours from the king' as it is possible to get – and closely conjunct Mercury in its domicile/exaltation. This dignified and highly angular Mercury casts a trine aspect into the terms of the directed ascendant as well as a sextile into those of the midheaven.

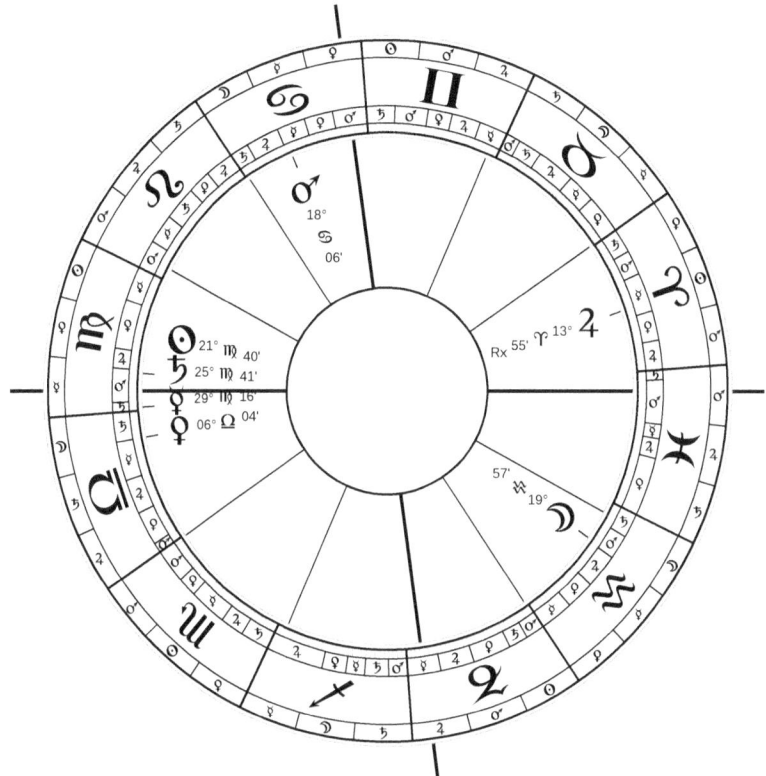

Figure 22: Native J, revolution 30.

At age 30 the directed ascendant perfected a trine with *natal* Mercury in the terms of Venus (7°–13°) in Aquarius, coinciding with the direction of the Sun to the conjunction of Venus with latitude. Mercury is a universal significator of learning and rules the seventh house of marriage; Venus is a universal significator of love and rules the tenth house of profession. In this year the native both married and obtained his doctorate. In the chart of the revolution (figure 22), Mercury and Venus are both highly angular in the first house, and occupy their respective domiciles; Mercury rules the year, and Venus is conjunct natal Mercury within a few degrees.

A third instance of Mercury trining the directed ascendant – in the revolution this time – occurred at age 31, with results very similar

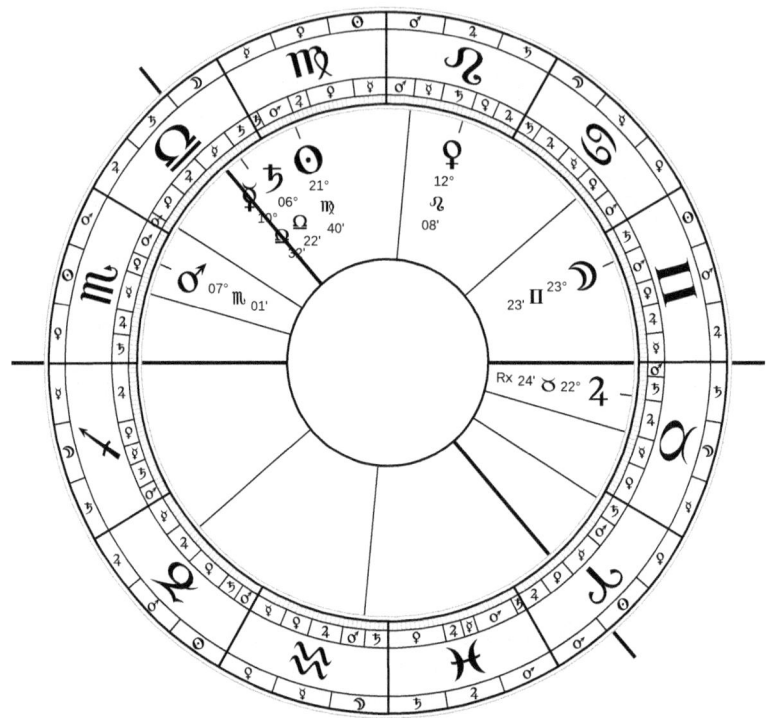

Figure 23: Native J, revolution 31.

to those at age 23 as one of the native's books earned him an award from a royal academy. In the revolution for that year (figure 23), Mercury has returned partilely to its natal position and is partilely conjunct the midheaven, from which it casts a trine aspect into the terms of Venus in Aquarius (still the division of the directed ascendant). As was the case at age 23, the tenth-house emphasis not only gives Mercury the power to act, but also confirms the nature of the benefic event. Comparing this figure with figure 22, Venus, despite being the divisor and also aspecting the directed ascendant, is much less conspicuous, whereas Mercury is as prominently placed as before or even more so. It is therefore not surprising that the significations of the promissor Mercury should correspond more strongly to events at age 31 than the significations of Venus.

JUDGING THE REVOLUTION FIGURE   109

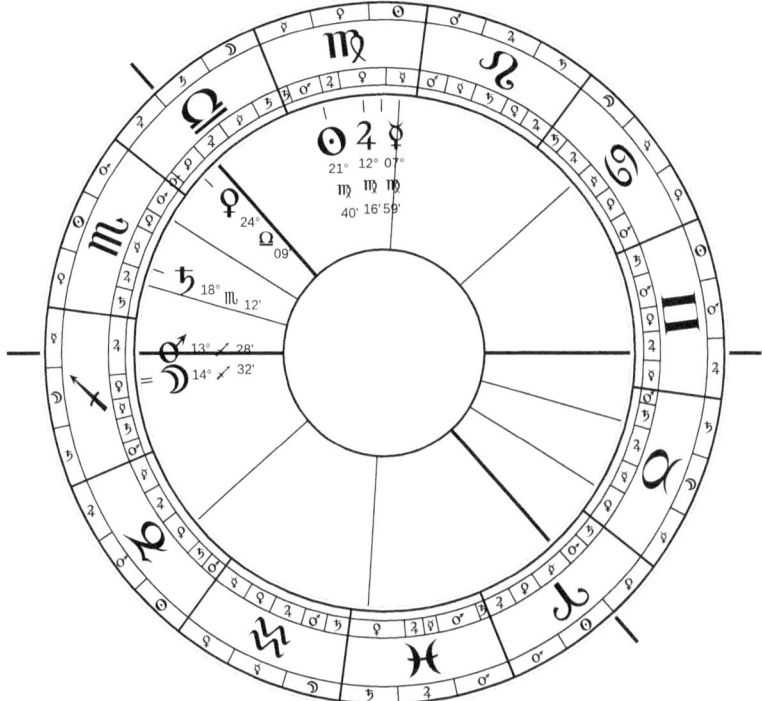

Figure 24: Native J, revolution 35.

The last year of this native's life that we examined in the context of honours and awards was age 35, when he was selected for a very competitive research fellowship. In the revolution for that year (figure 24) it is Venus, ruler of the natal tenth house, that is closely conjunct the midheaven in its own dignities of domicile and terms while casting a trine aspect into the terms of the directed ascendant, which where those of Mars at 20°–25° Aquarius. We thus see once again the pattern of a planet with the relevant significations, influencing the areas of the nativity activated by higher-level techniques, and enabled to do so in an effective way by being powerfully placed in the figure of the revolution. Having said that, however, there is a darker side to this particular revolution. We already touched on this in Chapter 7 and shall explore it further under our next heading.

Another look at loss of parents and friends

In the same nativity, as noted in Chapter 7 (p. 94), the annual profection of the ascendant had reached Scorpio at age 35, making Mars ruler of the year. At the same time, the ascendant was directed in this year through the terms of Mars (20°–25°) in Aquarius, so that Mars held double office as chronocrator. In the nativity (figure 19), Mars is in its fall on the cusp of the eighth house and rules the fourth and eleventh houses; in the revolution (figure 24), Mars is in the first house near the ascendant, indicating much power to act but also suggesting health problems. The latter are confirmed by Mars' tight configurations with the Moon (universal significator of the body and, in the nativity, ruler of the eighth house in the first) and Jupiter (ruler of the natal ascendant). Both configurations are separating, indicating that these problems had

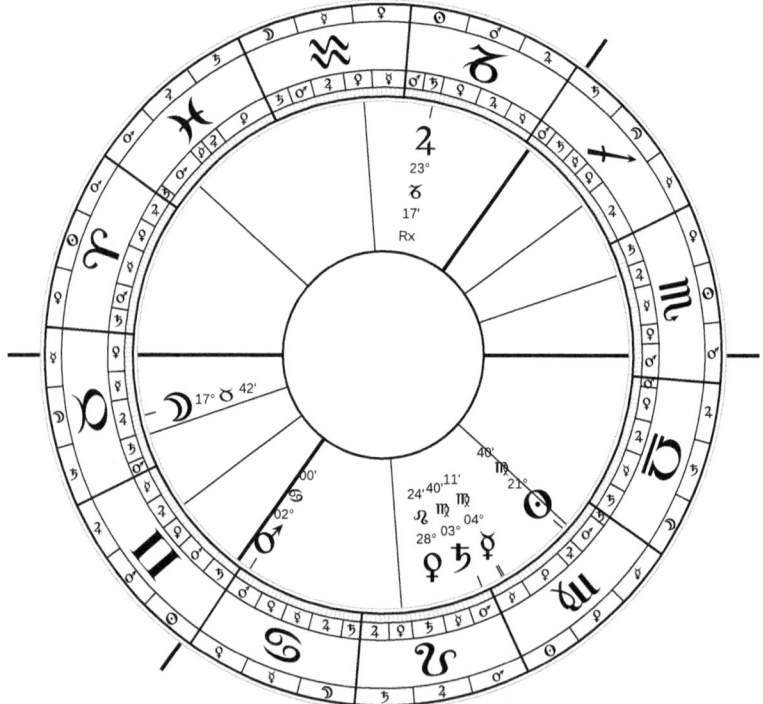

Figure 25: Native J, revolution 28.

already begun the previous year. That revolution, not shown here, had the Moon *applying* to the body of Mars, translating light from Venus as ruler of the year, and Venus itself applying by square to Saturn.

More traumatically, a close friend of the native died tragically and unexpectedly in this year, while another friend was mugged at knifepoint a week later. In addition to Mars ruling the eleventh house of friends in the nativity (and also in the revolution, although I attach less importance to that), we may note that Saturn is partilely conjunct the degree of the profection in the eleventh house of the revolution.

At age 28, as also discussed in the previous chapter (p. 94), Mars was likewise ruler of the year, as the annual profection had reached Aries. In that year the ascendant was directed to the opposition of Mars with latitude, once more making Mars a double chronocrator. In the revolution (figure 25), Mars has returned to its sign of fall and is strongly angular in the fourth house of parents, while also ruling the fourth house of the nativity. This was the year in which the native's mother died, also quite suddenly. The Moon was directed in the same year to the opposition of the Sun, to be followed by the opposition of Saturn with latitude.

Turning now to another nativity (figure 26) previously discussed in Chapter 7 (p. 90), we noted that the native lost his father at age 46. The annual profection of the ascendant had then reached Leo, making the Sun (universal significator of the father) ruler of the year. The Sun is natally in the eighth house, configured with Mars by opposition, and in the revolution (figure 27) this configuration is repeated by a close conjunction.

To these considerations we can now add that the ascendant was directed through the terms of Mars (0°–7°) in Scorpio, making Mars a joint chronocrator with the Sun and powerfully activating their configuration. Moreover, Saturn – ruling the natal fourth house of parents and conjunct the fourth house cusp of the revolution – was

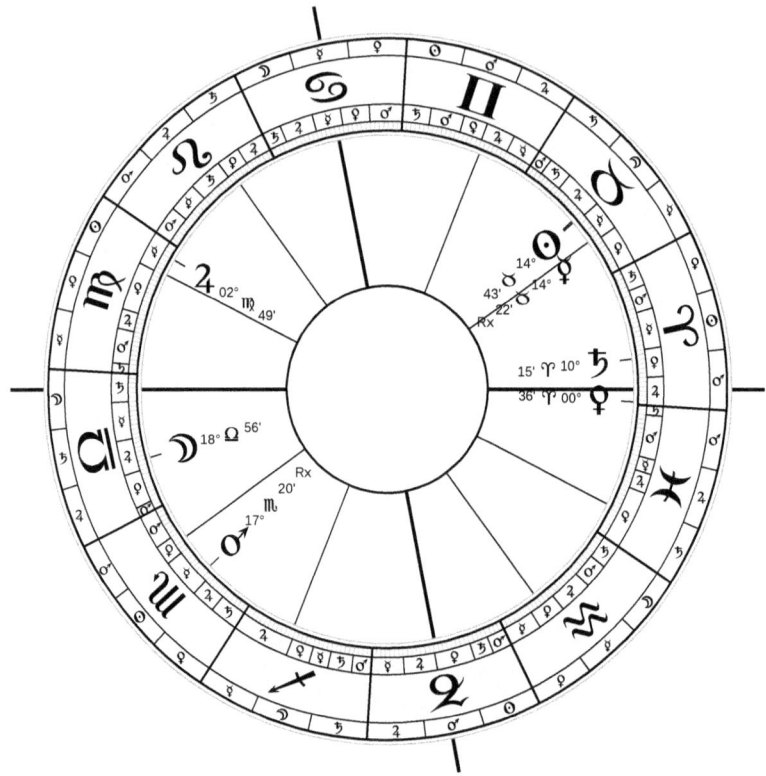

Figure 26: Nativity G.

just about to enter those terms by retrograde motion, in addition to aspecting the Sun/Mars conjunction in the tenth house. As will be discussed in Chapter 9, Saturn would play a crucial role in timing the event signified by these placements.

Conflicting indications

Our last re-examined example from Chapter 7 (p. 90) concerns the same nativity (figure 26) and illustrates Ptolemy's principle of fortunate events occurring in one area of life while another area is beset with misfortune. At age 34 the native made a major career advancement by completing his doctorate, but at the same time his marriage of ten years broke down. This, too, was a Leo profection year, making the Sun

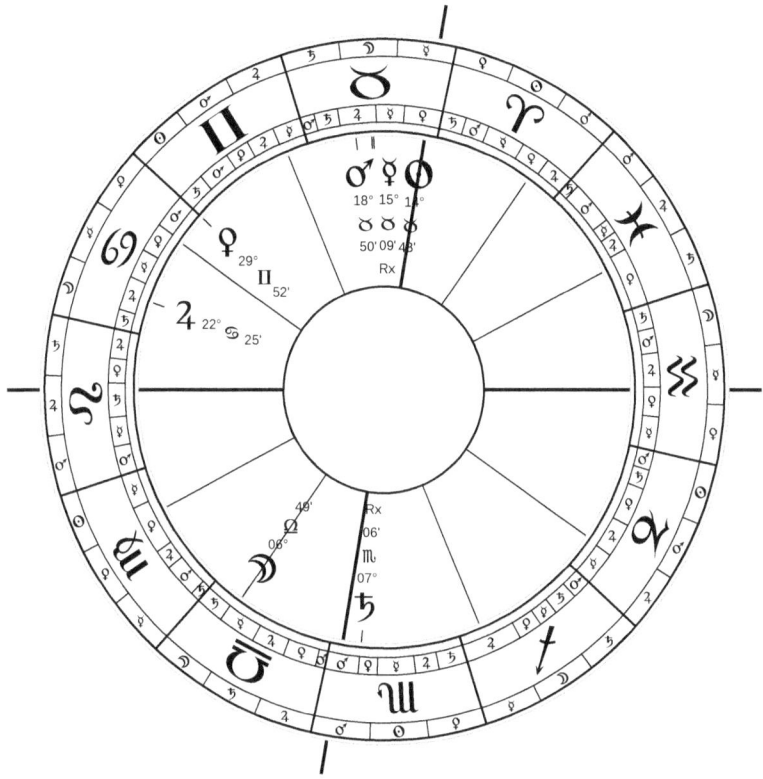

Figure 27: Native G, revolution 46.

ruler of the year and reactivating its natal opposition to Mars, ruler of the seventh house. The ascendant at this time was directed through the terms of Venus (21°–28°) in Libra, and the midheaven was in the terms of Mercury (18°–24°) in Leo, having recently perfected a sextile with the Moon, ruler of the tenth house in the first. In addition, the Moon itself was directed through the terms of Mercury (11°–19°) in Scorpio and was just about to perfect a conjunction with Mars *without* latitude (what I have called an 'aspect-point conjunction').

In the revolution (figure 28), we find Venus and Mercury – divisors of the ascendant and midheaven, respectively – conjunct in the tenth house and casting aspects into the directed terms of both angles (trines in the case of the midheaven). The Sun as ruler of the year is in the eleventh house, with the exalted Moon – ruler of the natal tenth house and promissor of the directed midheaven – applying to it by conjunction from the tenth. The Sun itself is applying by sextile to exalted Jupiter, above the horizon but still conjunct the ascendant degree within its own orb. These placements and aspects clearly point to a rise in status in this year, connected with the native's profession.

Simultaneously, however, Venus as divisor of the ascendant is afflicted by applying to the square of Mars, ruler of the natal seventh house placed in the seventh of the revolution. Mars also casts its other square aspect into the terms of the directed ascendant in late Libra. This emphasis on Mars and the seventh house strongly suggests marital

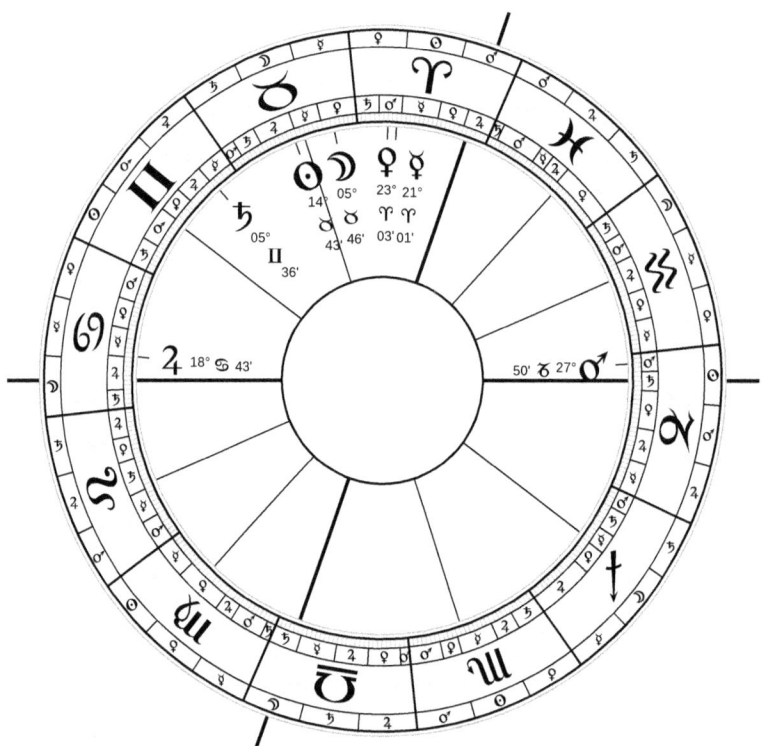

Figure 28: Native G, revolution at age 34.

conflict and separation. Venus in Aries being received by Mars may have prevented its more violent manifestations, but also confirms that Mars, which in addition holds the dexter end of the aspect and occupies its highest degree of exaltation, has the upper hand in the configuration.

Sometimes the conflicting indications may concern a *single* area of the chart or of the native's life, making prediction exceedingly difficult. One such instance related to the previous nativity (figure 19) was briefly discussed in my earlier book on directions. At that time I rather inclined towards Morin's practice of excluding the planetary terms altogether and compensating for the loss by using all planets (and house cusps) as potential significators, and my analysis of the directions

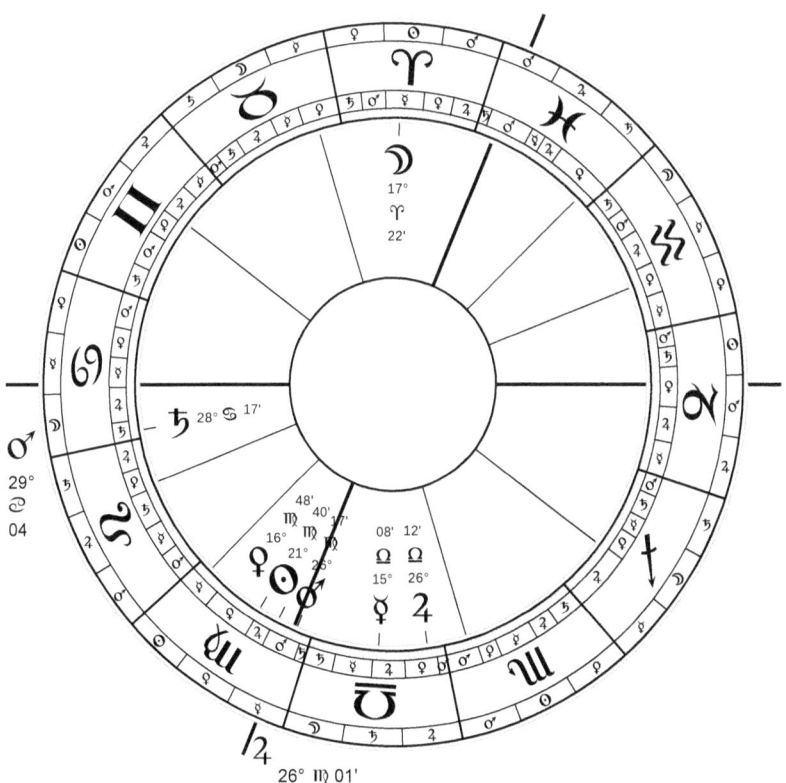

Figure 29: Native J, revolution at age 25 with natal placements outside the chart.

was made from that perspective. Over the past decade, however, I have gained great respect for the predictive usefulness of the terms and come to focus on the angles and luminaries as the most essential (though not the only) significators to be directed. Although I still believe the points made in my earlier analysis to be valid, I now consider some of them to be of only secondary importance.

The year in question was age 25, when the ascendant had just entered the terms of Mars (26°–30°) in Capricorn, simultaneously encountering the body of the Moon with latitude and the trine aspect of Jupiter. Jupiter was also the current divisor of the midheaven, and in the revolution (figure 29) it was present in the terms of Venus in Libra, through which the Sun – luminary of the sect – was directed. Natal Mars as well as revolution Mars, Jupiter and Saturn all cast aspects into the terms of the directed ascendant. The annual profection had reached Capricorn, making Saturn ruler of the year. All these planets were angular, as was the Moon (promissor of the ascendant).

What are we to make of such a confusion of indications? We may begin by attempting to sort them broadly into two classes:

Fortunate	Unfortunate
• Ascendant directed to the trine of Jupiter	• Ascendant directed through the terms of Mars
• Revolution Jupiter aspecting the terms of the directed ascendant	• Natal and revolution Mars aspecting the terms of the directed ascendant
• Revolution Jupiter present in the terms of the directed Sun	• Revolution Saturn aspecting the terms of the directed ascendant
• Midheaven directed through the terms of Jupiter	• Saturn ruling the year

The direction of the ascendant to the body of the Moon is more difficult to classify. In itself, the Moon is neither benefic nor malefic; it rules the eighth house of the nativity, suggesting some suffering, but in the revolution it occupies the tenth and applies next to Jupiter.

There is no denying the challenge inherent in judging cases of strongly mixed indications, but some definite statements can still be made. One such is that the sheer number of directions perfecting, and of the planets interacting with the directions in the revolution figure, signifies an eventful year. Secondly, powerful malefic and benefic indications being present simultaneously typically do not cancel each other out but rather result, where possible, in events of both types manifesting: success and failure, gain and loss, union and separation, and so on.

Various factors may contribute towards one or the other type of event predominating; but perhaps an even more important principle to note is that when an unfortunate event is indicated by the malefics, and the benefics involved are not numerous or powerful enough to prevent it, their significations will often show up as circumstances surrounding the event. Thus, Abū Ma'shar says that Jupiter participating by aspect when Mars is divisor, and being of poor condition (although this is not exactly the case here, Jupiter is outnumbered by the malefics), signifies problems caused by people of a Jupiter type: 'something detestable will affect him from administrators and the authorities, and it will impel him towards powerful people but they will be hostile towards him'.[1]

Abū Ma'shar's statement in fact accurately reflects some of the native's experiences in this year. In chronological order, the four main career-related events were: (1) A book the native had written was shortlisted for a prestigious award but did not win. (2) The native applied for a junior research fellowship, but his application was disqualified on what later proved to be incorrect grounds, as part of an intra-departmental power struggle. (3) The native was offered and accepted a seat in a government agency responsible for the development of science and scholarship. (4) The native made a second application for a fellowship equivalent to the first one and was successful. The year was thus ultimately one of success and honours, but with some initial disappointments and in the face of opposition 'from administrators and the authorities'.

With the clarity of hindsight, we may note that Saturn as ruler of the year forms a mutual reception with Jupiter (ruler of the natal ascendant and chronocrator of both angles as well as of the luminary of the sect), as they occupy each other's signs of exaltation while forming an applying aspect. While this factor may have been decisive, the mere prediction of both notable success (Jupiter) and much conflict (Mars) in this year, without stating definitely which would predominate, would still have constituted a perfectly valid and reasonably specific prediction.

One planet to rule them all

Although indications are not generally as tangled as in the case just discussed, directions often reflect the fact that life is a mixture of good and bad, some significators being under the influence of benefics while others are ruled by the malefics. But as Ptolemy notes, exceptions do exist:

> The subjects are unfortunate or fortunate in all respects at once, whenever either all or most of the directions are found in one and the same place, or if these are different, whenever all or most of the encounters occurring at the same times are similarly fortunate or unfortunate.[2]

Ptolemy speaks chiefly of encounters, that is, significators encountering the bodies or aspects of promissors as they move around the chart; but the influence of divisors is equally important. In the nativity of figure 26 above, starting from age 38, the ascendant, midheaven and Sun were all directed through the terms of Mars in Libra, Leo and Gemini, respectively. The Moon – which, although it is not the luminary of the sect, may reasonably be assumed to be the chief significator of life (hyleg) – was in the terms of Jupiter but had recently conjoined the body of Mars with latitude there.

Mars as the malefic contrary to sect is potentially the most harmful planet in the nativity, although tempered to some extent by the dignity of domicile. It rules the second house of finance and the seventh house of marriage, and age 38 in fact marked the beginning of a seven-year period of great financial difficulties for the native as well as prolonged legal and personal conflicts with his ex-wife, causing mental suffering and, eventually, physical ill health. Within this long period of misfortune, however, some years were still better than others. Unsurprisingly, the most fortunate years were those ruled by Jupiter, the benefic of the sect. Let us examine three of the years in this period, contrasting the two where Jupiter participated as ruler of the year with one in which the malefic influence was unmitigated.

In the revolution for age 38 (figure 30), when the ascendant had recently entered the terms of Mars (28°–30°) in Libra, we find Venus casting a trine aspect into those terms. As Venus occupies the twelfth house, this aspect by itself cannot be relied on to produce stable results; but it does alert us to the possibility of romance in that year of life – particularly as Venus was natally conjunct the cusp of the seventh house and Mars, the divisor, ruled it. The profection of the ascendant had reached Sagittarius, and Jupiter as ruler of the year was conjunct natal Mars in addition to their forming a close, applying trine with mutual reception in the revolution. In this year, the native began a long-term, live-in relationship which eventually matured into a second marriage. On account of Jupiter ameliorating the malefic influence of Mars, we

120   ANNUAL PREDICTIVE TECHNIQUES

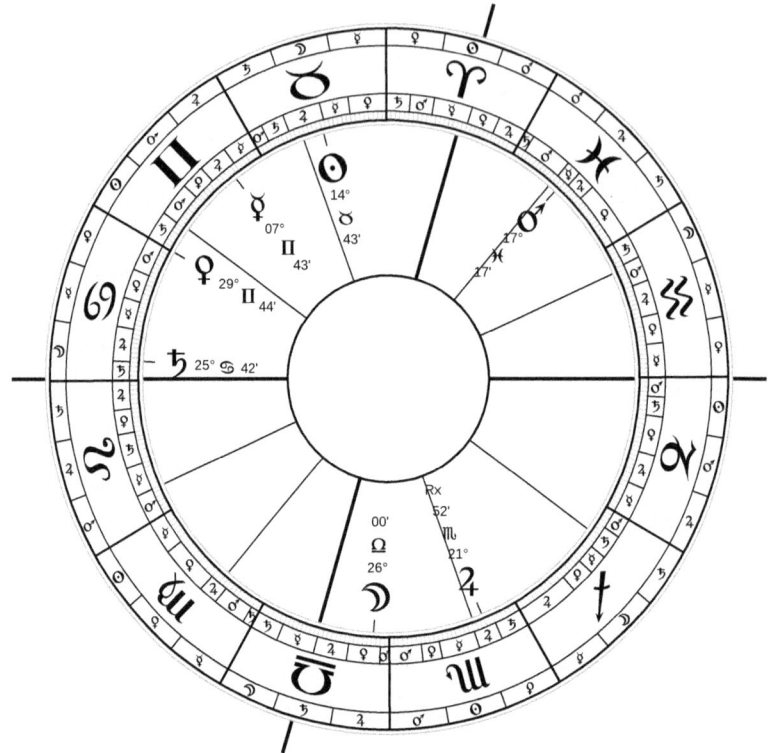

Figure 30: Native G, revolution at age 38.

thus find mixed indications for the seventh house this year: on the one hand, conflicts with an ex-spouse; on the other, a new relationship.

With regard to finances (second house), the situation was similar: although the native's employment came to an end, he was able for some time to secure additional income by private teaching. Another major event in this year was signified by the natal opposition of Mars with the Sun, ruler of the eleventh house of friends, which was naturally reactivated by the Sun returning to its natal degree. The event in question was a serious rift that occurred between the native and one of his closest friends and colleagues, involving another ex-partner of the native (seventh house again) and lasting several years.

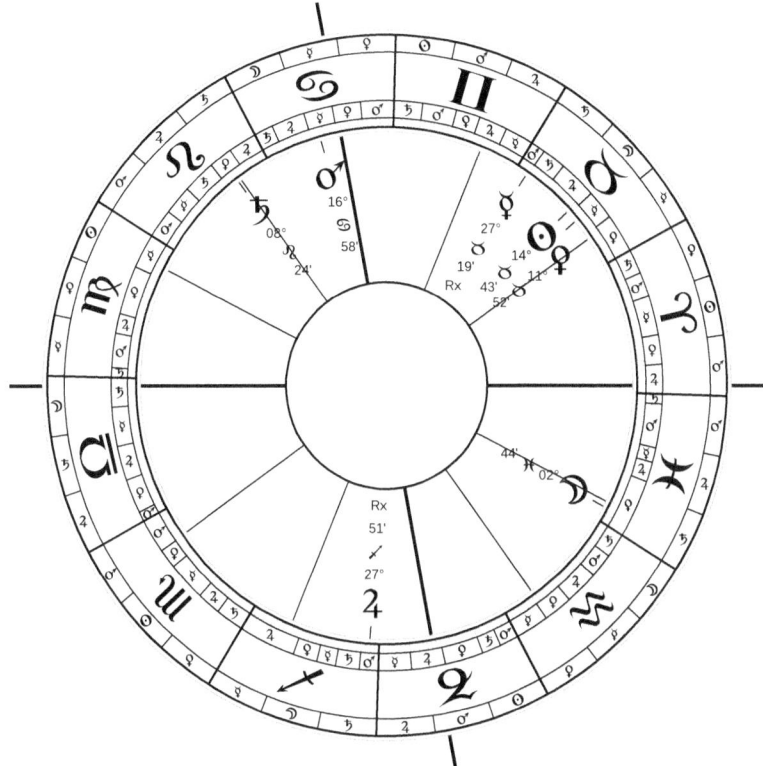

Figure 31: Native G, revolution at age 39.

In the revolution for age 39 (figure 31), Mars is prominent by angularity and made more malefic by occupying its fall (in addition to being occidental and contrary to the sect), while Saturn rules the year, which is thus dominated entirely by the malefics. Saturn, ruler of the year, rules the fourth and fifth houses of the nativity and is placed on the cusp of the eleventh house (thus opposite the fifth-house cusp) of the revolution. Its natal configuration with Venus, ruler of the ascendant, is repeated in the revolution as a separating square, with Venus placed in the eighth house. The most prominent event of this particular year of life was the native's ex-wife absconding with their children, thereby separating them from the native and initiating

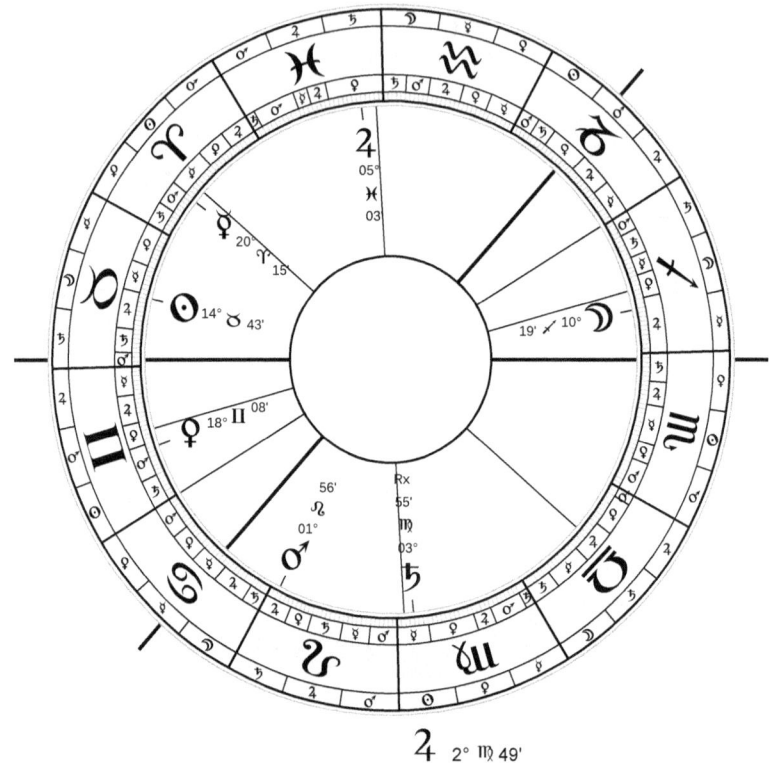

Figure 32: Native G, revolution at age 41 with natal placements outside the chart.

a drawn-out legal conflict. A second major event was the native himself moving house, arguably signified by the same separating aspect (the fourth house signifying the home). Both events can thus be related to the ruler of the year; the more unfortunate event was also causally linked with the significations of Mars, the predominant chronocrator (divisor and promissor) of the broader period.

The next time a benefic took up office as a chronocrator was at age 41, when the annual profection reached Pisces. In the revolution for that year (figure 32), the malefics still predominate, with Mars as divisor of both the primary angles casting a square aspect into the terms of the directed ascendant, which were now those of Mars (0°–7°)

in Scorpio. Saturn is also closely conjunct the natal position of Jupiter, the ruler of the year, and aspects revolution Jupiter with a separating but still tight opposition. Jupiter itself is, however, particularly well placed: of the sect, direct, oriental of the Sun, in the eleventh house (where it rejoices), and in dignity of domicile. The Moon in the seventh house also connects Jupiter with Venus by a translation of light, and Jupiter casts a trine aspect into the terms of the directed ascendant. Although the native's external circumstances did not change substantially in this year, it was marked by two fortunate events: first, his wedding (Venus, seventh house) to his partner of the past three years, and second, his reconciliation (Jupiter) with his estranged friend (eleventh house).

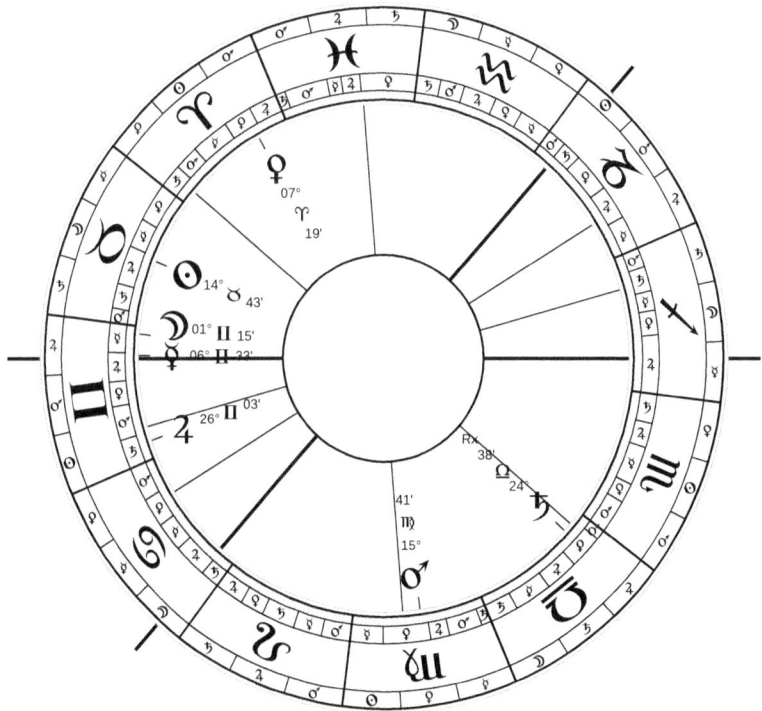

Figure 33: Native G, revolution at age 45.

Although the direction of the *ascendant* through the terms of Mars (in Libra and Scorpio) lasted a full thirteen years, the first chink of light appeared about halfway through that period, as the directed *midheaven* left the terms of Mars in Leo and entered those of Mercury (0°–7°) in Virgo, applying to the conjunction of Jupiter. It was another year and a half, however, before these chronocrators were sufficiently well-placed in a revolution to support a major change in the native's fortunes.

At the age of 45, the annual profection had reached Cancer, making the Moon – natal ruler of the tenth house placed in the first – ruler of the year. In the revolution (figure 33), the Moon (which has a good deal of southern latitude) is just below the horizon, about to rise, and applying to a conjunction with Mercury, divisor of the midheaven, which is dignified by domicile, highly angular in the first house (where it rejoices), co-rising with the benefic fixed star Castor (also of a Mercury nature), and configured by a close and applying sextile to Venus in the eleventh house of gain. Both Mercury and the Moon cast aspects into the terms of the directed midheaven; Jupiter, natally present in those terms, occupies the rising sign of the revolution but in the second quadrant house of wealth – and, incidentally, conjunct the Lot of Fortune.

In that year, the native was awarded a three-year research grant that meant a return to academic employment. In fact, his project proposal was approved by both the major funding bodies to which he had applied, giving him a choice between them – another instance of powerful significators in double-bodied signs indicating a repeated event. This also illustrates what was said in Chapter 4 about the duration of effects being contingent on both astrological and non-astrological factors: once the three-year project had been approved, it was not necessary for the next two revolutions to be equally favourable in order for the native to keep his employment. In the absence of malefic

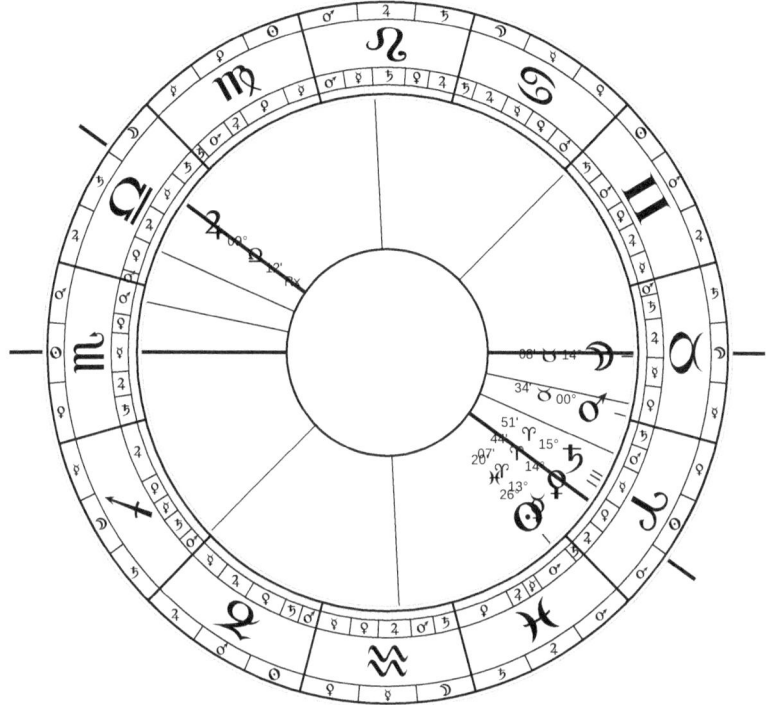

Figure 34: Nativity H.

configurations threatening a premature end to the project, it could be expected to run its course, and so it did. It was, however, followed by another two years without gainful employment, corresponding to the ascendant being directed through the last few degrees of Mars' terms.

On the wings of love

After these extended discussions of two nativities introduced in previous chapters, we now turn to some new and briefer examples. The first is the nativity of a woman who, after living with her parents up to the age of 37, looking after them and other family members, suddenly moved a thousand kilometres away to be with the man she loved (figure 34).

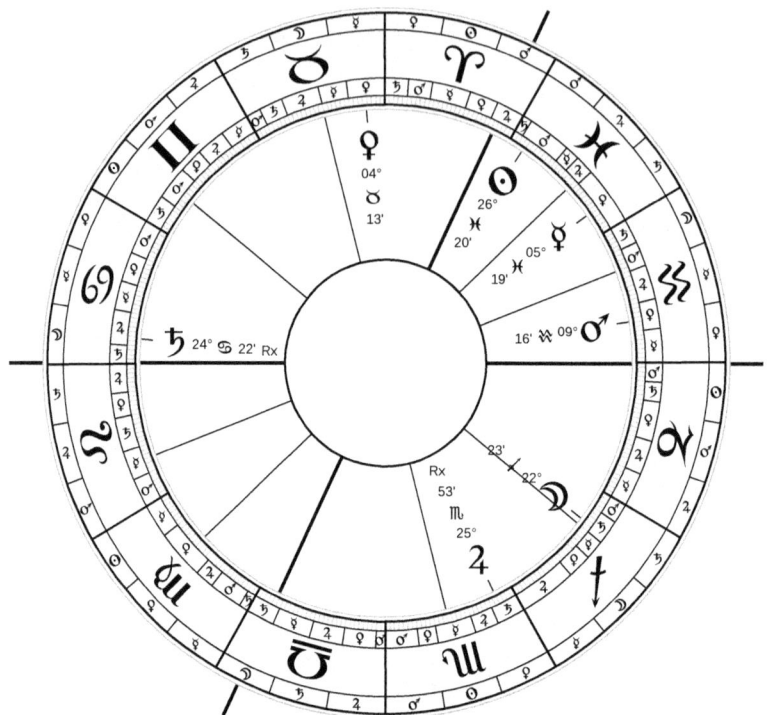

Figure 35: Native H, revolution at age 37.

The directed ascendant in that year had just entered the terms of Venus (12°–17°) in Sagittarius, where it would encounter the trine aspect of Venus itself as well as those of Mercury and Saturn. Venus is not only a universal significator of love and romance, but also rules the seventh house of marriage and partnership; its natal conjunction with Mercury and Saturn agrees well with a late marriage to a man whose acquaintance she had made in an academic context.

In the figure of the revolution (figure 35), Venus as divisor is angular in the tenth house in addition to being dignified by domicile in Taurus and in its own terms. While it should thus be fully able to bring forth its significations in this year, Venus also applies by square to Mars in the seventh house, suggesting some sort of obstruction affecting marriage or relationships – possibly an obstruction originating with the native herself, as Mars rules the natal ascendant. The annual profection had reached Sagittarius, making Jupiter ruler of the year. Being a benefic, unafflicted and reasonably well-placed both in the nativity and in the revolution, Jupiter generally bodes well for the year; but being retrograde at both times, it also indicates the possibility of delays, instability and repetition.

Some seven months into the year, the native bought a flight ticket and went to the airport, but was prevented by her fear of confined spaces from actually boarding the plane. Determined not to be ruled by her fear, she then decided to seek professional help, worked assiduously, and within two months had sufficiently mastered her phobia to be able to make the journey not just once but three times in quick succession, the last time moving permanently. The transits surrounding these events are quite instructive and will be discussed in the next chapter.

Annus horribilis

The delayed move was not the first problem that Mars had caused in the life of this native. Only the year before, when the ascendant was still directed through the terms of Jupiter (0°–12°) in Sagittarius, Mars was casting an opposition aspect into those terms while Jupiter itself was retrograde in the sixth house of illness and injury in the revolution (figure 36). As the native was 36 years old, the annual profection had returned to the natal ascendant in Scorpio, making Mars ruler of the year; and in addition to ruling the first house of the nativity, Mars was closely conjunct the revolution ascendant, having just risen above the horizon in the daytime – both factors contrary to its sect, and therefore increasing its harmful tendencies.

In the revolution, Mercury was just about to enter Pisces, its sign of fall, where it would form an applying square with this Mars – a configuration that proved highly relevant to events during the year. The first thing to go seriously wrong was a dental procedure: for reasons that

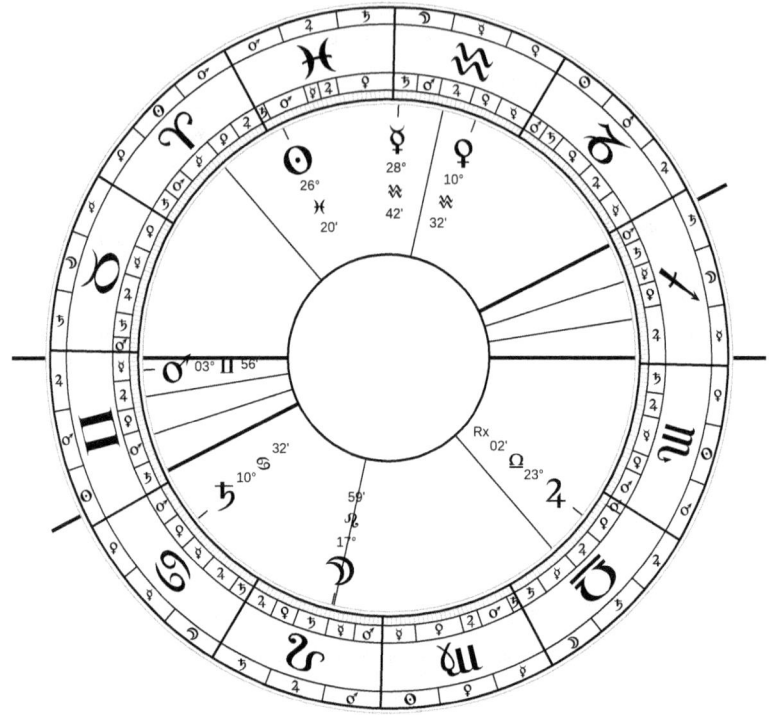

Figure 36: Native H, revolution at age 36.

were never made clear, the effects of the local anaesthetic applied did not wear off as they should, and the native spent nearly a month with no sensation in her lower jaw. (Surgeons and surgery are traditional significations of Mars combining with Mercury.)[3] Next, the native was a mature student, having returned to university for her master's degree, and generally did very well in her studies; but in the final term, she was greatly distressed when her crucial thesis did not receive the high marks that she had been led by her supervisor to expect. Finally, just hours before the thesis defence, during which the native came under attack from an over-zealous opponent, she also by mistake received an email with highly unwelcome information that would affect her negatively for a long time to come. We thus see afflictions with both first-house themes (body and health) and Mercury themes (education and communication) in this year.

A fated wedding

Our next example is the nativity of a woman who requested a birth time rectification after being told by another astrologer that her ascendant ought to be sidereal Libra rather than Virgo, which would imply a later birth time than that stated in her records. Having examined the indications of the radix as well as of her primary directions and revolutions, I was satisfied that the ascendant was indeed Virgo, and that the recorded birth time was reasonably correct – the true time

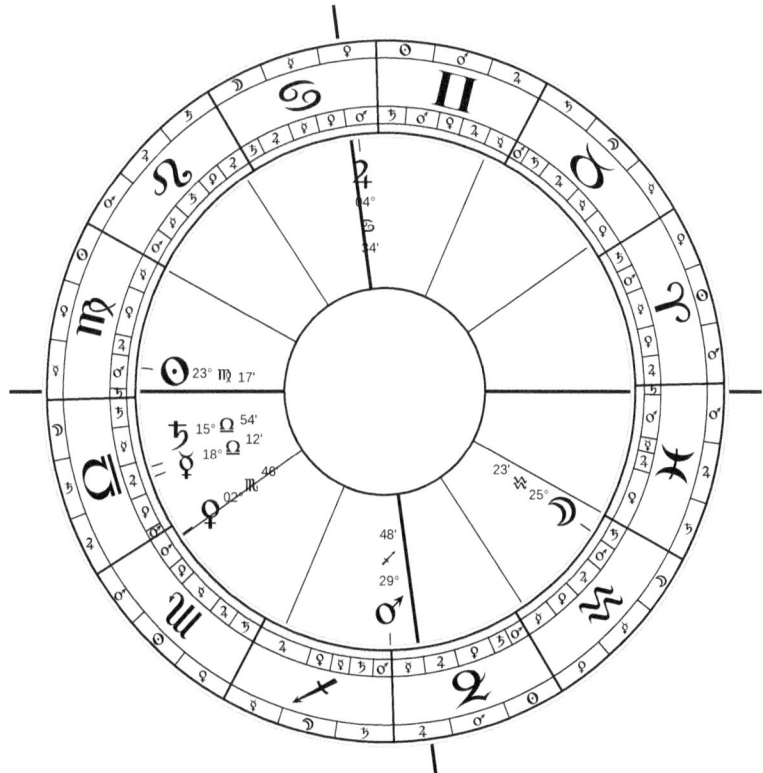

Figure 37: Nativity C.

possibly being two or three minutes *earlier*, but no more. I give the unaltered chart (figure 37).

Among the first questions I asked the native was whether she was happily married to a particularly successful, wealthy man. The reason was the extraordinarily well-placed Jupiter on the midheaven as ruler of the seventh house: of the sect, oriental of the Sun, angular, exalted, and with Venus on the cusp of the second house applying to it by trine. This conjecture was confirmed. If Libra had been rising, the seventh house would have been ruled by malefic Mars, which is contrary to the sect, occidental, cadent, without major dignity (though in its own terms) and unaspected by the benefics. The contrast could hardly have been greater.

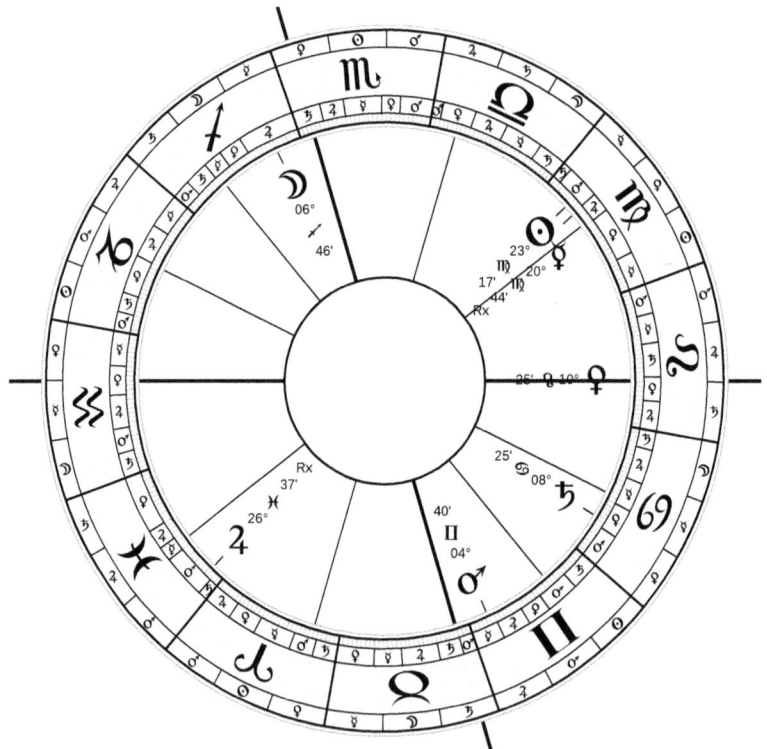

Figure 38: Native C, revolution at age 21.

The timing of this wedding, just two days before the native's twenty-second birthday, is what particularly interests us here, and further confirms the correctness of the birth time. The happy event had in fact been planned for a later date but was brought forward to ensure the presence of the native's prospective mother-in-law, who was seriously ill.

The ascendant at age 21 was directed through the terms of Mercury (6°–14°) in Libra, and Mercury was also ruling the year, making it the most important chronocrator. In the revolution (figure 38), this Mercury is in its dignity of domicile and exaltation, but retrograde and therefore seemingly separating from the opposition of Jupiter. Shortly afterwards, however, Mercury stationed (without ever leaving the orb of Jupiter's aspect), resumed application and perfected the aspect. Jupiter not only rules the natal seventh house, but is actually conjunct the natal seventh-house cusp by transit, in its own domicile. The opposition aspect, though frequently seen in conflicts and unfortunate events, is not necessarily evil, particularly when formed by benefics in dignity or with mutual reception: it signifies coming 'face to face' with something for better or worse, and I have often seen it in connection with marriage or romantic relationships.

In this case, the separation turning to application may relate to the sudden change of plans. To my mind, however, the most striking feature of the revolution figure is Venus exactly on its seventh cusp, casting a sextile aspect into the terms of the directed ascendant. With Venus already favourably configured with the ruler of the seventh house in the nativity, such a placement positively demands a wedding, the start of a major relationship, or some similar event. There simply was no way the native could avoid getting married this year!

Although I should not have ventured to predict it, we may also note with perfect hindsight that the circumstance of the mother-in-law's illness precipitating the wedding is reflected by the Moon, ruler

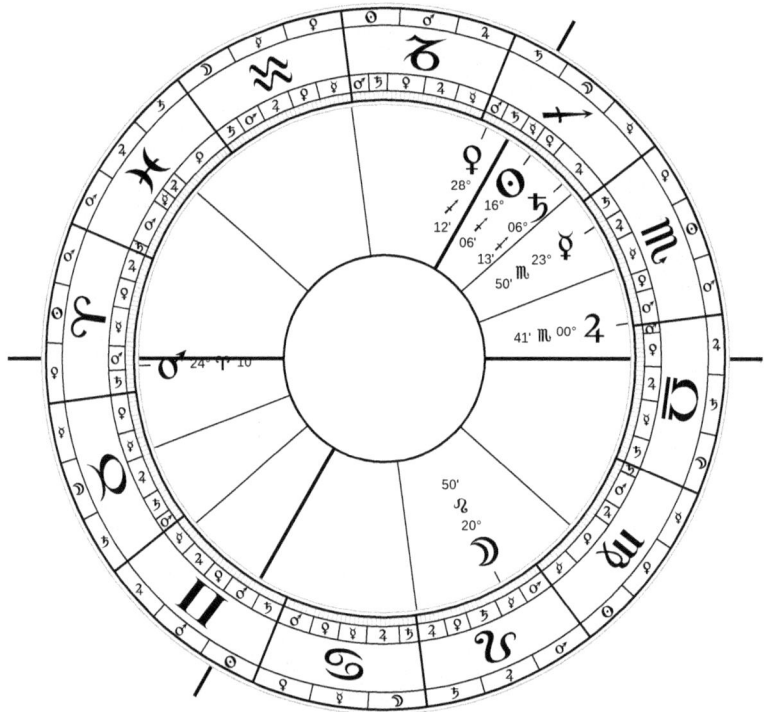

Figure 39: Nativity E.

of the natal tenth house, now occupying the tenth and casting a sextile aspect into the terms of the directed ascendant in Libra while applying by trine to Venus. The tenth house, being the fourth from the seventh, signifies parents-in-law, and the Moon separating from its opposition with Mars agrees with an ongoing illness.

Death from two perspectives

We next come to an unfortunate event illustrated by two nativities: that of a man with congenital lung disease who died from pneumonia at age 37, and that of his mother, who found him dead in his home later the same day. The male nativity (figure 39) was briefly discussed in my earlier book on directions, but we shall make a somewhat more detailed study of it here.

Traditional methods of delineating length of life, and the nature and circumstances of death, are a complex matter that would require a book of its own, but typically centre around the identification of the hyleg or chief significator of life. Briefly stated, there are two main possibilities in this case. According to the view of most Arabic authorities (based largely on Dorotheus and Vettius Valens), the succedent Moon would be hyleg, taking precedence over the cadent Sun although the latter is the luminary of the sect. According to the rules given by Ptolemy, however, Mars – conjunct the ascendant and having dignity of domicile and terms there – is most qualified to be hyleg. (Ptolemy, incidentally, was not alone in allowing a non-luminary planet to be hyleg: we know that Balbillus, who lived a century earlier and was thus a contemporary of Dorotheus, did the same.)

As it happens, both these potential significators were directed to evil aspects, perfecting within days of each other, at the age of 37: the Moon to the opposition of Mars with latitude, and Mars to the opposition of Saturn with latitude. Regardless of which planet we find to be the more convincing hyleg, there is thus no doubt that this year was a highly critical one. Also coincidentally, both the Moon and Mars (as well as the ascendant) were passing through the terms of Jupiter, which thus becomes a major chronocrator. The annual profection was in Taurus, making Venus ruler of the year.

The most salient feature of the revolution (figure 40) is the Moon in the eighth house of death, partilely conjunct the natal ascendant and some 2° from natal Mars, ruler of the first and eighth – thus opposite its own directed position, repeating the contact made by direction. The Moon further applies by sextile to Saturn in the sixth house; and as the Moon has most recently separated from Venus by square, this application also constitutes a translation of light between Venus (ruler of the

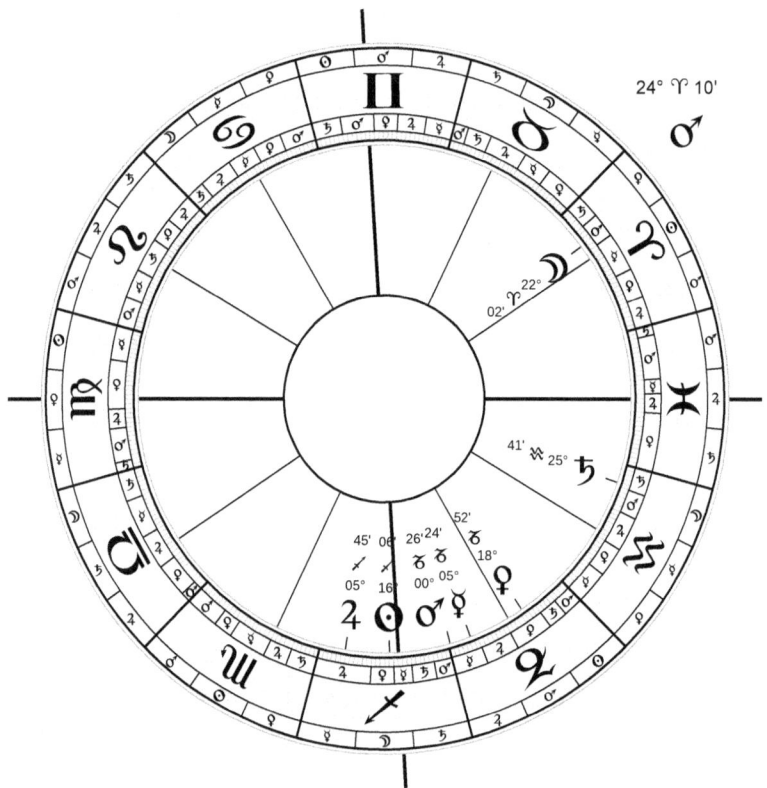

Figure 40: Native E, revolution at age 37 with natal placements outside the chart.

year) and Saturn. Mercury, ruler of the natal sixth house, appears to be separating from the other possible hyleg, Mars, but in fact stationed before leaving its orb and proceeded to perfect the conjunction.

We now turn our attention to the nativity of the mother (figure 41), where the Moon as ruler of the ascendant is in its fall in the fifth house of children, while Mars as ruler of the fifth house closely opposes the ascendant itself (and forms an applying square with Mercury, ruler of the Lot of Children). At age 56, the Moon had recently entered the terms of Venus (14°–22°) in Capricorn, where Mars is located, and was approaching the body of Mars with latitude (perfecting at age 58),

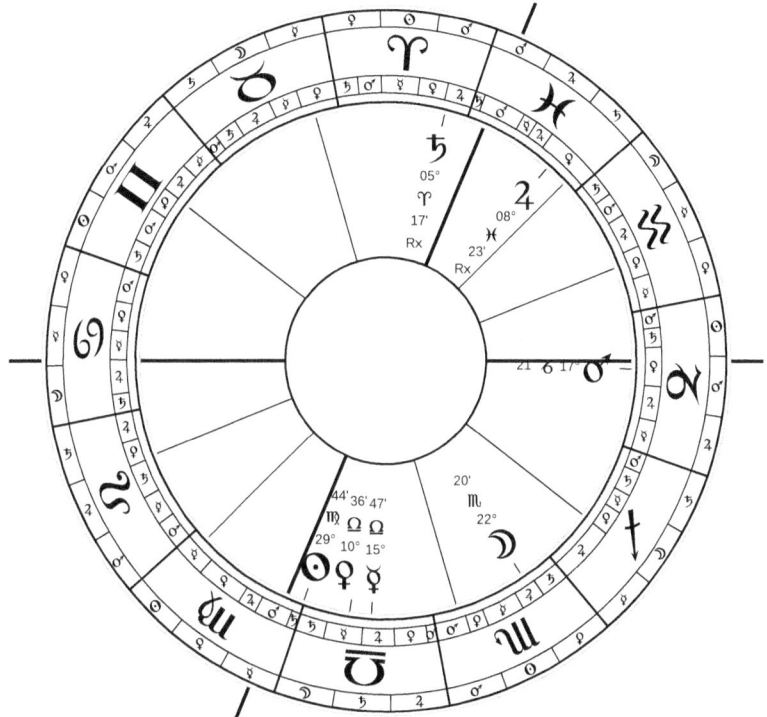

Figure 41: Nativity B.

while the ascendant was directed through the terms of Mars in Leo. Mars was thus doubly activated as chronocrator. The annual profection was in Pisces, making Jupiter ruler of the year.

The chart of the revolution (figure 42) clearly illustrates how misleading the usual approach of reading a 'solar return' as a separate horoscope can be. Not only is Venus exactly on the ascendant, but five out of seven planets occupy their domiciles. Yet, according to the native, this was the worst year of her life.

The solution to this apparent conundrum lies, of course, in the consideration of the directions and chronocrators. The directed ascendant, which is in the terms of Mars – ruler of the natal fifth house of children – at 26° of Leo meets with a partile opposition from

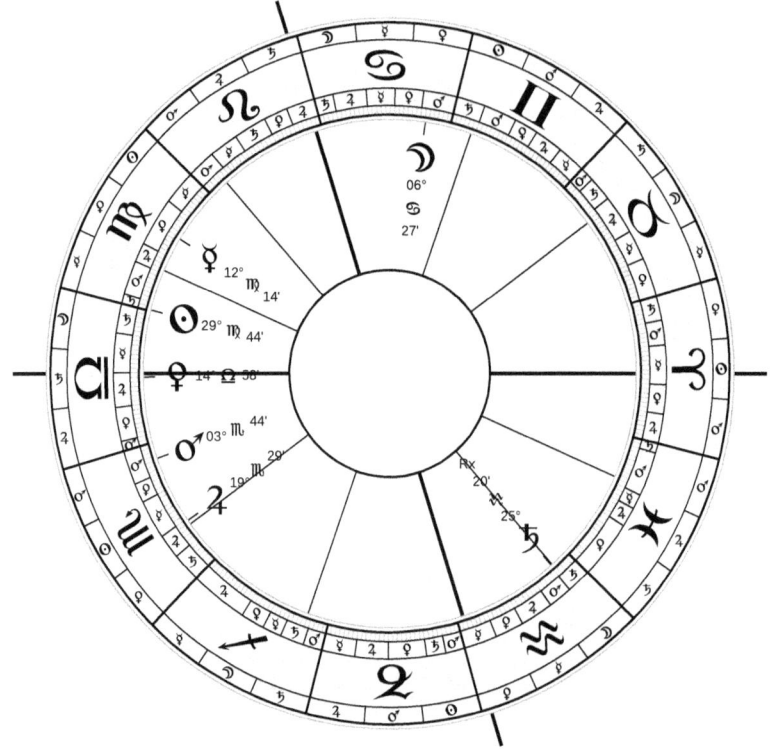

Figure 42: Native B, revolution at age 56.

Saturn, ruler of the natal eighth house, placed exactly on the cusp of the fifth house in the revolution. Further, Jupiter as ruler of the year and universal significator of children, conjunct the fallen natal fifth-house Moon, forms a mutually applying square with this Saturn, while Mars is closing in on Jupiter from the opposite side. Abū Ma'shar actually states as an example scenario that 'if Jupiter was the lord of the year or the lord of the division, and in the revolution he was with Saturn under the earth, it indicates the death of children'.[4]

Decline and drowning

Another sad but astrologically instructive case is the nativity of a man who in his early twenties abandoned a military career for an austere life of religious devotion, but who later began to suffer from a debilitating mental illness and eventually drowned, alone and most likely deliberately, shortly after turning 47 years old (figure 43).

Saturn, present in the ascendant and having dignity of exaltation and triplicity there, meets Ptolemy's criteria for a non-luminary planet to be hyleg. The fallen Moon in Scorpio forms what appears to be a rather wide opposition to Mercury in the eighth house; but when latitude is taken into consideration, the distance decreases considerably, so that they are nearly on the same 'horizon' – with the result that Saturn was directed to the opposition of Mercury with latitude at age 47, followed by the body of the Moon with latitude at age 48. (Some might prefer to view the Moon as significator or hyleg and Saturn as

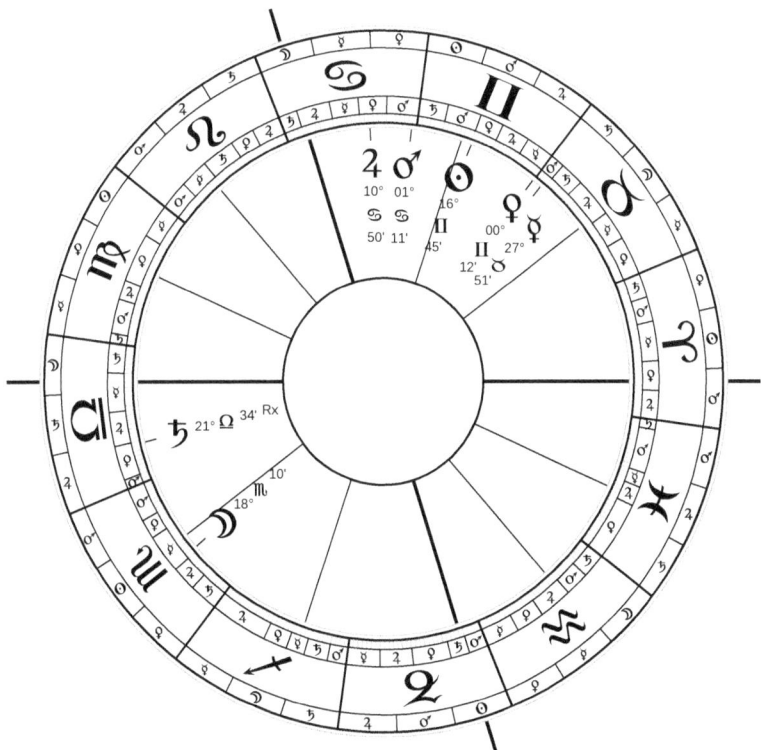

Figure 43: Nativity D.

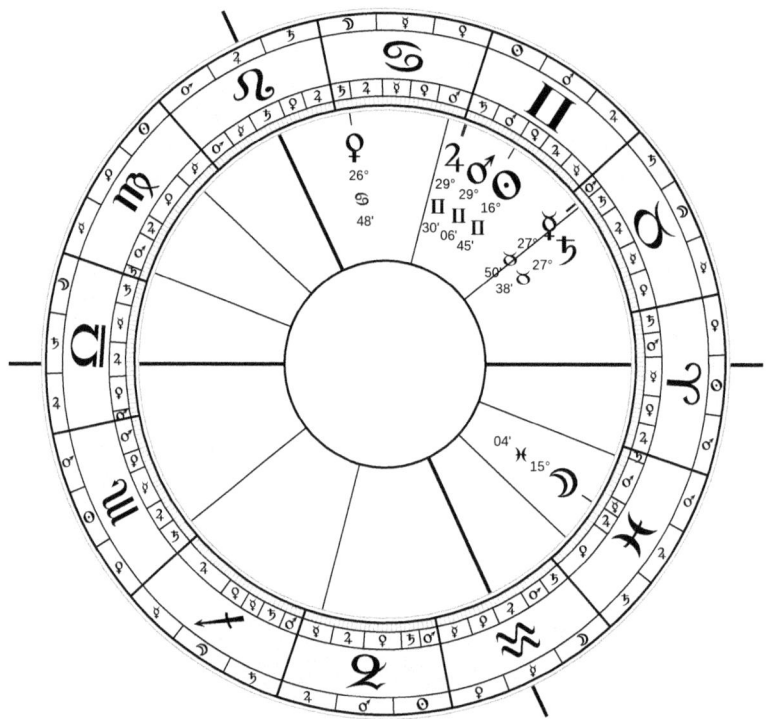

Figure 44: Native D, revolution at age 47.

promissor, making this a converse direction; but that would obscure the key role played by Mercury.)

In fact, although one swallow does not make a summer, this is one instance in which the position-circle method of Placidus – known as directions under the Placidean pole of the significator – gives results striking enough to merit a separate mention: the two directions here occur within two months of each other, the second falling almost exactly on the native's forty-seventh birthday, and are followed a few months later by the direction of Saturn to the fixed star Scheat, commonly associated with drowning – though I have not been able to determine how old that association is or where it originates.[5]

Irrespective of the precise method of direction employed, the annual profection had come to Virgo, making Mercury – the *anaereta*, or life-threatening promissor – ruler of the year. In the revolution (figure 44), Mercury has not only returned to its natal degree, but also to the eighth house, very near the cusp, where it is partilely conjunct Saturn itself. These placements leave the malefic tendency of Mercury for this year of life in no doubt whatever.

The revolution ascendant

As mentioned in Chapter 5, Perso-Arabic astrologers such as al-Andarzaghar and Abū Maʿshar, and the Indian Tājika astrologers who followed them, gave much importance to the ascendant of the revolution and to any planets in it, including planets present there in the nativity. My own view, based on experience, is that the rising sign of the revolution, its ruler and occupants do not qualify as chronocrators in their own right, but can reinforce themes already indicated by the chronocrators.

To illustrate, let us return to nativity G (figure 26) and examine the native's revolution for age 30 (figure 45). In that year, the annual profection had reached Aries, making Mars ruler of the year, while Venus – occupying Aries in the nativity – was divisor of the ascendant. The figure of the revolution has Cancer rising with its ruler, the Moon, in the fifth house in Scorpio, and a major event in the native's life during this year of life was the birth of a daughter, who incidentally had Scorpio rising in her own nativity.

This example may seem compelling, but unfortunately things are rarely that simple. We may note that Venus as divisor of the ascendant was natally conjunct Saturn, ruler of the fifth house, in Aries, a configuration now activated by the annual profection reaching Aries. Moreover, in the revolution, angular Jupiter was partilely conjunct this natal Venus and also partilely configured with revolution Mars as

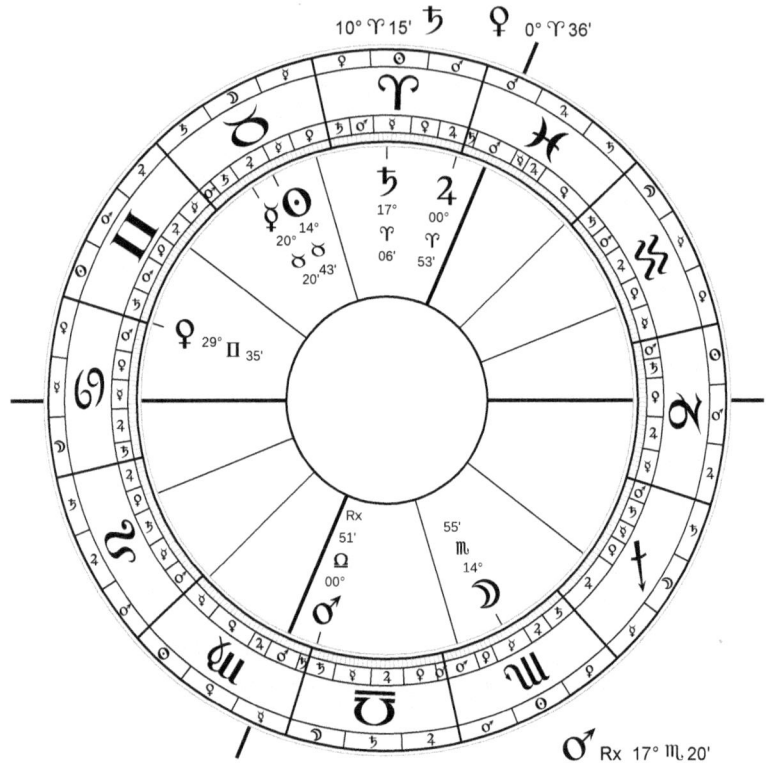

Figure 45: Native G, revolution at age 30 with natal placements outside the chart.

ruler of the year. Finally, the Moon in the fifth house was conjunct *natal* Mars within a few degrees. Without these more fundamental indications in place, the event might not have occurred at all.

Another look at some of the revolutions of the same nativity already examined above will serve to drive home the point. The next time the native had Cancer rising in a revolution was at age 34 (figure 28), when exalted Jupiter was conjunct the ascendant near the natal midheaven and the Moon itself was exalted in the tenth house. In that year the native advanced his career by completing his doctorate; but the Moon was also configured to the ruler of the year (the Sun) by an applying conjunction. At age 41 (figure 32), when the native remarried, Venus ruled the revolution ascendant and was configured to the Moon in the seventh house by an applying opposition; but the Moon was in fact connecting Venus with Jupiter, ruler of the year, by a translation of light. Finally, at age 46 (figure 27), when the native lost his father, the Sun (besieged by the malefics) ruled the revolution ascendant but was itself ruler of the year as well.

Letting the chart speak
In some nativities, particularly with signs of short ascension rising, there is so much going on by direction alone that in many years the figure of the revolution takes a back seat. We looked at one such case in our discussion of directions as a stand-alone technique in Chapter 6 (p. 71). When a year is marked by one or more major directions while nothing much seems to be happening in the revolution – no planets or aspects present in the terms of the directed significators; chronocrators not prominently configured with other planets – it is best to listen to the chart and focus on the directions as the area of greatest activity. Nevertheless, it is always worth bearing in mind which planet rules the year, as the results indicated by directions will often be channelled through its significations, and also to note the general strength or weakness of the chronocrators in the revolution.

Figure 46 is a nativity where directions, particularly those of the ascendant, follow rapidly on each other. Its most striking feature is the opposition of the two malefics along the ascendant-descendant axis without the mitigating aspect of either benefic. Although the opposition is a separating one, Mercury is reconnecting Mars with Saturn through a translation of light (separating from one planet while applying to the other). In fact, because the changeable Mercury assumes the nature of the planets with which it is configured, its presence with the malefics increases the potential for trouble.

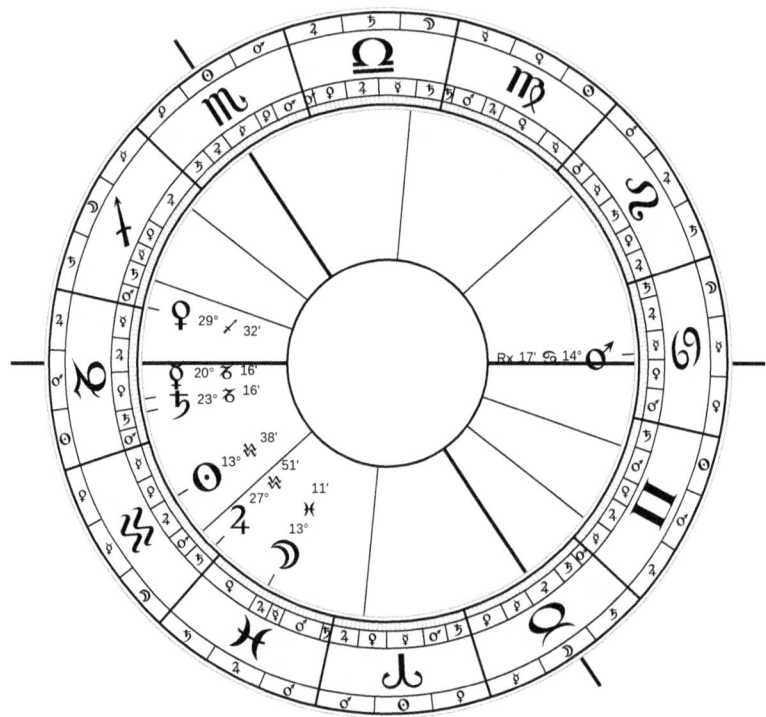

Figure 46: Nativity F.

Latent malefic configurations are the astrological equivalent of time bombs, manifesting as concrete events when the planets involved are activated as chronocrators. It is important to note, however, that difficult configurations in a nativity emphatically do not mean that the native is a bad person! Although character delineation does have a place in traditional astrology, the chart *as a whole* is not regarded as a map of the native's psyche but as a latent representation of his or her entire life – and in real life, bad things do happen to good people.

The most dramatic activations of this particular configuration took place when the ascendant was directed through the terms of Mercury and, especially, Mars in Aries, encountering the natal squares of Mars, Mercury and Saturn in turn. It is pertinent to add that the native, who is himself a practising astrologer, believes his actual time of birth to have been some five minutes earlier than the officially recorded time (the basis of the charts shown here). I personally agree with this conjecture, which would tighten the time frame of the directions discussed here; but it would not alter the chronocrators active during the events in question.

At the age of 36, the ascendant was directed through the terms of Mercury (12°–20°) in Aries, in which the square aspect of natal Mars falls. Mercury rules the sixth house of illness, and in the revolution, Mars again cast an aspect into the same terms by opposition. The annual profection of the ascendant had returned to the rising sign Capricorn,

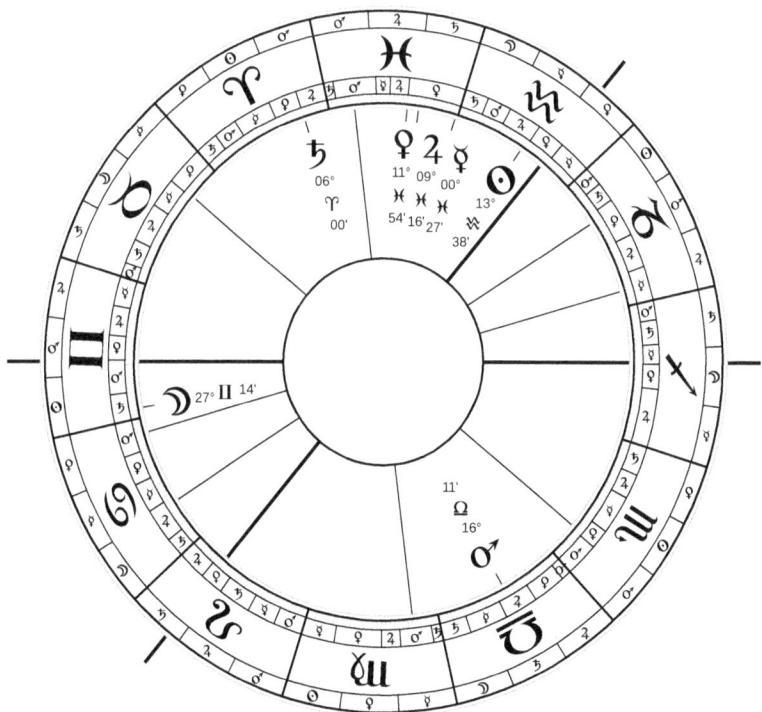

Figure 47: Native F, revolution at age 36.

making Saturn ruler of the year; the natal Mercury-Saturn conjunction in Capricorn was squared within a few degrees by revolution Mars. In that revolution (figure 47), both Mercury and Saturn were in their fall, and although Mercury seemed to be applying to the dignified benefics, it never perfected the conjunction but instead turned retrograde and entered under the beams of the Sun. Towards the end of this year, the native's skin suddenly and inexplicably erupted with fluid-filled blisters in the course of a few hours, covering his entire body with the exception of the hands, feet, face and genitals. The attack was so severe that the native doubted his skin would ever return to normal, and neither of the two physicians he consulted had ever seen anything like it. Fortunately, the condition was eventually completely cured by homoeopathic means.

The full impact of the malefics was, however, felt at the age of 40 with the direction of the ascendant through the terms of Mars (20°–25°) in Aries, the squares of Mercury and Saturn falling in them. The profection of the ascendant had reached Taurus, making Venus ruler of the year and lending a definite Venus flavour to the forms taken by the malefic events. The first of these was partly anticipated: the native, noting an unfavourable transit coming up, feared an accident of some kind and thus resolved to stay indoors for a few days to minimize the risk. Instead, what happened around the expected time was an acute and extremely painful attack of kidney stones, severe enough to require hospitalization. The placement of Venus in the twelfth house of the nativity seems particularly relevant here. (Traditional sources vary somewhat in assigning the kidneys to Libra, ruled by Venus, or to Scorpio, ruled by Mars; Vettius Valens explicitly relates kidney stones to both these signs.[6] In this case, Mars and Venus were both active as divisor and ruler of the year, respectively.)

Serious as this episode was, later events the same year proved far worse, while also relating to the placement of Venus as ruler of the year in the seventh house of marriage and relationships in the revolution

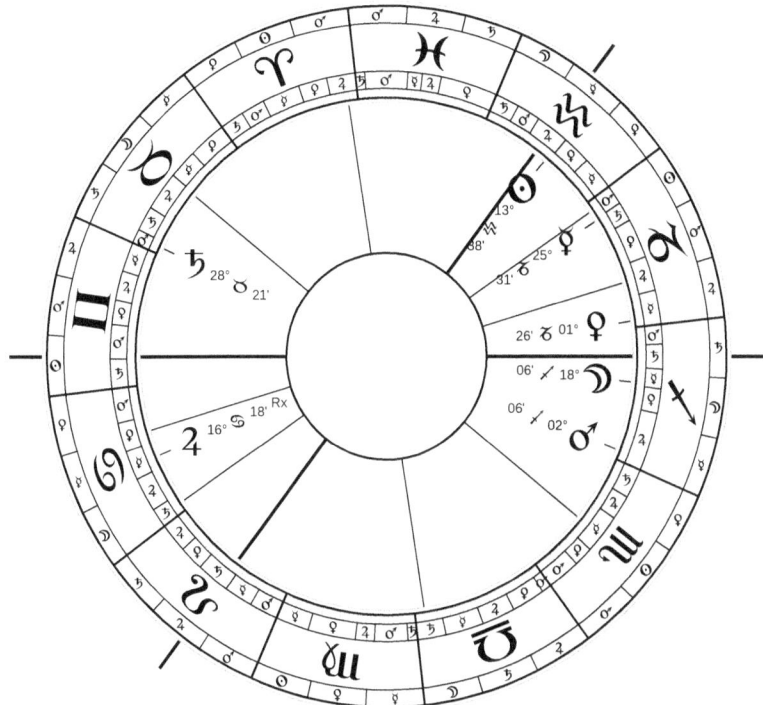

Figure 48: Native F, revolution at age 40.

(figure 48). The year before, the native had begun a passionate whirlwind romance, including plans of marriage, with a woman who unfortunately turned out to be seriously mentally unbalanced. The ruler of that year was Mars, and we may note the debilitated status of Mars (retrograde and in its fall) in the seventh house of the nativity. The native was forced to sever the relationship and even left the country for some months. On his return, however, his former lover refused to accept that their relationship was at an end. This volatile situation came to a head when, frustrated in her attempts to rekindle the flame, she physically attacked the native with an axe, screaming that she was going to dismember him.

Escaping by the skin of his teeth and severely shaken, the native considered reporting the incident to the police but decided against it for compassionate reasons. Not long afterwards, he was therefore shocked to find himself charged instead with assault on the woman in question. Instructed by his defence counsel not to bring up details of the relationship in court, he could only stand by incredulous as a female judge declared him guilty on no other evidence than the statement of his axe-wielding ex-girlfriend (although suspending his sentence). On that day, in the native's words, 'something died inside him', and he lost all faith in the judicial system.

Not only were these events horrible to live through as they occurred, but the trauma they set off remained with the native for many years, shaping his life to no small extent. In Chapter 4 I mentioned the views of the Renaissance astrologer Johann Schöner on the duration of the effects of directions, and it seems relevant here to quote him verbatim:

> When [a direction comes] to Saturn, then it seems that the evil fortune given by Saturn lasts for many years, as for example it happens that someone is made unfortunate and imprisoned and becomes ill and suffers several other infortunes not only in that year in which the direction to Saturn happens, but also he will suffer through ten or twelve years these tribulations in turn.[7]

Such delineations naturally apply only to cases of severe affliction, which is what we are seeing here. In addition to the series of directions to the squares of the malefics falling in the terms of the malefics, the ascendant was directed in the same period to the fixed star known as the Southern Scale or Claw (of the Scorpion) and considered by the ancient astrologers to be of the combined nature of Mars and Saturn. To the natural significations of violence, animosity and danger to life and property associated with the two malefics, the square of Mercury (especially in the terms of mendacious Mars) adds the particular meanings of false accusations and miscarriages of justice.

Reversals of fortune

As our closing example for this chapter, let us contrast the preceding nativity (and our directions-only example in Chapter 6) with one where signs of long ascension are rising, resulting in directions through the terms that last for many years. Here we clearly need to correlate the native's life history not only with the directions, but also with profections and revolutions, to form a nuanced understanding of the astrological indications for each year.

Figure 49 is the chart of a native whose life has taken some unusual turns. The nativity has definite indications of misfortune, the most important perhaps being that both the luminaries (the Sun and Moon) are placed in the cadent sixth and twelfth houses without the aspect of either benefic. The Sun – which, as the birth was diurnal, is both the luminary of the sect and the chief significator of the father – also has Mars, the malefic contrary to the sect, rising just before it.

But there are positive indications as well. Saturn in the second house, although a natural malefic, is of the sect and exalted, indicating good fortune – particularly regarding finances – with time and effort. It is also the participating triplicity ruler of the sect light, which relates to the native's overall standing in life, and becomes all the more important as the other two rulers (the Sun itself and Jupiter) lack the impact and stability needed to provide much support. Further, Mercury and the Moon – universal significators of the mind or soul – are in Saturn's terms and apply to Saturn (in the case of the Moon, by trine and with reception), giving it great influence over the native's character. Saturn also incidentally rules the Lot of the Daimon, sometimes translated as Spirit, which is conjunct the Moon. Such placements foster the constructive qualities of Saturn, such as introspection, profound

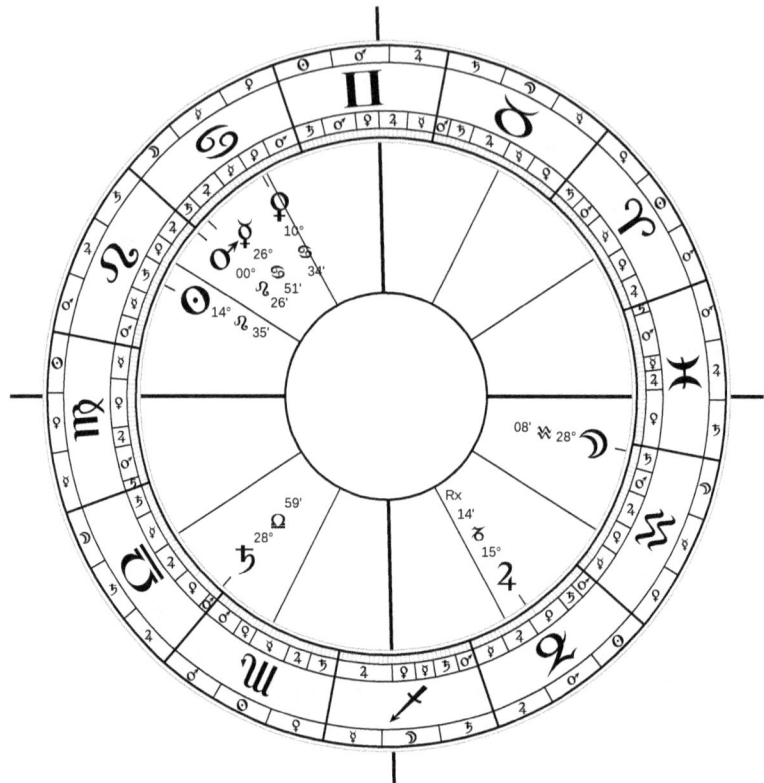

Figure 49: Nativity L.

thinking, reserve, solitariness, steadfastness, austerity, self-discipline and hard work. With a superior square from Mercury, intellectual and academic endeavours would be particularly favoured. Another fortunate indication is that of Venus, ruler of the second and ninth houses – the latter associated with travel, learning and religion – which is well-placed in the eleventh, in the minor dignities of terms and triplicity. Venus is also received by its exaltation ruler Jupiter, although Jupiter itself, being retrograde and in its fall, may be considered ultimately too weak to assist in the affairs of Venus (a condition known as 'return of light').

When the native was seven years old, with Mars ruling the year, his father died suddenly and unexpectedly of a brain aneurysm. Over the following ten years, the native grew up in poverty and in a socially disadvantaged environment, seeing his peers take to drug-dealing and other crime. He had no contact with his extended family; his mother was neglectful and misappropriated his inheritance; his elder siblings, who were in and out of institutional care, physically abused him. The native suffered much with ill health (as might be expected from Mercury, ruler of the ascendant, applying first by square to Saturn as ruler of the sixth house and then by conjunction to Mars as ruler of the eighth), especially from severe asthma exacerbated by his mother's chain-smoking. His own life was in danger more than once, and one of the mother's boyfriends died before his eyes as a result of diabetic shock.

After he was forced to leave home at age 17, the native's life gradually improved. He eventually secured a university degree, left North America to travel extensively in Asia, and found himself, a decade later, ordained as a Buddhist monk. Perhaps owing to the debility of Jupiter, the religious life proved a disappointment, particularly with regard to the native's preceptor and the local monastic community, and lack of spiritual and material support made him leave the monkhood after less than two years. Returning to the west and to academia, he was accepted into a doctoral programme at a respected university, successfully completed a doctorate within three years, and is now fashioning a career for himself as a scholar. Let us examine a few revolutions that have marked important turning points along this eventful journey.

The summer when he was 17 was described by the native as the most dreadful time of his life. He had taken a job at a fast-food restaurant but was forced to give it up after suffering a severe asthma attack due to the smoke from the kitchen. He was then told by his mother to move out, leaving him without either home or income. At this low point the native was saved by the charity of a female friend and her parents, who for some months put him up rent-free in their basement.

In the revolution figure for this year (figure 50), five out of seven planets are in their major dignities of domicile or exaltation. Unfortunately for the native, the chief chronocrators for the year are the remaining two planets: Mars (divisor of both the ascendant and the Sun) and Saturn (ruler of the year and divisor of the midheaven). This demonstrates the importance of knowing which parts of the revolution figure are in fact activated at a higher level in the predictive hierarchy. In addition to being malefics and lacking major dignity, both chrono-

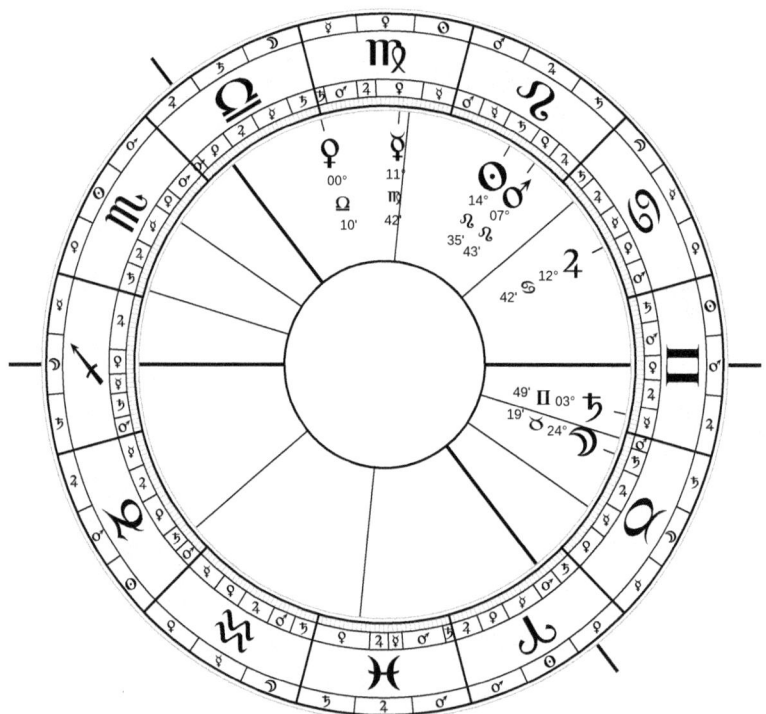

Figure 50: Native L, revolution at age 17.

crators also occupy unfortunate houses, reinforcing their natal rulerships: Mars, ruler of the eighth house in the nativity, is in the eighth of the revolution, while Saturn, ruler of the sixth house, now occupies the sixth.

The assistance of a female friend is indicated in the revolution by Venus applying to Saturn (the ruler of the year) with a trine aspect. Venus is just minutes of arc into Libra, its domicile, and thus commits its strength to Saturn – although, as Venus itself is cadent in the ninth house, its ability to help is somewhat limited. Saturn also has multiple dignities in early Libra and could thus be said to receive Venus; but as its own position in the sixth house is even weaker, it can hardly assist Venus at all.

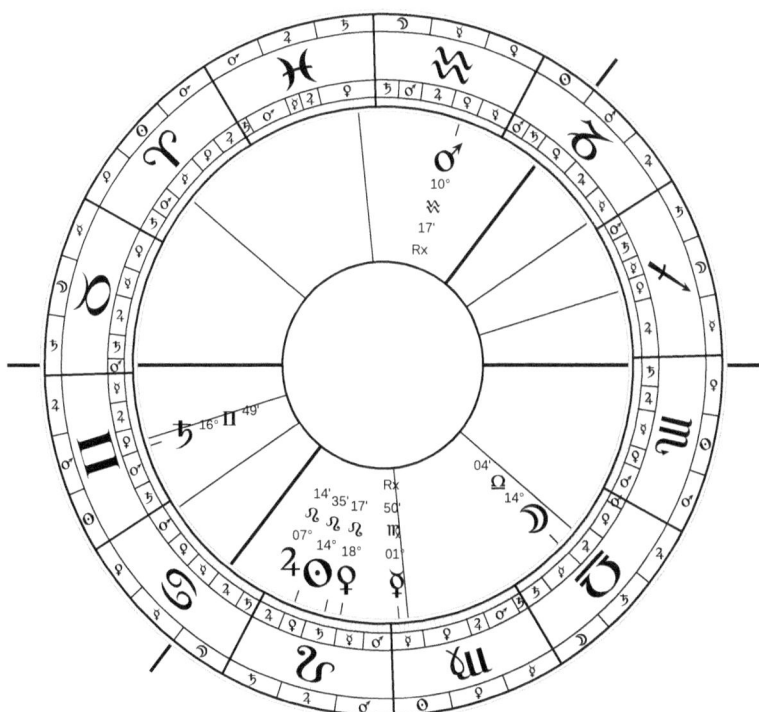

Figure 51: Native L, revolution at age 18.

152 ANNUAL PREDICTIVE TECHNIQUES

The next year, age 18, Mars continued as divisor both of the ascendant and of the Sun, but Jupiter ruled the year. In the revolution (figure 51), these two chronocrators are both angular and applying to one another by opposition. This is good for the significations of Mars, which are favoured by the aspect of the benefic, though less so for those of Jupiter. In this year the native began his university studies but without much success. He did, however, get a job as a security guard (consistent with Mars in the tenth house of work) and also took up the martial art of jujutsu, in which he did well. With Jupiter ruling the fourth house of the nativity and occupying the fourth of the revolution,

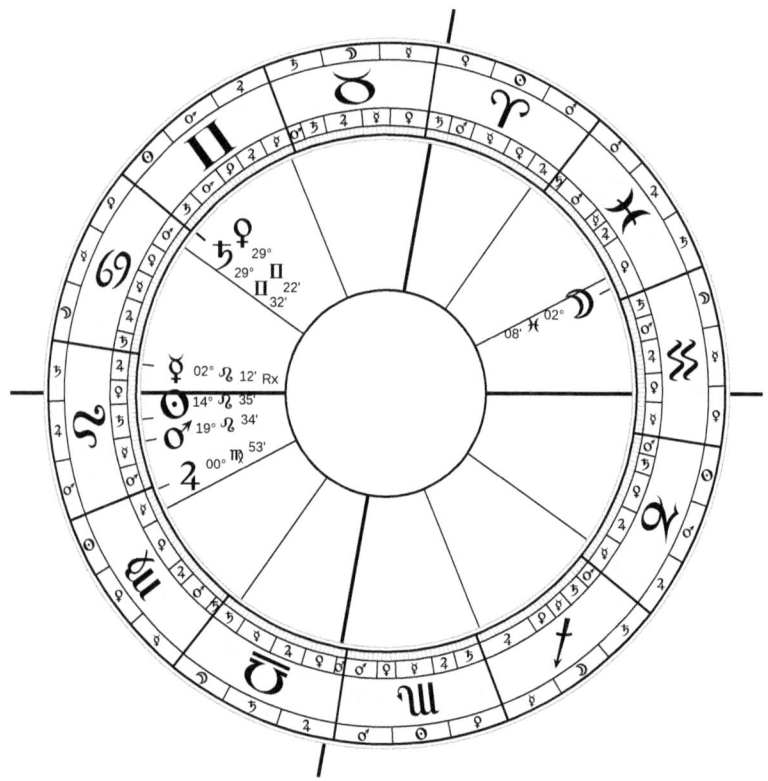

Figure 52: Native L, revolution at age 19.

the native was now able to rent a flat of his own. This greatly improved his quality of life, although the amenities were primitive and the neighbourhood less than salubrious, as indicated by Jupiter in its fall in the nativity and opposed by Mars in the revolution.

The native's second year at university, at age 19, was much better. The directed midheaven in the terms of Saturn (24°–30°) in Gemini had recently perfected a trine with exalted Saturn, and in the revolution (figure 52), Saturn itself was now partilely conjunct Venus in those terms in the eleventh house. Mars, which ruled the year in addition to continuing as divisor of the ascendant, was also strongly placed in the first house of the revolution – under the Sun's rays but in Leo, where the Sun received Mars by applying to it – and Mercury in the revolution was conjunct the natal position of Mars. As Mars is both a universal significator of travel and ruler of the natal third house, it is not surprising that the native travelled to Japan for a few weeks towards the end of this year, having already taught himself some Japanese. By this time the midheaven, too, had entered the terms of Mars.

Over the next few years the native continued his education, graduating when the ascendant was directed to the sextile of Mercury at age 23. Internally this period was still stressful, as he was dealing with the traumas of his childhood and experiencing feelings of 'extreme rage and hatred' (signified by Mars) towards his family; but he found solace in Stoic and Buddhist writings. At age 21, with Mercury ruling the year, the native had returned to Japan for a year of study abroad; three years later, as Mercury again took up the rulership of the year, he once more relocated to Japan after graduating, to pursue an MA degree in Buddhist Studies.

In the revolution for age 24 (figure 53) we find Jupiter casting a trine aspect into the division of the ascendant. Although Jupiter itself – cadent, retrograde and in its fall – is not able to give much in the way of external support, it agrees with an inclination towards wisdom and

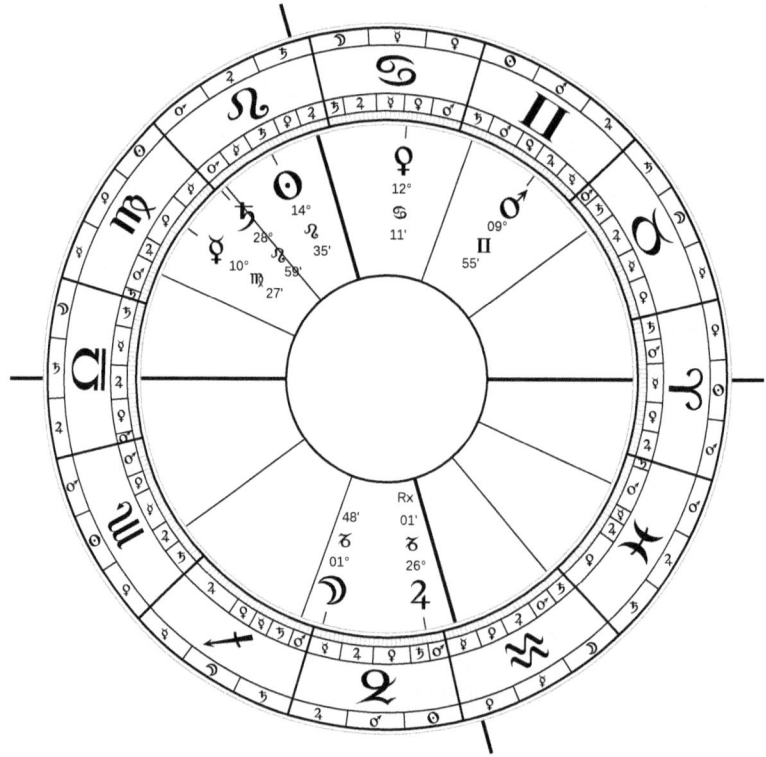

Figure 53: Native L, revolution at age 24.

religion. Mercury as ruler of the year and promissor of the ascendant is exalted in the eleventh house, in the degree of the natal ascendant, and receiving Mars (still divisor of the ascendant and the midheaven) by an applying aspect, all of which contributes to the native's academic success. The aspect in question being a square, and the position of Mars in the eighth, probably reflect his inner turmoil at this time. Mercury applies to Mars in the nativity as well, and one might speculate that this original application of the ruler of the ascendant across a sign boundary is what particularly indicates going abroad when Mercury and Mars become joint chronocrators.

The following year marked an important astrological change as, after more than a decade, the directed ascendant finally left the terms of Mars at age 25 and entered the terms of Saturn (28°–30°) in Virgo. In the revolution (figure 54), Mars itself is present in the former terms, while Venus, which also rules the year, is at the very end of the latter. Within weeks of this shift, the native travelled to India for the first time and visited the pilgrimage site of Bodh Gaya, where the Buddha is said to have attained his awakening. Sitting near the famous Bodhi tree, he felt 'a sense of relief, like I could let go of a lot of anger'. After several years of not speaking to his mother at all, the native called her up and sought a reconciliation. In addition to the ascendant changing terms, the Moon was directed to the sextile of Jupiter this year – an aspect that is reinforced by repetition in the revolution, where both

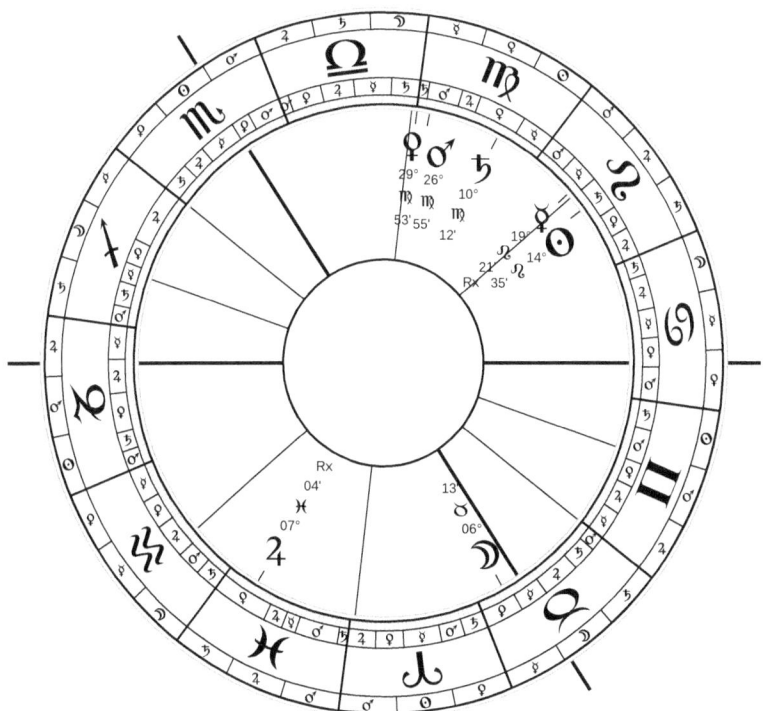

Figure 54: Native L, revolution at age 25.

planets are also dignified and closely aspect the new divisor (Saturn). The Moon being a universal significator both of the mother and of the mind, this direction accurately reflects the positive change in the native's emotions as well as in his attitude towards his mother.

The native's engagement with Buddhism led, at age 27, to the next major event in his life: becoming a monk or *bhikkhu*. The ascendant at this time was still directed through the terms of Saturn – universal significator of monastics, hermits and ascetics – in Virgo, and the ruler of the year was Jupiter, which has an affinity with religious practices and teachers. While Saturn is exalted both in the nativity and in the revolution, the condition of Jupiter at the two times differs

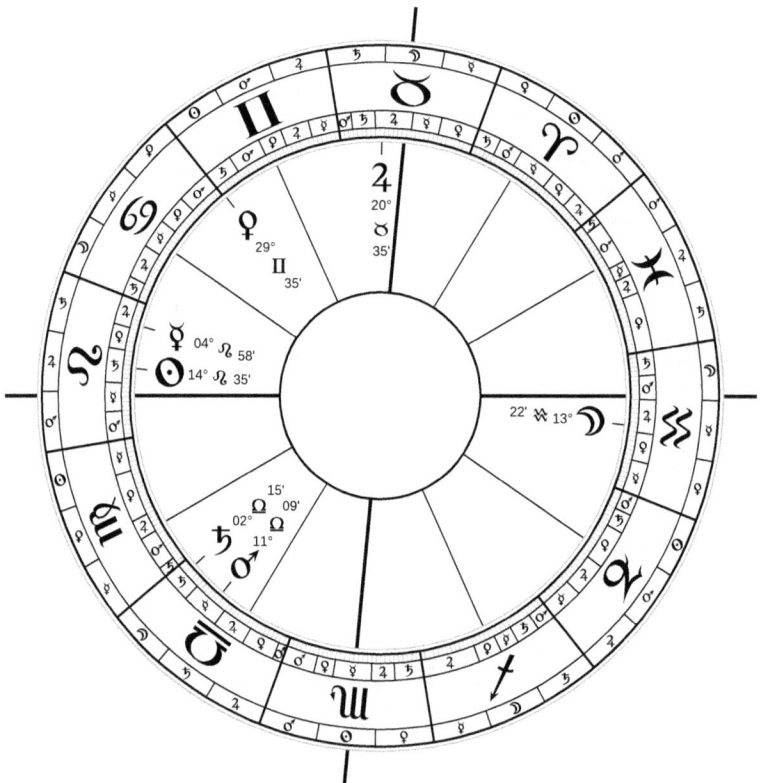

Figure 55: Native L, revolution at age 27.

considerably. In the revolution (figure 55) it is conjunct the midheaven, in its own terms, oriental and of the sect, confirming its ability to manifest its significations. However, these features did not entirely compensate for the underlying weakness of natal Jupiter, retrograde and in its fall: as it turned out, the preceptor-monk conducting the ordination ceremony did not adhere to traditional forms, leaving the native feeling 'like an impostor'; nor did this senior monk fulfil his promises of arranging formal training for the native, who instead was used for cheap labour and to enhance the former's status.

The next two years in the native's life contrast sharply, which is particularly interesting as both are dominated by a single planet: Saturn, which is divisor of the ascendant as well as ruler of both years. The two revolution figures are best studied side by side.

The former year (age 28) was emotionally stressful: the native felt 'spiritually broken' and was involved in conflicts both within and outside his own monastic community. He suffered from dysentery and believed that some persons he had upset were attempting to harm him by magical means. Somewhat ironically, life as a Buddhist monk was also proving financially impracticable for a foreigner, and the native struggled to keep afloat. In the revolution (figure 56), Saturn, though still exalted, is in the twelfth house, associated both with loss and – like the sixth house natally ruled by Saturn – with illness and enemies; it is further afflicted by a fallen Mars, ruler of the natal eighth house, applying with a superior square. Near the end of this difficult year, as transiting Mars was about to conjoin Saturn, the native was travelling through Nepal and made offerings at two shrines dedicated to the elephant-headed deity Gaṇeśa. Shortly afterwards, following a dream in which Gaṇeśa led him to safety from a pursuing mob, he began to regain his health and received sufficient funds to return to Japan.

The following year (age 29) began with a decision to leave monastic life, announced within days of the revolution. During this

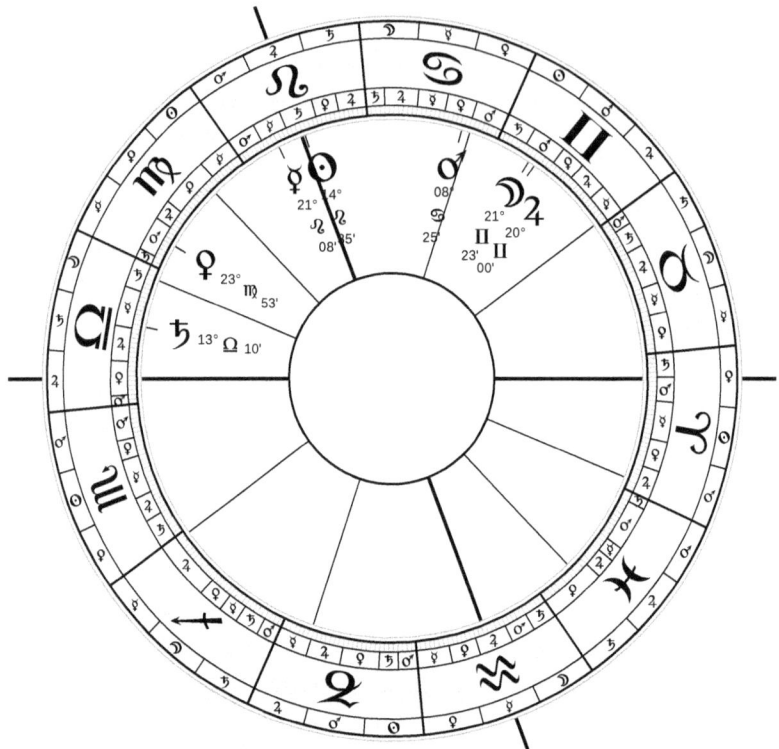

Figure 56: Native L, revolution at age 28.

year, in the native's words, 'everything just blossomed'. He was awarded a major scholarship that solved his financial problems, was accepted into the doctoral programme at a prestigious European university and returned to the west. He also visited his family again after an absence of eight years and tried, albeit with limited success, to make peace with his mother. What accounts for these largely positive changes?

On the level of directions, the ascendant had moved, during the previous year, from the terms of Saturn in Virgo into the terms of Saturn (0°–6°) in Libra, where it encountered the aspect of natal Mars (fortunately a sextile rather than a hard aspect), perfecting just weeks before the native's twenty-ninth birthday.

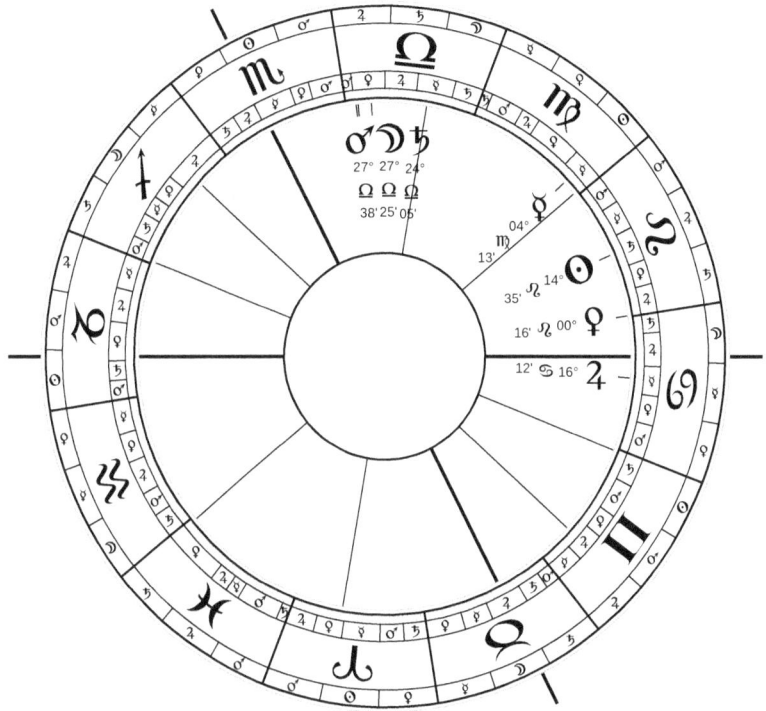

Figure 57: Native L, revolution at age 29.

In the revolution for that year (figure 57), we find benefic Venus partilely on natal Mars, thus casting a sextile into the same terms. Saturn is still in Libra, within a few degrees of its natal position, but in the ninth quadrant house (tenth equal house). The Moon and Mars partilely conjunct near natal Saturn presumably reflect the issues with the mother; more importantly, Mars separating from Saturn in the revolution suggests recent hardships coming to an end. Where Mars had been in the previous revolution, we now have exalted Jupiter applying to the likewise exalted Saturn with a superior square. Saturn's other sect-mate, the Sun, similarly applies to it by sextile from its domicile, so that both planets commit their strength to Saturn. This demonstrates how even the malefics, when dignified and well-configured, can signify positive and constructive events.

❧ ☙

The last three chapters have tried to show how to identify major events and overall trends in a given year of life by integrating universal chronocrators (primary directions), annual chronocrators (profections) and the figure of the revolution. In the next and final chapter we address the question of how to identify particular times within a single year.

Endnotes
1. Transl. Dykes 2019b: 323 f.
2. Ptol. *Tetr.* IV 10, transl. Robbins 1940: 457 (translation modified).
3. See, for instance, Ptol. *Tetr.* IV 4,7, transl. Robbins 1940: 387.
4. Transl. Dykes 2019b: 344 (translation modified).
5. Robson 1923: 206 seems to be the source of most or all popular references to this association.
6. See Vett. Val. II 37, transl. Riley 2010: 48.
7. *Opusculum* IV 10, transl. Hand 1994: 90.

9
Critical Times and Periods Within a Year

PINPOINTING THE TIME of an expected event, or even just predicting general ups and downs over the course of a year, is perhaps the most difficult part of annual prediction. It is not unlike having landed in a vast city and trying to pick your way through the maze of streets that looked so neatly laid out from the air. Nevertheless, it is often possible to identify in advance, at least broadly and conjecturally, the times at which themes and events signified by the chronocrators in a year will manifest.

The most important factor in subdividing a year of life would be the ascendant or another major significator changing terms by direction, which may happen at any time during a year; but in most nativities, most years will lack such a shift, and in any case we often want a way of breaking the year up into more than just two parts. Abū Ma'shar presents a bewildering array of methods for this purpose – many of which seem quite impracticable, and bring to mind ar-Rijāl's colourful description of Abū Ma'shar as 'a man gathering firewood in the dark'[1] – but in my experience, the most consistently reliable tool is real-time transits. In fact, other techniques used for subdividing a year may function less reliably not because they are in themselves invalid, but because they are so far down the predictive hierarchy that they can be trumped by a powerful transit.

General indications of early or late events

As mentioned previously, separating aspects in the figure of the revolution can signify events that are already wholly or partly in the past. A logical extension of that principle would be for the distance (in time or space) within which *applying* configurations perfect to be an indication of how soon the event signified will manifest. Although I have not seen this explicitly stated by any ancient author, my own experience suggests that such is indeed the case: an aspect that is partile or quite close to perfecting in the revolution is more likely to correspond to an early event, whereas an aspect that is far from perfecting, formed across sign borders, and/or involves a planet changing direction, may manifest closer to the end of the year.

We have already seen examples of this above. In the revolution of the man who drowned within weeks of his forty-seventh birthday (p. 138), Mercury, which was both the promissor (anaereta) and ruler of the year, was partilely conjunct Saturn on the cusp of the eighth house; both planets were also partilely conjunct *natal* Mercury. Conversely, in the revolution of the woman whose wedding was brought forward so as to take place at the very end of her twenty-second year of life (p. 130), Mercury – once more ruler of the year, and also divisor of the ascendant – first seemed to be separating from Jupiter (ruler of the seventh house) but eventually changed direction and perfected the aspect after some weeks. More instances will be discussed below.

Identifying key transits

As noted in Chapter 4, the most important transits are those *of* the chronocrators and *to* the directed places of the significators; and to these we may add transits to the natal places of the chronocrators. This is as true of the ongoing transits during the year as it is of the 'freeze-frame' transits at the time of the revolution – but with the important additional consideration of the varying velocities of the planets: the transit of the Moon, which covers some 13° of the ecliptic per day, obviously cannot be used analogously to that of Saturn, which on average travels the same distance in a year.

As also mentioned previously (in Chapter 5), Abū Maʿshar at the very end of his treatment of transits in annual prediction states as a rule that if a transit configuration occurs between two planets that were already configured in the nativity, it signifies an event with an old cause; if the planets were configured only in the revolution, the cause is recent; and if neither, the cause is unknown. Turning this principle around, if two planets are configured in the revolution (and even more surely if they were also configured in the nativity), the event signified by that configuration may be expected to occur when it repeats in transit. It is not entirely clear to me whether Abū Maʿshar was talking about a real-time aspect between two transiting planets or about one planet transiting the revolution placement of another, but in my own experience, the former is the more common scenario.

Like real-time aspect configurations, the real-time zodiacal dignity or debility and solar phases of the planets involved are important in judging the effects of transits. In particular, the stations of the five non-luminary planets – turning retrograde (first station) and direct again (second station) – often quite literally signify turning points, that is, definite changes for better or worse.

A final question is whether transits to the revolution itself – through its houses and over its planets and aspect points – are astrologically meaningful. Abū Maʿshar, unsurprisingly, wants transits to be considered relative to not just two, but three sets of houses: those of the nativity, the profection, and the revolution. This is not something I would personally recommend, but I have seen appropriate transits both through houses and to planetary positions in the revolution just a little too often to dismiss them. I do, however, consider them something of

Example revisited: on the wings of love

In the previous chapter (p. 125) we examined the nativity of a woman who, as the ascendant was directed through the terms of Venus (ruler of the seventh house) with the trine of Venus falling in them, conquered her fear of flying in order to start a new life with her new-found partner (figure 58). As discussed in that chapter, Venus in the revolution was powerfully placed but applying by square to Mars in the seventh house. Let us now consider the transits.

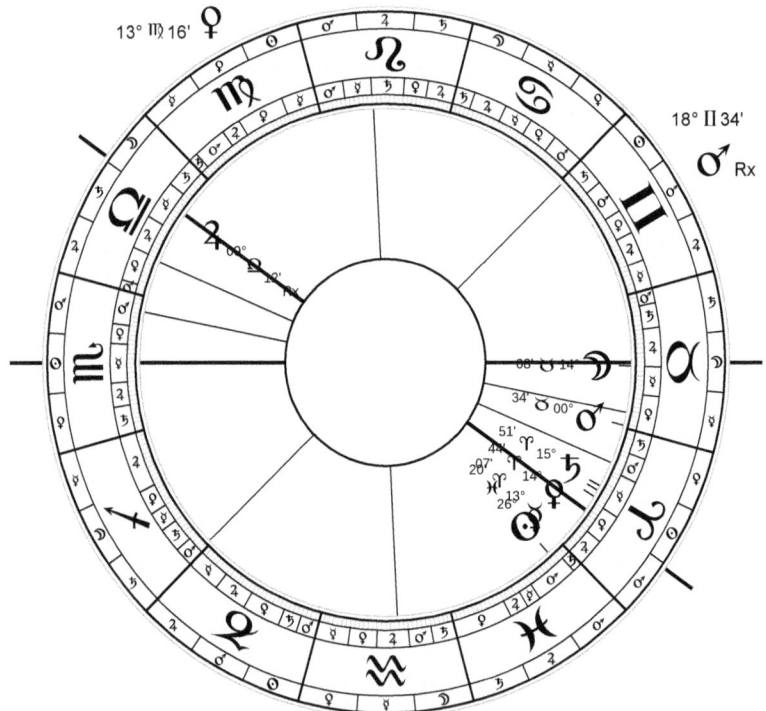

Figure 58: Nativity H, noon transits on 15 November, 2007.

The native's initial, abortive attempt to make her cross-country journey took place around mid-November of 2007. Although the exact date is not on record, we may note that Venus was transiting Virgo – its sign of fall – from 3 November to 29 November and repeating its square to transiting Mars in the revolution, coming within the latter's orb on 12 November. On 15 November, Mars underwent its first (retrograde) station in Gemini, opposite the sign of the profection, and the transiting square perfected on 20 November. We thus see three principles of transit interpretation coming together: first, that the results of aspect configurations in the revolution may manifest when the same planets are configured by transit; second, that the real-time

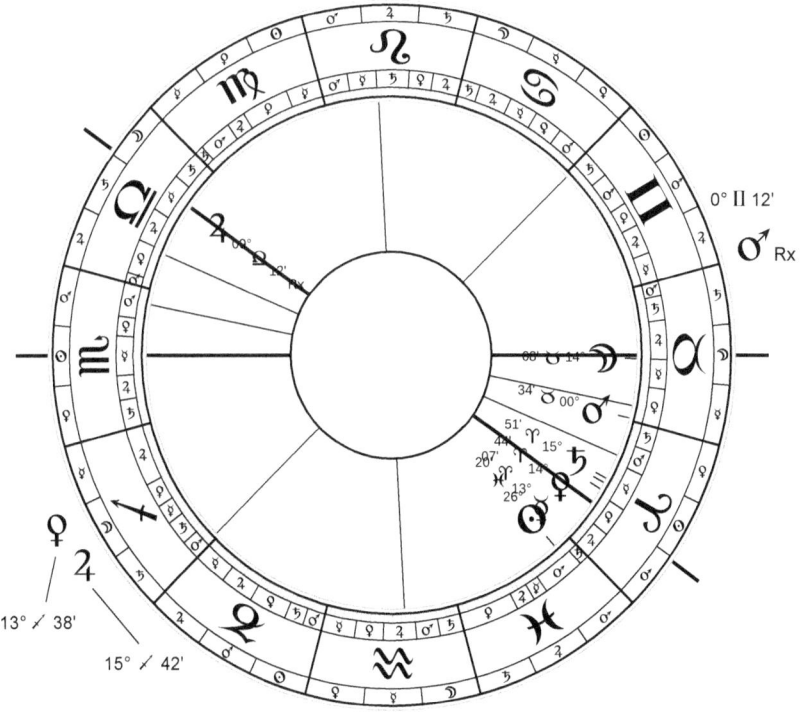

Figure 59: Nativity H, noon transits on 30 January, 2008.

dignity or debility of a planet affects its action in transit; and third, that the transiting stations of chronocrators or of planets configured with them often indicate critical times.

About two months later, the native made her first successful flight across the country on 14 January, 2008. This was less than 24 hours after transiting Jupiter, ruler of the year, had entered the terms of Venus in its own domicile Sagittarius, which was also the sign of the profection, and from where it closely trined natal Venus. The native briefly returned home to settle her affairs before moving permanently on 30 January. The day before this final journey, transiting Venus had entered the same terms in Sagittarius and was now applying to conjoin Jupiter there (figure 59). Again, we see several important transit principles at work, as the two chief chronocrators activated both the division (the terms of a directed significator, in this case the ascendant in 12°–17° Sagittarius) and the sign of the profection.

This latter transit also meant that *natal* Venus as both promissor and divisor was doubly activated by trine aspect, which merits a separate mention: if Venus and Jupiter had transited the same degrees in Pisces, for instance, they would still have activated the division in Sagittarius by casting their aspects into it, but would not have been in any aspect relationship with natal Venus in Aries, which would have lessened their impact somewhat. The very fact of the two benefic chronocrators conjoining in transit also indicates a positive event; furthermore, both planets were in their own dignities by sign and terms, respectively. Finally, the date on which the move was finalized also coincided with the second (direct) station of transiting Mars.

The critical role of stations

While major events can definitely take place without planets stationing in transit, such stations do seem to figure in a disproportionate number of cases. In Chapters 6 and 7 we looked at the chart of an elderly man who broke both his legs in two successive accidents (pp. 82, 89). Only the date of the first accident is known, although the second one reportedly took place within a month or two. The astrological indication of the double event was Mars partilely conjunct the directed ascendant and afflicting Jupiter – divisor and ruler of the year – by a partile square at the time of the revolution, both planets occupying double-bodied signs and Jupiter being retrograde. Mars also aspected *natal* Jupiter with a slightly wider square.

After separating from Jupiter following the birthday, Mars ingressed into Libra where it stationed in early March, 2014; within a few days, Jupiter too stationed and turned direct. Mars then re-entered Virgo in retrograde motion and once more began applying to transit

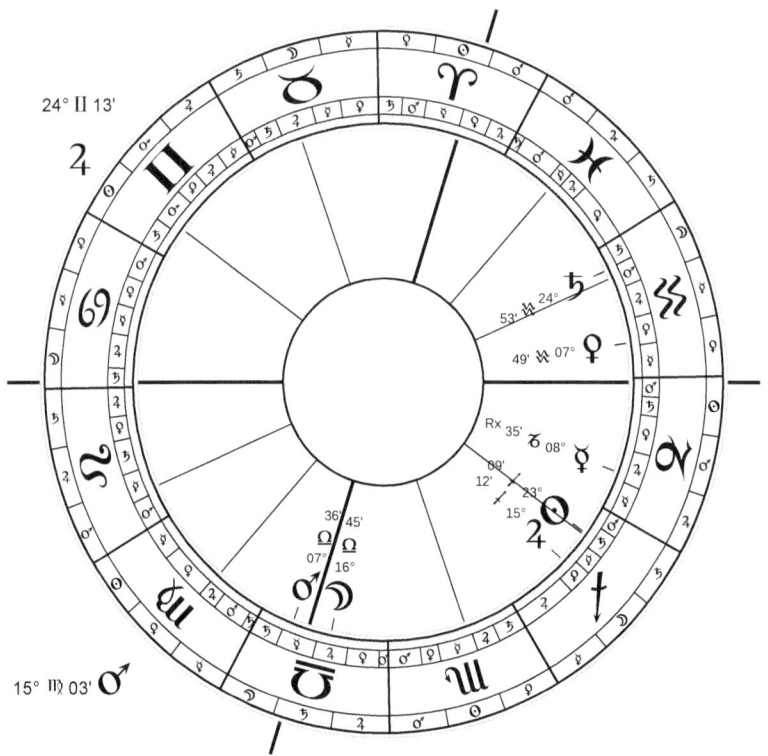

Figure 60: Nativity A, noon transits on 20 May, 2014.

Jupiter by square; but the accident occurred only on 20 May, when Mars stationed for the second time, in partile square to Jupiter in the nativity (figure 60) and in partile opposition to the Moon in the revolution.

Another nativity discussed in some detail in previous chapters is that of a scholar recognized by several awards early in his career. The transits at age 23 are particularly interesting: in the revolution for that year (shown on p. 106), exalted Mercury was conjunct the Sun on the midheaven, casting a trine aspect into the terms of the directed ascendant in Capricorn. The promissors strong in a double-bodied sign (Virgo) suggest a repeated event related to literary or academic achievement. A few months into this year, transit Jupiter stationed near the same degrees in Virgo, in trine to the directed ascendant (22°–26°). While it was transiting this area (the exact date is unavailable), the native was informed that he had been selected for an award relating to his previous work. Some five months later, Jupiter again transited the same degrees, this time in direct motion. At that time, a new work by the native was published. The symbolism of these transits – looking back and forward, respectively, as it were – seems highly appropriate.

A darker example found in Chapter 8 is that of a single death seen from the perspective of two nativities: that of the man who died and that of his mother, who found him (p. 132). In the male nativity, there were two possible choices for the hyleg or chief significator of life, namely, the Moon or Mars. Both of these, along with the ascendant, were directed through the terms of Jupiter at the time, making Jupiter an important chronocrator, and the native died within 24 hours of its first station, on 5 May, 1996. It is also worth noting that although Mercury was not a major chronocrator, it too had stationed less than a day before Jupiter, in the eighth house of the revolution (figure 61), in which it ruled the ascendant and was afflicted by Mars (seemingly separating but in fact about to retrogress and perfect the conjunction).

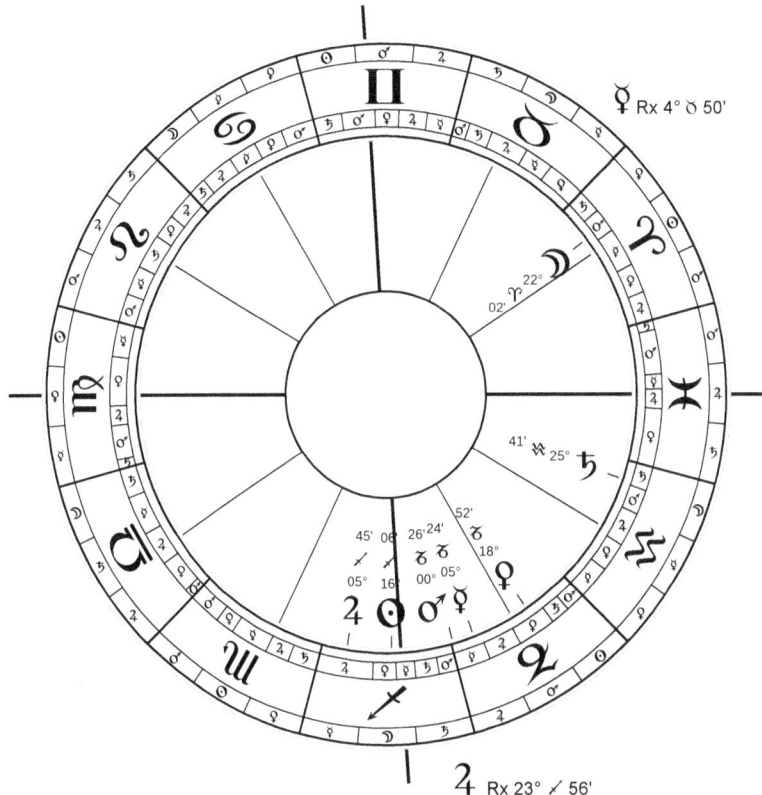

Figure 61: Native E, revolution at age 37 with morning transits for 5 May, 1996.

For the mother, too, Jupiter – universal significator of children – was an important chronocrator by ruling the year; as discussed in the previous chapter, it was also afflicted by both malefics in her revolution and conjunct the fallen Moon in the fifth house of her nativity. It is therefore not surprising that Jupiter stationing in transit should mark the time of the tragic event from the mother's perspective.

Twenty years later, this native passed away herself (an event not discussed above). Without going into the vexed question of the hyleg and longevity procedures, we may note that the profection in that year had reached Scorpio, making Mars ruler of the year. In the revolution (figure 62), the profection degree (not shown) was partilely conjunct the fallen Moon, universal significator of the body and ruler of the first house of the nativity; they were also within a few degrees of the fallen *natal* Moon. The Moon in the revolution is further separating from Saturn (ruler of the eighth house in the nativity) and configured with Mars by a partile square; but Mars itself is partilely conjunct Jupiter, a mitigating factor. What actually happened was that the native, whose general health was quite debilitated, began to suffer from a severe and protracted illness within weeks of her seventy-sixth birthday but partially recovered and stabilized, contrary to her doctors' expectations. About halfway through the year, Saturn and Mars both stationed in Scorpio; a few months later, the native died suddenly in her sleep within 24 hours of Mars' second station, on 1 July, 2016.

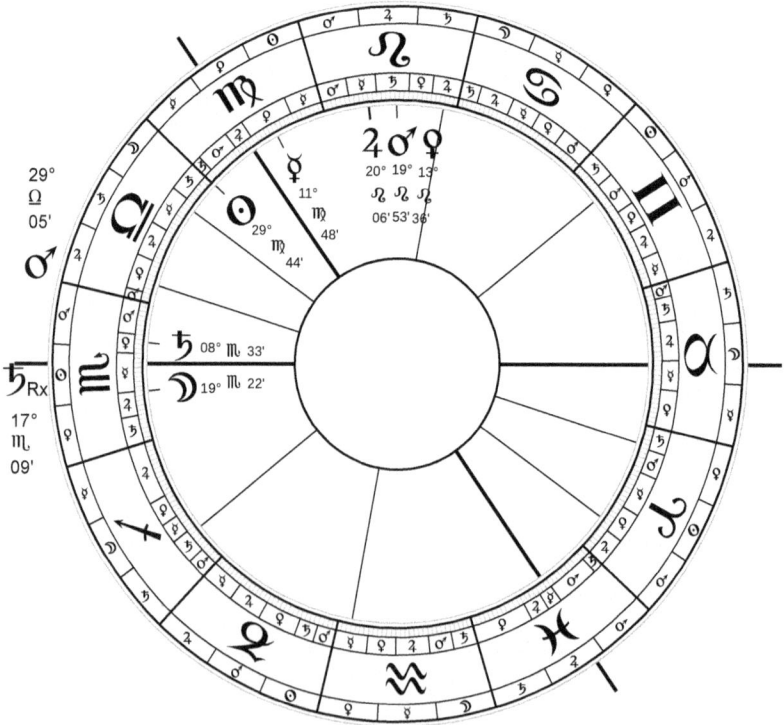

Figure 62: Native B, revolution at age 76 with night transits for 1 July, 2016.

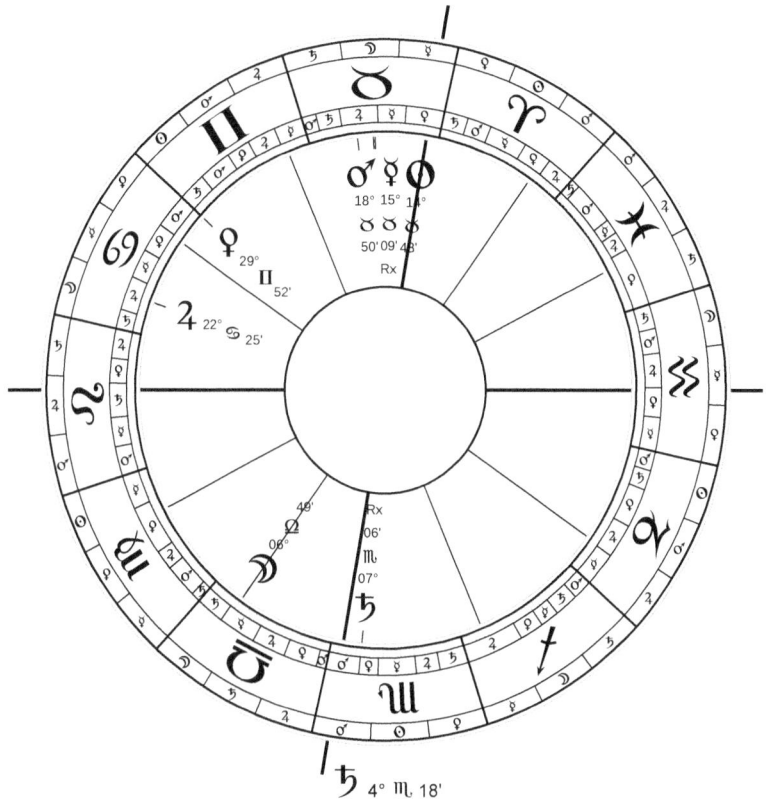

*Figure 63: Native G, revolution 46
with noon transits for 4 August, 2015.*

As a final instance, for now, of chronocrators stationing in transit (though many more could easily be added), let us look at the example from Chapters 7 and 8 (pp. 93, 111) of the native who lost his father at the age of 46 (figure 63). In addition to the Sun, natally in the eighth house, ruling the year and being afflicted by Mars both in the nativity and in the revolution, the directed ascendant was in the terms of Mars in Scorpio, conjunct the revolution IC (quadrant fourth-house cusp, signifying parents) and retrograde Saturn. On judging this revolution, I stated that while I *hoped* nothing serious would happen to the native's parents, *if* it did, it would probably be around the time of Saturn's second station on 2 August, 2015. On 3 August, the native's father (aged 78) was unexpectedly taken severely ill, admitted to hospital and diagnosed with sepsis – that is to say blood poisoning, highly pertinent for Saturn in the terms of Mars. On the next day, he died.

Transits as intensifying factors

In Chapter 8 we discussed some dramatic events in the life of the native of figure 64. I also mentioned that the native, who is himself a practising astrologer, believes his actual time of birth to have been a few minutes earlier than the time recorded. This conjecture is supported by events at age 53, related below. In addition to the importance of chronocrators stationing by transit, this example demonstrates how transits *to* chronocrators and to the directed places of significators – particularly the transits of slow-moving and/or stationing planets – may intensify an event, even when the transiting planet (in this case, Mars) is neither a chronocrator nor closely configured with the chronocrators in the revolution.

According to the official time of birth, the ascendant was directed in that year through the terms of Jupiter (14°–22°) in Taurus and about a degree past the square of the Sun, which as ruler of the eighth house in the first (by quadrant division) indicates potential danger to life. A birth time five minutes earlier would make that aspect perfect at age 53 instead, with the ascendant still in the terms of Mercury (8°–14°). The annual profection of the ascendant having reached Gemini, Mercury (ruling the sixth house of illness) was also ruler of the year.

The native first became aware of the impending dangerous configurations in the early part of the year. Within a few weeks he began to experience chest pains and irregular pulse and naturally suspected some trouble with his heart (a universal signification of the Sun). The discomfort intensified as transiting Mars – not itself a chronocrator – gradually slowed and then stationed in Scorpio in mid-April, within

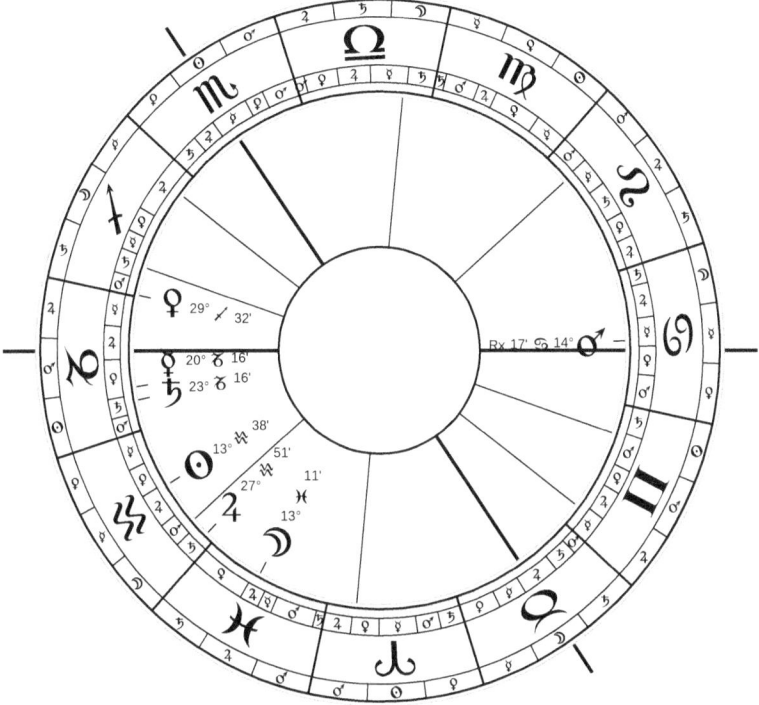

Figure 64: Nativity F.

two degrees of a square with the natal Sun and opposite the directed ascendant. Previous negative experiences of hospitals and conventional medicine made the native unwilling to seek professional help, but he did ask for my astrological judgement of his current year of life. After examining the revolution carefully, I gave it as my opinion that while the transit of Mars might be dangerous, the year did not look fatal.

A potentially critical point in time was the upcoming station of Mercury, ruler of the year and probable divisor of the ascendant, on 28 April, 2016. The native lived alone, and on the day of the station I contacted him to see how he was. He related having felt a great pressure in his chest and weakness in his left extremities for several days but said that he was now feeling better after resting and taking herbal supplements to dilate the blood vessels. Unfortunately, on returning home from a walk the same evening – just as Mercury was stationing, and only hours after our conversation – the native began suddenly to experience extreme chest pain with violent palpitations. He passed out while sitting on a chair in his living room and, when he came to after an unknown period of time, found himself lying on the floor next to the overturned chair, drenched in sweat and with a feeling of severe bruising in his chest. Despite this he chose not to call for medical help once he was able to get up, but simply dragged himself to bed. Although he remained weak and exhausted for some time, his chest

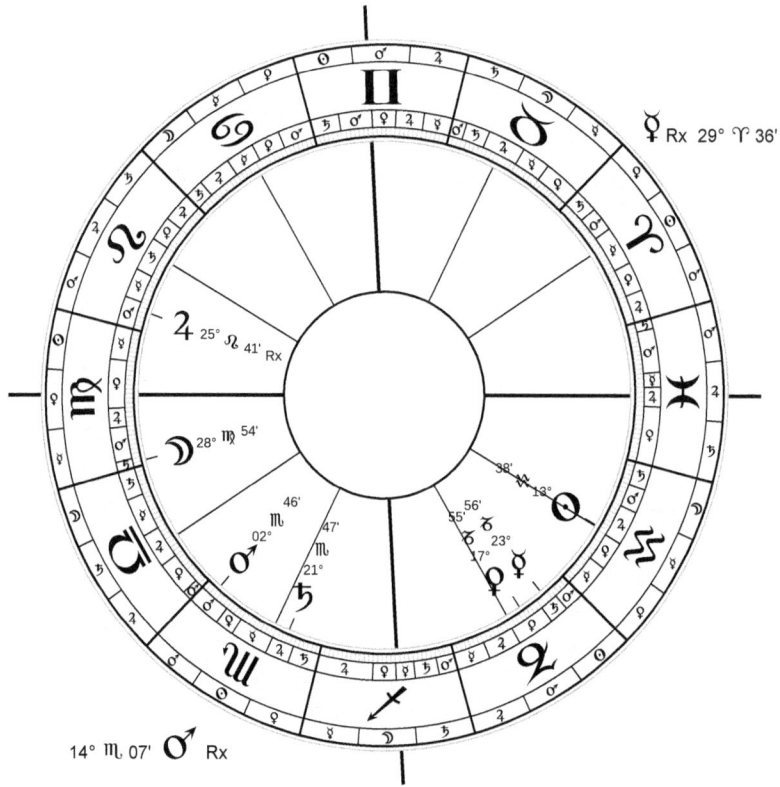

Figure 65: Native F, revolution at age 53 with evening transits on 28 April, 2016.

too painful for him to lift even the smallest object, he did survive the ordeal, which was almost certainly a myocardial infarction.

In the revolution for age 53 (figure 65), the Sun as promissor of the ascendant occupies the sixth house of illness. An argument could be made for Jupiter recently having become divisor, as it is poorly placed in the revolution – retrograde in the twelfth house, in a mutually applying square with Saturn – but as Jupiter was not clearly involved by transit at the time of the event, I rather incline to the view that the birth time should be adjusted slightly, tightening the time frame of the malefic direction and making Mercury divisor as well as ruler of the year. In either case, it seems clear that transiting Mars played a part not only in timing but in intensifying the evil results indicated by direction.

In a sequel to this event, the next time that Mercury ruled the year, which was at age 56, the native suffered once more from a potentially life-threatening condition caused by a blood clot – this time in the form of an ischemic stroke – but survived again. In the revolution for that year (figure 66), Mercury is in its fall in Pisces and within a degree of a sextile to Venus; but that aspect never perfects to the minute. Instead, Mercury stations and begins applying to a conjunction with the Sun, ruler of the natal eighth house occupying the eighth of the revolution. Although distant and outside the orb of either planet, this is the first application that Mercury actually perfects – which again agrees with the principle of wide aspects, particularly those involving changes of sign and/or motion, signifying events late in the year.

By this time, the directed ascendant had definitely moved into the terms of Jupiter in Taurus, where it encountered the sextile aspect of the fallen Mars. In the revolution, the Moon (universal significator of the body generally) cast an opposition aspect into those same terms from its sign of fall. Mars itself, powerfully angular, formed a partile square to its own natal position and a close square to natal Mercury,

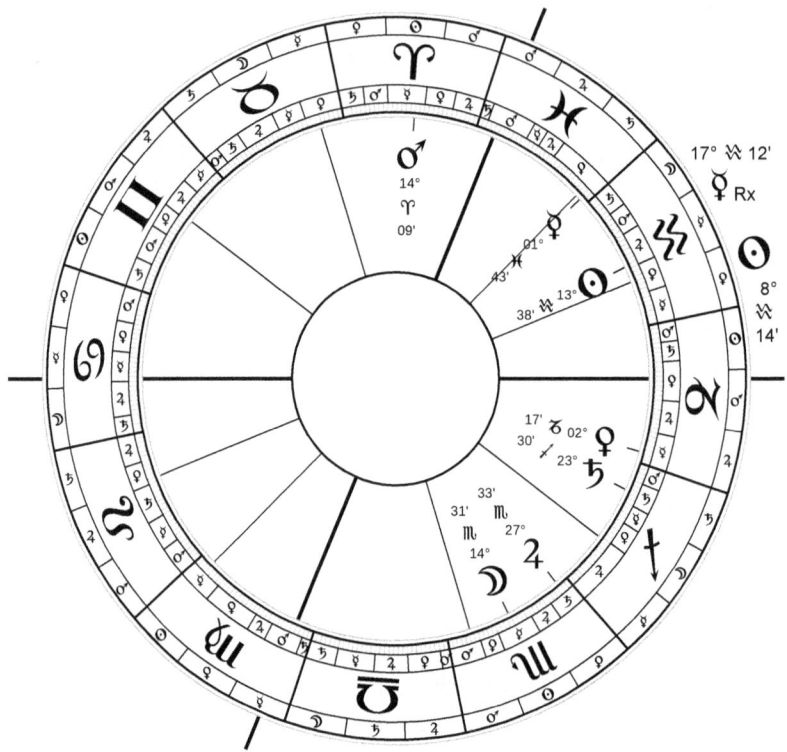

Figure 66: Native F, revolution at age 56 with noon transits on 21 February, 2020.

ruler of the year, thereby reactivating their configuration by opposition in the nativity. Given their sudden nature and relation to blood, strokes are typically associated with Mars, particularly in Aries, which signifies the head. On 17 February, 2020, Mercury again stationed in transit and began to apply to the radical Sun by retrograde motion while casting a square into the terms of the directed ascendant; four days later, the native suffered his stroke. It is interesting to note that at the times of both these dangerous events, Mercury as ruler of the year had recently stationed in the eighth house of the revolution.

Repeating indications and transit triggers

Staying with the same nativity a little longer, let us examine a less traumatic type of event and see how repetition may give us a clue as to which transits to look out for. At age 54, the native had just bought a house in the country and relocated there, but had not yet sold his flat in town. In the space of just eight days, and with no causal links between the two events, he suffered water damage first to his now unoccupied flat and then to his new house. The ascendant at this time was directed through the terms of Jupiter in Taurus, where the IC or cusp of the fourth house (signifying the home) falls in the nativity, and

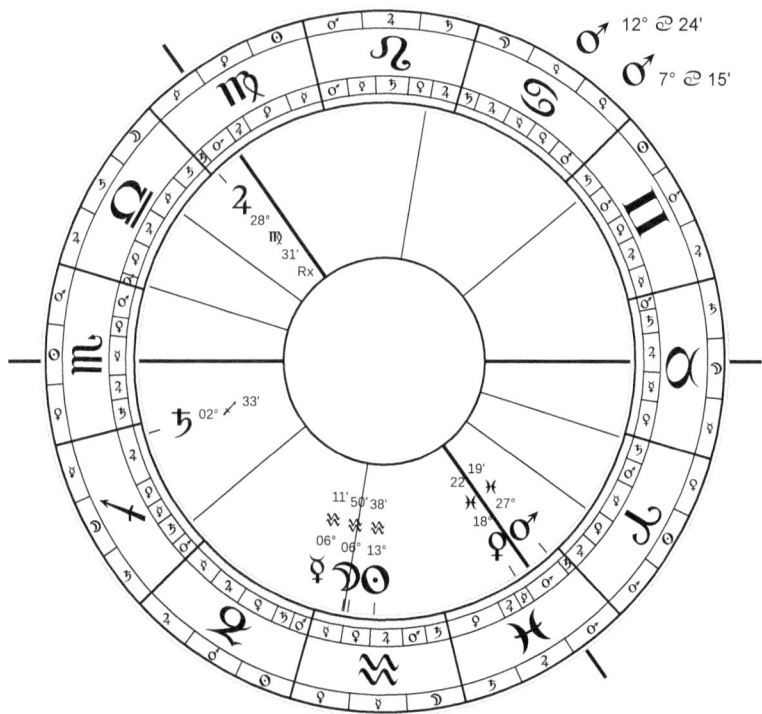

Figure 67: Native F, revolution at age 54 with noon transits on 22 and 30 July, 2017.

into which Mars in its fall in the watery sign of Cancer casts a sextile aspect. By profection, the ascendant had reached Cancer, emphasizing this connection and making the Moon ruler of the year; the Moon itself is in Pisces, another water sign.

In the revolution for this year (figure 67), Mars as promissor of the ascendant is likewise in Pisces, in the fourth house, and forming a close and mutually applying opposition with Jupiter, the divisor of the ascendant. We thus see Mars influencing (a) the division, or terms of the directed ascendant; (b) the divisor Jupiter; and (c) the sign of the profection; we also see a recurring emphasis on water signs and the fourth house. In addition, Mars and Jupiter both occupy double-bodied signs, suggesting the possibility of a repeated event. A harmful event (Mars being a malefic) involving water and the fourth house is likely to be a flooding of some sort, and the significator returning by transit to its natal position in its sign of fall, which is also activated as the sign of the annual profection, would clearly be one potentially critical time. This, in fact, was what happened: both floodings took place as Mars transited Cancer close to its own position in the nativity.

The greater and lesser conditions

As briefly discussed in Chapter 7, some modern practitioners believe that profections were originally used in a manner that either ignored degrees entirely or 'jumped' exactly 30° on each birthday. As there is no actual statement to that effect in the early sources, this belief is based wholly on an argument from silence, assuming that degrees were never used in ancient astrology unless explicitly stated – a position which I personally find unconvincing. Be that as it may, by the eighth century ʿUmar aṭ-Ṭabarī explicitly taught the use of profections as a continuous motion, using both the ascendant of the nativity and that of the revolution. In the medieval Latin translation of ʿUmar's work (the Arabic text has not yet been edited or translated into modern languages), the former technique is called the *maiora esse* or 'greater condition', while the latter is known as the *minora esse* or 'lesser condition'. Both these methods of continuous profection are also included in Abū Maʿshar's arsenal of techniques for timing events within a year.² I have occasionally found them useful, although they do need to be considered together with real-time transits and can be overridden by major transits of the types discussed above.

The greater and lesser conditions may be regarded as a system of major and minor planetary periods. The greater condition begins from the profected position of the natal ascendant on the day of the revolution and proceeds at a rate of 30° per year along the ecliptic (that is, in the zodiac), which is to say 2°30′ per month or some 12.175 days per degree – in the sexagesimal format used by Abū Maʿshar, 12;10,30 days. If the profected ascendant encounters the body or aspect of a planet, that planet becomes a chronocrator up to the time of the next encounter. Abū Maʿshar adds that if there is no planet or aspect in the terms where the ascendant is, the ruler of the terms itself is the chronocrator.

The profection of the lesser condition works in the same way as the greater but begins from the ascendant of the *revolution* and proceeds at a rate of 360° per year, which is to say 0°59′08″ per day (the mean daily motion of the Sun through the zodiac). These profections, too, are made in ordinary ecliptical degrees, *pace* Dykes: Abū Maʿshar mentions that the daily rate is an approximation because ideally, in his view, it should follow the true daily motion of the Sun (which can vary from the mean by a few minutes of arc either way depending on the time of year); but there is no indication that either he or ʿUmar intended for this method to be used with ascensional degrees, that is, as a form of primary direction. If you want to use the true solar rate of motion, simply note the exact distance of the Sun from the ascendant – or vice versa, whichever is more convenient – in the revolution and apply the same distance to the Sun's transit throughout the year to find the current position of the profected ascendant.

It is not entirely clear from either ʿUmar's or Abū Maʿshar's description whether the profected motion, particularly of the greater condition, takes place through the figure of the nativity, of the revolution, or both. Kūshyār ibn Labbān (971–1029) in his introduction to astrology is a little more explicit and seems to advocate using both, but with certain provisos.[3] Planets in the nativity are more powerful than those in the revolution, but only if they are *also* angular in the revolution; natal malefics that are not angular in the revolution signify hardships that can be overcome. Two or more indications in the revolution can also trump a natal indication, especially if the planets in the revolution are angular. Finally, malefics in either figure may be counteracted by aspects from benefics, unless the malefics are more powerfully placed than the benefics. Kūshyār makes no mention of the terms but only of the bodies and aspects of the planets – and, from the beginning of a sign up to the first planet or aspect, the ruler of the *sign* as ruler of a period.

To illustrate the method, let us look at the first example discussed in this chapter (p. 164), of the woman prompted by love to move across the country despite her fear of flying. By ordinary annual profection, as used in ʿUmar's greater condition, the ascendant had reached Sagittarius in that year, starting at 14°54′ (the same degree and minute as the ascendant in the nativity). It then progressed at a rate of 12.175 days per degree, completing a full sign or 30° in 365.25 days. Table 2 shows the times during that year in which the profected ascendant entered the various terms and encountered the bodies and aspect points of the planets in the nativity and the revolution, respectively.

When the native made her first, failed attempt to get on a plane, she was about 219 days into her current year of life (give or take a few days, as the exact date is not on record; the figure is for 15 November).

As seen from the table, the profected ascendant was then in the terms of Mercury in Capricorn, having most recently met with the trine of Mars in the nativity. It is worth noting that Mercury in the revolution was in its fall in the eighth house. If we want to know the exact degree of the profection, we simply divide 219 by the daily rate of 12.175 days, yielding just under 18°, and count these off from the starting point in Sagittarius. Exactly 60 days later, the native completed her first journey successfully; the profection at that time had recently entered the terms of Jupiter, which was the ruler of the year. On the day in question, Venus was transiting the position of Jupiter in the revolution within 2°.

Longitude	Terms	Nativity	Revolution	Days
14°54′ ♐	♀	△ ♀		0
15°51′		△ ♄		11
17°00′	☿			25
21°00′	♄			74
22°23′			☌ ☽	91
26°00′	♂			135
26°20′		□ ☉		139
0°00′ ♑	☿			183
0°34′		△ ♂		190
4°13′			△ ♀	235
5°20′			✶ ☿	248
7°00′	♃			269
9°12′		□ ♃		295
13°07′		□ ☿		343
14°00′	♀			354
14°44′		□ ♀		363

Table 2. Greater-condition periods for native H with starting dates in days into the year of life (rounded to whole numbers) at age 37.

The lesser condition is calculated in the same way, except that the starting point is the ascendant of the revolution figure (which was 29°44′ in Cancer) and the total distance travelled 360°. A complete table of these profections would run to several pages, but we can calculate the exact positions for the two dates in question by multiplying the number of days by the daily rate of 0°59′08″ and adding the result to the starting point. For the failed attempt, this will give 5°34′ Pisces, partilely conjunct the fallen Mercury in the eighth house of the revolution; for the successful attempt, it will give 4°42′ Taurus, partilely conjunct the dignified Venus in the tenth house. Alternatively, we may note that the ascendant of the revolution was exactly 123°24′ ahead of the Sun and add that distance to the daily transit positions of the Sun, which will give figures within a few degrees of those just mentioned.

Although my confidence in these methods is, for the reasons stated above, not absolute, in principle there is another useful side to fine-grained timing techniques. Sometimes we know the *time* of a planned event – such as a test, an interview, a competition or the announcement of a decision – in advance, but are less sure of the outcome. In such cases the techniques can be used in reverse, as it were, to determine whether a fortunate or unfortunate event is more likely to take place on the date in question.

Primary directions from the revolution?

As already mentioned, neither ʿUmar's nor Abū Maʿshar's description of the techniques just discussed contains any mention of distances measured in degrees of ascension – in other words, of primary directions applied to the figure of the revolution. In an earlier part of his work, however, Abū Maʿshar does make such a reference in passing:

> And you make the degrees of direction in the root of the
> nativity be years, but in the revolution of years months

and days, and in the revolutions of months [you make them be] days and hours.[4]

The context of this sentence makes it clear that Abū Maʿshar is speaking of actual (primary) directions calculated by oblique, direct or mixed ascensions; but the mention appears only in the third book, dealing with directions in general, and does not recur in the ninth book on timing techniques within a year, which is where the greater and lesser conditions (or, in Dykes's translation of Abū Maʿshar's terminology, 'mighty days' and 'small days', respectively) are discussed.

I am not aware of any preserved early examples of directions applied to revolution figures. In the Renaissance period, however, some astrologers wanted to do away with the purely symbolic motion of profections and replace them with the more naturalistic method of directions adapted for use within a single year. The best-known proponent of this approach was Morin, who devoted two chapters of his *Astrologia Gallica* to it.[5] For those who wish to experiment with them, some astrology software, such as the freeware Morinus, calculates primary directions from the revolution using the rate of 0°59′08″ per day to cover a full 360° in a year. Should you prefer to try out Abū Maʿshar's suggestion of a degree for a month, you can use the same function but ignore all directions with an arc above 12°. My own experiments with directions in the revolution (examining both tropical and sidereal figures in a spirit of open-minded investigation) have, however, not been encouraging.

Monthly and daily profections and revolutions

The methods explored so far for narrowing down times within a year are all based on manipulating the figure of the nativity or the annual revolution. A different approach is to devise additional figures or layers of interpretation. The latter include monthly and daily profections:

just as each zodiacal sign is equated with a single year in annual profections, so in monthly profections each sign is allotted a month, making the zodiac as a whole correspond to a year; and in so-called daily profections, the entire zodiac is equated with a month (so that each sign really corresponds to two days and a fraction).

Monthly and daily profections are discussed by both Ptolemy and other Greek-language authors, but their methods of calculating them differ. Ptolemy advocated a month of 28 days, which Abū Maʿshar explicitly rejected as he believed it to be based on the lunar cycle; in its place he proposed a wholly solar month based on the transit of the Sun in increments of exactly 30°.[6] But Abū Maʿshar had almost certainly misunderstood Ptolemy: there is no lunar month of 28 days – the Moon completes a revolution of the zodiac in approximately 27.3 days, and a synodic cycle with the Sun in 29.5 days, and such imprecise approximations of observable phenomena would have been uncharacteristic of the naturalist Ptolemy. Rather, Ptolemy's figure appears to be based on the division of a solar year into *thirteen* (not twelve) months, to form a continuous motion with the annual profections.

If there were only twelve profection months in a year, then an Aries year would begin with an Aries month and end with a Pisces month. This would be followed by a Taurus year starting with a Taurus month, making the monthly profection proceed directly from Pisces to Taurus, omitting Aries. To avoid such gaps, an extra month is needed; and dividing a year of approximately 365.25 days by 13 yields a month of just over 28 days (thirteen 28-day months come to 364 days). Other authors, such as Paul of Alexandria, do seem to advocate twelve monthly profections to a year, which would give a month of approximately 30½ days.[7] This, too, is rejected by Abū Maʿshar.[8] It is probably not a coincidence that these two calculation models correspond to the two ways of deriving the so-called dodecatemoria or twelfth-parts of a sign, one of which actually yields thirteen divisions (the first and last being assigned to the sign itself). Both models are attested from Babylonian times and are present in both Greek and Sanskrit sources.

If the received text of the *Tetrabiblos* is correct, however, Ptolemy was not entirely consistent, as the duration of his 'daily profections' is given as 2⅓ days (corroborated by Abū Maʿshar). This corresponds to a further division of 28 days by *twelve* signs, although thirteen would be required to make the daily profection continuous with the monthly one. The latter alternative would come to approximately 2⅙ days; but although there is some variation in the manuscript sources, no variant seems to support that figure.

Just as the greater-condition technique consists of a continuous *annual* profection from the nativity, equating one year with 30°, so some astrologers, including Kūshyār ibn Labbān, describe a continuous *monthly* profection which equates one year with 390° (thirteen signs), making one day correspond to 1°04′04″. This is close to the rate of the lesser condition but calculated from the ascendant of the nativity rather than that of the revolution. To give just one calculation example, in the nativity discussed above (native H), the profection of the ascendant on the thirty-seventh birthday had reached 14°54′ in Sagittarius. The successful journey took place some 279 days into that year, corresponding to an arc of 297°54′. Adding that arc to 14°54′ in Sagittarius brings us to 12°48′ in Libra.

In addition to profections of various kinds, medieval and Renaissance astrologers sometimes advocated the use of separate revolution figures cast for every month or even day. Not everyone was convinced of their usefulness, however, and Kūshyār wrote:

> Many astrologers go into details concerning the operation in the revolution so that they revolve it month by month, week by week, and day by day. Even if this is part of the art ⟨of astrology⟩, it is one of the branches which

are far from the bases, and generalization of the teaching in it concerning its judgment is impossible but they are dependent on coincidences, even though papers are filled with them.[9]

The most common time to use for casting a monthly revolution figure is the moment at which the Sun enters the same degree, minute and second of arc that it occupied in the nativity, but in each of the twelve zodiacal signs. In other words, these are true solar months, as distinct from synodic months (calculated from one New or Full Moon to the next), Ptolemy's 28-day months, etc. This is the method prescribed by Abū Ma'shar and followed by the Indian Tājika astrologers. Similarly, 'daily' revolutions are cast for the moment at which the Sun enters its natal minute and second in each *degree* of the zodiac – which means that there are only 360 such revolutions in a solar year, not 365.

I have not personally found these monthly or daily revolutions to be astrologically useful. I do see some value in the monthly profections of Ptolemy, which I regard as a continuous motion where rulership is handed over from one planet to the next at thirty-degree intervals, on the same principle as annual profections; but I would echo Ptolemy's remark that real-time transits 'to the places of the times [...] play no small part in the prediction of the times of events'. When a new sign becomes activated by monthly profection, planets occupying it in the nativity and/or the annual revolution come into focus (more so if they are already activated as chronocrators at a higher level), as do the ruler of the sign and transits through the sign. There may even be some validity to casting a chart for the beginning of each monthly profection, though that is not a practice mentioned by Ptolemy and such a figure would, in any case, be far down the predictive hierarchy.

Example: transits and monthly profections

To illustrate the combined use of monthly profections and transits – while acknowledging that the transits of major chronocrators can often be effective even when not activated on this level – let us take another look at the nativity of the award-winning scholar (p. 168), focusing on an event that was not discussed above.

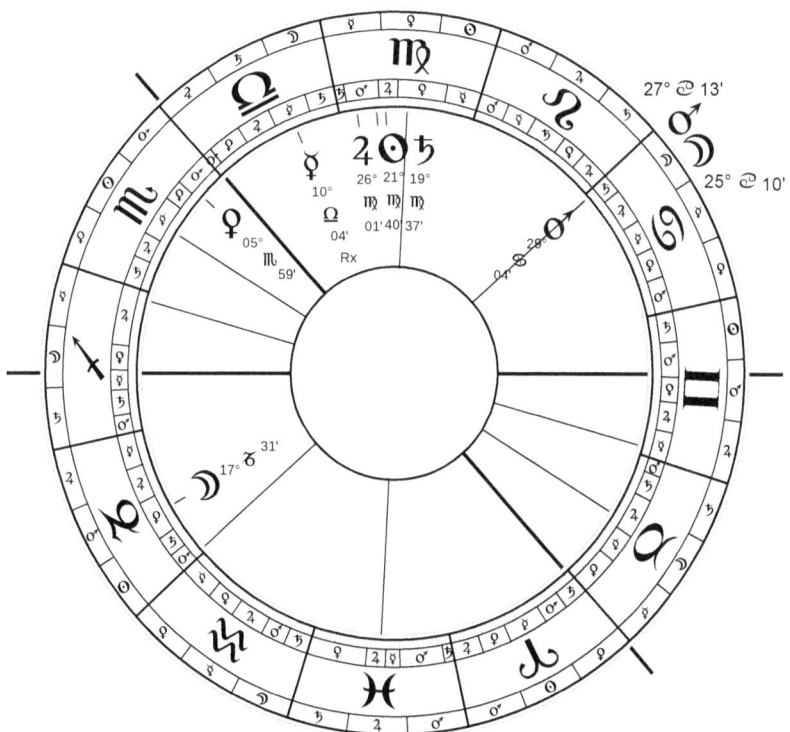

Figure 68: Nativity J, evening transits on 30 September, 2013.

Although age 31 was overall a successful year for the native, it ended on a jarring note as he took a bad fall while walking home from town late one night and was severely concussed – a relatively minor event in itself, but its after-effects were felt on and off for many months. The profection of the ascendant in this year had reached Cancer, making the Moon ruler of the year. In the nativity (figure 68), Mars is in its fall

188   ANNUAL PREDICTIVE TECHNIQUES

at the end of Cancer. In the revolution (figure 69), there are no planets in Cancer, and the Moon forms no applying aspects at all until leaving Gemini, after which it first perfects a square with Saturn and shortly afterwards a trine with Mars. This agrees with what was said above about aspects that are wide and/or involve changes of sign indicating events that take place later in the year.

At the time of the accident, transiting Mars had returned partilely to its natal position in Cancer (the sign of the annual profection), where the Moon as ruler of the year was applying to conjoin it within a few degrees. It may also be relevant to note that the directed ascendant had by this time shifted from the terms of Venus in Aquarius to those

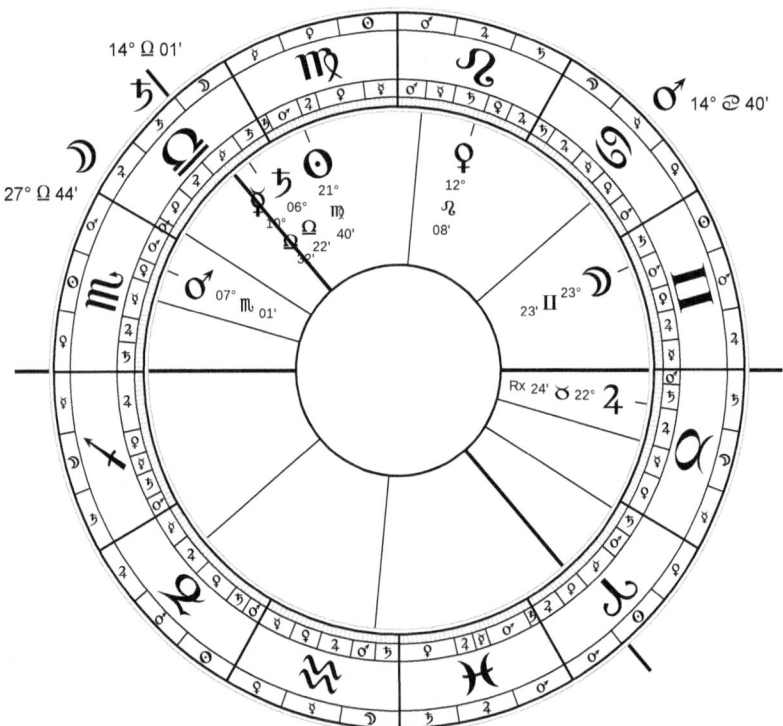

Figure 69: Native J, revolution 31 with transits for the beginning of the last (Cancer) month.

of Jupiter, and that in the revolution, Jupiter – the new divisor of the ascendant and ruler of the first house in the nativity – was in its first (retrograde) station in the sixth house of illness and injury.

Coming now to the monthly profections, in Ptolemy's thirteen-month scheme the first and the last month of the year both belong to the sign of the annual profection – in this case, Cancer – but the transits during the two months will naturally differ. In the annual revolution itself, which was the start of the first Cancer month, there were no transits through that sign; nor was its ruler, the Moon, applying to any other planet. By contrast, at the commencement of the second Cancer month, Mars was transiting Cancer (its fall) in the eighth house of the revolution and was further afflicted by a partile square from Saturn (figure 69). The Moon, ruler of the month as well as the year, was in a partile square with *natal* Mars in Cancer (cf. figure 68). We may regard these placements as setting the scene for the accident which was then triggered by the transiting conjunction of the Moon and Mars.

Tājika *daśā* systems

For timing events, classical or pre-Islamic Indian astrology relies chiefly on systems that divide a life into blocks of time assigned to the planets or, sometimes, zodiacal signs. The most common name for such blocks is *daśā* 'period, condition', and *daśās* may be divided fractally into subperiods (*antardaśā*), subsubperiods (*pratyantardaśā*), and so forth. The *daśā* systems found in the earliest Sanskrit texts probably have Hellenistic roots, but in the medieval period, methods based on the position of the Moon with respect to the twenty-seven indigenous asterisms or *nakṣatras* became popular. A common feature of all *daśā* systems is a lack of the sense of motion that is characteristic of many Hellenistic astrological procedures: there is no 'sending out' of any point to move around the horoscope, just a fixed succession of periods.

The Indian authors who introduced and developed Tājika or Sanskritized Perso-Arabic astrology explicitly contrasted traditional *daśā* systems with annual revolutions, which they said allow for subtler and more detailed predictions. Despite this, however, the *daśā* model was so ingrained that they reinterpreted the Perso-Arabic timing techniques as miniature *daśā* systems, most likely by mistake. Several of these Tājika *daśās* seem to be based on the greater or lesser conditions of ʿUmar, perhaps as described with some variations by different Arabic sources. This includes the systems known as *tāsīra* (from the Arabic *tasyīr* 'sending out', mostly used to denote directions but sometimes also profections) or *haddā-daśā* (from the Arabic *ḥadd*, plural *ḥudūd* 'terms'), but the most common system is called *pātyāyinī* 'going by subtraction' and arranges the planets and ascendant in order of longitudes within their respective signs. The original source presumably did so in order to determine the order in which the profected ascendant would make contact with each planet or its aspect point. I shall not go into the details of the Tājika reinterpretations here, as I believe them to be based on misunderstandings, but they are discussed in my translation of Balabhadra's *Hāyanaratna*.

Other Tājika *daśās* are based on pre-Islamic Indian techniques that have been resized for use within a single year. The 'natural periods' (*nisarga-* or *naisargika-daśā*) described by Varāhamihira in the sixth century[10] and the *vimśottarī daśā* known to all modern students of Indian astrology are both based on a total cycle of 120 years, and the duration of each planet's period in either system is therefore multiplied by 3 to give its length in *days* in a 360-day year. (This manner of calculation does not mean that the year was considered to consist of 360 actual days; rather, these are 'solar days', defined as the time taken by the Sun to transit 1° of the ecliptic. Solar days were then converted to standard 'civil days' as necessary.) For reasons that are not entirely clear, the miniature *vimśottarī* periods are sometimes referred to in

Tājika works by the Arabic word *mudda*, which, like the Sanskrit *daśā*, simply means 'period'.

Sign	Beginning	Ruler	Solar days
♈ ♌ ♐	0°00'	Ketu	21
♈ ♌ ♐	13°20'	Venus	60
♈ ♌ ♐	26°40'	Sun	18
♉ ♍ ♑	10°00'	Moon	30
♉ ♍ ♑	23°20'	Mars	21
♊ ♎ ♒	6°40'	Rāhu	54
♊ ♎ ♒	20°00'	Jupiter	48
♋ ♏ ♓	3°20'	Saturn	57
♋ ♏ ♓	16°40'	Mercury	51

Table 3: The nakṣatra *rulers and their periods (*mudda-daśā*).*

For readers not familiar with Indian *daśās*, table 3 lists the extensions of the standardized *nakṣatras* or asterisms and their rulers in the *viṃśottarī* system (repeating three times in the zodiac), along with the durations of the periods assigned to each planet (including the lunar nodes, Rāhu and Ketu) in the context of annual revolutions. Tājika texts give some counterintuitive rules for calculating the *muddas*, such as using the position of the Moon in the nativity (not the revolution) and a non-proportional method for calculating subperiods. To illustrate the method briefly, focusing on major periods, our concussed academic's Moon was at 17°31' Capricorn in the nativity, in an asterism ruled by the Moon itself. The Moon would therefore rule the first *daśā* of the first year of life. In his second year of life (beginning when he turned one year old), the first period would be ruled by Mars; the year after that, the first period would belong to Rāhu, and so forth. As the native turned 31, the first *daśā* ruler would be Saturn, and the remainder of that period on the day of the revolution would correspond to the distance yet to be covered by the natal Moon in its asterism (the extension of the asterism as a whole being 13°20′). As there were 5°49′ left of the natal asterism, which ends at 23°20′ Capricorn, we thus get 5°49′ / 13°20′ × 57 ≈ 25 'solar days' remaining of Saturn's *daśā*, followed by the *daśās* of Mercury, Ketu, and so on, until Saturn's *daśā* begins for the second time around 32 days before the next birthday. The accident therefore took place in the (second) *mudda-daśā* of Saturn.

Again, details of subperiods and so forth are found in my translation of the *Hāyanaratna*. I do not use these Tājika techniques myself, but for those who wish to experiment with them, Indian astrology software designed to calculate annual revolutions (known in Sanskrit as *varṣaphala*) typically includes one or more *daśā* systems.

Summing up

To summarize what has been said in this chapter, the most useful and important ways of dividing a year of life into smaller parts are, in my experience and in descending order:

Directions changing terms. If the ascendant or another important significator in the nativity moves into a new set of terms during the year, making a new planet its divisor, that shift can signal a major change. The state of the divisor both in the nativity and in the revolution should be considered.

Indications of late or early events. Events that are indicated by an applying configuration between two (or more) planets in the revolution often take place early in the year if the aspect/conjunction is partile or very close to perfecting. Conversely, an aspect that is applying but not yet within orb, or that will only perfect after one or both planets change sign or motion (turning direct or retrograde), often signify an event towards the end of the year. A close but separating aspect may signify an ongoing situation that began prior to the revolution.

Real-time transits. Transits of the chronocrators and to the directed terms of the significators, to the natal places of the chronocrators, and through the sign of the annual profection are the most consistently reliable tools for timing events closely. Look out for repeating configurations between planets already configured in the revolution, and for the transits of planets repeatedly activated by direction and profection. Even planets that are not activated as chronocrators may be important by either intensifying or obstructing/mitigating an event if they transit points that are activated by other techniques. The real-time dignity or debility of transiting planets should be considered, and above all their stations: a major chronocrator stationing in transit often indicates a turn for better or worse. Tracking transits through the houses of the revolution, and over the positions of the planets in it, may provide additional insights.

The greater and lesser conditions. The continuous annual profection of the ascendant of the nativity at a rate of 30° per year (that is, 12.175 days per degree) can be tracked to see which terms it is passing through and which planets it is making contact with, in the nativity or revolution and/or by transit. The ascendant of the revolution can be similarly profected at a rate of 360° per year (0°59′08″ per day or, alternatively, in tandem with the real-time transit of the Sun). Both these conditions are, however, subordinate to and therefore less consistently reliable than major transits, particularly transit stations.

Monthly profections. At the bottom of my personal list of trusted techniques are the monthly profections of Ptolemy, dividing the year into thirteen equal months of just over 28 days assigned to the zodiacal signs (beginning and ending with the sign of the annual profection). These may add emphasis to placements in and transits through the sign being activated and to the planet ruling it. I do not use either the continuous monthly profection (1°04′04″ per day) or the so-called daily profection.

Endnotes

1. Quoted in Burnett and Yamamoto 2019: I 4, n. 21.
2. For ʿUmar's treatment of the techniques, see Dykes 2010: 32–35. For Abū Maʿshar's treatment, see Dykes 2019b: 634–637 (omitting the content in pointy brackets and in the footnotes, which is based on a misunderstanding).
3. See Kūshyār III 20,11–12, transl. Yano 1997: 221.
4. Transl. Dykes 2019b: 287.
5. See *Astr. Gall.* XXIII 15–16, transl. Holden 2002: 99–117.
6. For Ptolemy's views, see Ptol. *Tetr.* IV 10,20, transl. Robbins 1940: 453; for those of Abū Maʿshar, see Dykes 2019b: 563.
7. See Paul. Al. 31, transl. Holden 2012: 69 f.
8. See Dykes 2019b: 563.
9. Kūshyār III 20,13, transl. Yano 1997: 223.
10. See *Bṛhajjātaka* 8.9, transl. Vijnanananda 1979: 161.

Appendix I
Zodiacal dignities and aspect orbs

Terms

♈	♃	6°	♀	12°	☿	20°	♂	25°	♄	30°
♉	♀	8°	☿	14°	♃	22°	♄	27°	♂	30°
♊	☿	6°	♃	12°	♀	17°	♂	24°	♄	30°
♋	♂	7°	♀	13°	☿	19°	♃	26°	♄	30°
♌	♃	6°	♀	11°	♄	18°	☿	24°	♂	30°
♍	☿	7°	♀	17°	♃	21°	♂	28°	♄	30°
♎	♄	6°	☿	14°	♃	21°	♀	28°	♂	30°
♏	♂	7°	♀	11°	☿	19°	♃	24°	♄	30°
♐	♃	12°	♀	17°	☿	21°	♄	26°	♂	30°
♑	☿	7°	♃	14°	♀	22°	♄	26°	♂	30°
♒	☿	7°	♀	13°	♃	20°	♂	25°	♄	30°
♓	♀	12°	♃	16°	☿	19°	♂	28°	♄	30°

Table 4: Egyptian terms (rulers and ending degrees).

Indian Tājika sources reverse the order of the terms of Venus and Jupiter in Gemini, and of those of Mars and Saturn in Sagittarius, possibly as a result of textual corruptions.

Triplicities

	Diurnal	Nocturnal	Participating
♈ ♌ ♐	☉	♃	♄
♉ ♍ ♑	♀	☽	♂
♊ ♎ ♒	♄	☿	♃
♋ ♏ ♓	♀	♂	☽

Table 5: Joint rulers for each sign triplicity.

Most Indian Tājika sources misunderstand or reinterpret these rulerships (known in Sanskrit as *trirāśi* or *trairāśika*). For details, see Gansten 2018.

Exaltation and fall

	☉	☽	☿	♀	♂	♃	♄
Exaltation	♈	♉	♍	♓	♑	♋	♎
Fall	♎	♏	♓	♍	♋	♑	♈

Table 6: Signs of exaltation and fall for the seven planets.

Orbs of aspect

☉	☽	☿	♀	♂	♃	♄
15°	12°	7°	7°	8°	9°	9°

Table 7: Orbs of aspect or conjunction (to either side) for the seven planets.

Appendix II
Primary directions formulae

These formulae are meant for readers who do not have access to software calculating primary directions, or who prefer to make their own calculations. Please note that the algorithms for directing a non-angular point are based on the proportional semi-arc method of Ptolemy used throughout this book (and by most ancient and medieval astrologers). The position-circle methods that became popular in early modern Europe are not described here. For fuller instructions and explanations I refer the reader to my earlier book *Primary Directions: Astrology's Old Master Technique*.

    The following descriptions assume directions by direct motion, where the symbolic progress of the significator *forward* through the zodiac is accomplished by rotating the rest of the chart across it with the primary motion. For directions by converse motion, simply read 'significator' for 'promissor' and vice versa. All traditional directions, whether direct or converse, are performed *with* the primary motion and thus perfect *after* birth. The concept of prenatal directions did not exist prior to the nineteenth century.

Required data
To calculate any direction, you need to know:
- the terrestrial latitude (Φ) of the place of birth;
- the right ascension of the midheaven (RAMC) or local sidereal time (LST);
- the obliquity of the ecliptic (ε);
- the *tropical* longitudes (λ) and, optionally, latitudes (β) of the heavenly bodies involved (the Sun never has latitude).

Tropical longitude is another way of saying 'ecliptical distance from the intersection with the equator'. This is relevant because primary directions are based on the equatorial system of daily rotation. It has no bearing on the question of where the zodiac begins and does not imply that directions are a 'tropical technique'.

The RAMC is the LST expressed in degrees, each hour equalling 15°: for example, if the LST is 01:45:42, the RAMC will be 26°25′30″. The obliquity of the ecliptic is slowly decreasing, but a value of 23°26′30″ (or 23.44) will be correct to within half a minute of arc for births over the past century.

Calculating declination (δ) and right ascension (RA)

Astrology software typically gives the declinations and right ascensions of the celestial bodies (*with* latitude for the bodies outside the ecliptic), but it is also possible to calculate these values from the data listed above. For the Sun or another point *without* latitude (or if you do not want to consider latitude for planets but only their ecliptical projections), use the formulae below.

$$\delta = \sin^{-1}(\sin \varepsilon \times \sin \lambda)$$

If the result is a negative value, the point in question has southern declination. Next, to find the right ascension, we first calculate the equinoctial distance (ED):

$$ED = \tan^{-1}(\cos \varepsilon \times \tan \lambda)$$

RA	= ED	if $\lambda < 90°$
RA	= ED +180°	if $90° < \lambda < 270°$
RA	= ED + 360°	if $\lambda > 270°$

For planets or other points *with* latitude, use these formulae:

δ = $\sin^{-1}$ (sin ε × sin λ × cos β + cos ε × sin β)

ED = $\cos^{-1}$ (cos λ × cos β / cos δ)

RA = ED   if λ < 180°
RA = 360° - ED   if λ > 180°

This procedure is reliable except when λ is very close to 0°/360° or 180°, in which case the actual body of the planet may be on the opposite side of the equator. The correctness of the RA may be verified with the following formula, allowing a very small margin (less than 1″) for rounding errors:

sin RA × cos δ = cos ε × sin λ × cos β - sin ε × sin β

If the two values do not match, subtracting the presumptive RA from 360° will give the correct RA.

Directing the midheaven or a point on it

These directions are performed in right ascension (RA) or culminating times. The arc of direction is known as the meridian distance (MD) of the promissor:

MD = RA promissor - RAMC

To direct the *lower* midheaven (IC) or a point on it to a promissor, simply find the direction of the upper midheaven (MC) to the opposite point. For example, to direct the Sun located on the IC to the conjunction of Venus in the fifth house, calculate the direction of the MC to the point in the eleventh house exactly opposite natal Venus.

Directing the ascendant or a point on it

These directions are performed in oblique ascension (OA) or rising times. The arc of direction is known as the horizontal distance (HD) of the promissor. To calculate it, we first need to know the oblique ascension of the ascendant:

OA Asc = RAMC + 90°

We then need to know the oblique ascension of the promissor, which we find by calculating its ascensional difference (AD):

AD   = $\sin^{-1} (\tan \delta \times \tan \Phi)$

OA   = RA - AD   for births in the northern hemisphere
OA   = RA + AD   for births in the southern hemisphere

HD   = OA promissor - OA Asc

To direct the *descendant* or a point on it to a promissor, calculate the direction of the *ascendant* to the opposite point. For example, to direct the Sun located on the descendant to the conjunction of Jupiter in the ninth house, calculate the direction of the ascendant to the point in the third house exactly opposite natal Jupiter. (This manoeuvre saves us the trouble of introducing oblique descensions, OD, as a separate category.)

Directing a point not conjunct an angle

Over the years I have taught students two methods of calculating the proportional semi-arc directions described by Ptolemy. One is more commonly used today, the other is based on ancient and medieval sources. Which is perceived as easier seems to depend on the student, so I give both methods here. As this is the most complex sort of direction,

I also give an example, in the form of the direction *Sun to the opposition of Jupiter with latitude* in the nativity of Lisa Marie Presley (see p. 88).

Modern method (proportional semi-arcs)
The horizon and meridian divide the celestial sphere (and thus the chart) into quadrants. The time spent by a planet or point in any quadrant is called a semi-arc (SA): diurnal if it is above the horizon, nocturnal if below the horizon. The two diurnal semi-arcs (DSA) are always exactly equal, as are the two nocturnal semi-arcs (NSA); but a diurnal and a nocturnal semi-arc are typically of unequal extension. Determine the extension of the significator's current semi-arc and its proportional distance (PD) within it as follows:

DSA = 90° + AD
NSA = 90° - AD

or, alternatively:

SA = HD + MD (treating both these values as positive numbers)

DSA = 180° - NSA
NSA = 180° - DSA
PD = MD / SA

> **Example:** As the Sun in Presley's nativity is in the western half of the chart, we use its opposite point as significator and direct that to the *conjunction* of Jupiter. This opposite point falls below the horizon; its AD is 12°33′ and its NSA is therefore 77°27′. Its MD (measured from the IC) is 71°48′; its PD is thus 71°48′ / 77°27′.

Next, determine the SA for the promissor in the same quadrant and its projected position (PP) within that quadrant when the direction perfects:

PP   = SA promissor × PD

> **Example:** Jupiter in Presley's nativity has an NSA of 81°48'. We calculate 81°48' × (71°48' / 77°27') = 75°50'.

Finally, the arc of direction is the difference between this projected position and the MD of the promissor in the nativity. Which is subtracted from which depends on whether the promissor is moving away from or towards the meridian by primary motion; but as the arc should be a positive number, the simple rule is always to subtract the lesser value from the greater:

arc   = PP - MD if the promissor is moving away from the meridian
arc   = MD - PP if the promissor is moving towards the meridian

> **Example:** Jupiter in Presley's nativity has an MD of 50°50'. Subtracting this from the PP, we get 75°50' - 50°50' = 25°00'. This is the arc of direction, corresponding to exactly 25 years by the so-called key of Ptolemy.

Ancient/medieval method (mixed ascensions)

This method is identical to the previous one up to the calculation of the proportional distance, PD. (Actually, the ancients and medievals divided a semi-arc into six 'hours' and adjusted the other calculations accordingly, but I have eliminated those steps.) We then measure the distance between significator and promissor twice:

RA distance   = RA promissor - RA significator
OA distance   = OA promissor - OA significator

> **Example:** Jupiter in Presley's nativity has an RA of 155°35′, and the point opposite the Sun has one of 134°37′, making a distance of 20°58′ in RA. Similarly, Jupiter has an OA of 147°23′, and the point opposite the Sun has one of 122°04′, making a distance of 25°19′ in OA.

Next, find the difference between the two, subtracting the lesser from the greater, and use it to determine what is known as the *equation*:

difference   = RA distance - OA distance   if the RA is greater
difference   = OA distance - RA distance   if the OA is greater

equation   = difference × PD

> **Example:** In Presley's nativity, the difference between the two distances is 25°19′ - 20°58′ = 4°21′. We calculate 4°21′ × (71°48′ / 77°27′) = 4°02′, which is the equation.

Finally, the arc of direction is found by adding the equation to, or subtracting it from, the RA distance so that the result is a value somewhere *in between* the RA distance and the OA distance:

arc   = RA distance ± equation

> **Example:** In Presley's nativity, the distance in RA is less than that in OA. We therefore add it to the equation: 20°58′ + 4°02′ = 25°00′. The arc of direction is thus identical to that found by the modern method.

Please note that the modern method described above assumes that the promissor already occupies the same quadrant as the significator. If they should be located in adjacent quadrants, that procedure must be modified. If, for instance, the significator in Presley's nativity were located *above* the horizon rather than below it, we should first have to calculate Jupiter's remaining distance below the horizon (its HD). This HD would then be added to Jupiter's arc from the horizon up to the proportional distance (PD) corresponding to the location of the significator.

Directions through the terms

To find when a significator enters the terms of a planet in any sign, treat the starting point of those terms like a promissor (without latitude). Remember that if you are using a sidereal zodiac, you first need to convert the starting point of the terms to tropical format. For example, if you want to know when a significator will enter the terms of Jupiter in sidereal Pisces (12°–16°), and the precessional value (*ayanāṃśa*) on the date of birth was 23°30′, you add that value to 12° Pisces. This will give a tropical λ of 5°30′ to be used like a promissor. You then calculate the direction by the appropriate procedure: right, oblique or mixed ascensions, depending on where your significator is located.

Appendix III
Software settings for traditional directions

A growing number of astrology applications offer primary directions as part of their predictive techniques. To ensure that these are calculated in a traditional manner, as used in the examples discussed in this book, follow the guidelines below.

General settings

A number of settings typically available in astrological software, while not specific to the technique of primary directions, will still affect the directions produced. Not all applications include all the variables listed here, and those that do may differ somewhat in their layout, but the available options should be easy to find. Relevant settings may include:

Choice of zodiac

Choose sidereal or tropical zodiac and, if sidereal, your desired precessional value (*ayanāṃśa*). This will affect the directions through the terms (in addition to the sign placements of planets and houses, and the length of year used for revolutions). Early Hellenistic astrologers such as Dorotheus and Vettius Valens, Persian astrologers such as al-Andarzaghar and some of the early Arabic-language astrologers such as Sahl ibn Bishr all used sidereal values, as did the Tājikas and other Indian astrologers; Ptolemy, later Byzantine and Arabic astrologers and the medieval European tradition used tropical values.

Terms (bounds, confines)

Some software offers a choice between different systems of terms, including Ptolemaic and Chaldean. The predominant system in Late Antiquity, the Perso-Arabic, Tājika and medieval European traditions, however, was the so-called Egyptian or Dorothean terms.

Parallax

Correction for lunar parallax will affect all directions involving the Moon, more so the closer it is to the horizon (ascendant or descendant) in the chart. Choose parallax correction, or topocentric position, to calculate the Moon's longitude as seen from the actual place of birth; geocentric position for an imaginary point in the centre of the earth.

Lots, syzygy, nodes and stars

Other points that you may want to use in working with directions include significators such as the Lot of Fortune and perhaps other lots, and the syzygy or prenatal lunation; and promissors such as the lunar nodes and/or fixed stars. With regard to stars, the chief questions are which ones to include and whether to consider their latitudes. Ptolemy used a fixed formula for the Lot of Fortune, while other authors used different formulae for day and night births. The traditional way of calculating the lunar nodes is typically designated as 'mean nodes'.

Direction-specific settings

The settings particularly related to primary directions also vary from one application to another. Figure 70 shows the main dialogue box from the traditional version of the freeware Morinus with my basic choice of settings for directions in direct motion.

Starting from the top left-hand corner, the method of direction called *Placidus (semiarc)* is the traditional Ptolemaic one used throughout Late Antiquity and the Middle Ages. The method of position circles developed by some Arabic astrologers and popularized in Europe in the fifteenth century is called *Regiomontanus*, while *Placidus (under the pole)* is a position-circle variant closer to the Ptolemaic system. Although *Campanus* is given as a separate method of direction, no such system really exists: other than so-called mundane aspects, which were never mentioned by either author, there is no difference between Regiomontanus directions and those attributed to Campanus.

The set of options directly below relate to the type of aspects used. Only zodiacal aspects were used prior to the seventeenth century. I have still ticked *Both* in order to include conjunctions and oppositions with latitude (identical to 'mundane' conjunctions and oppositions),

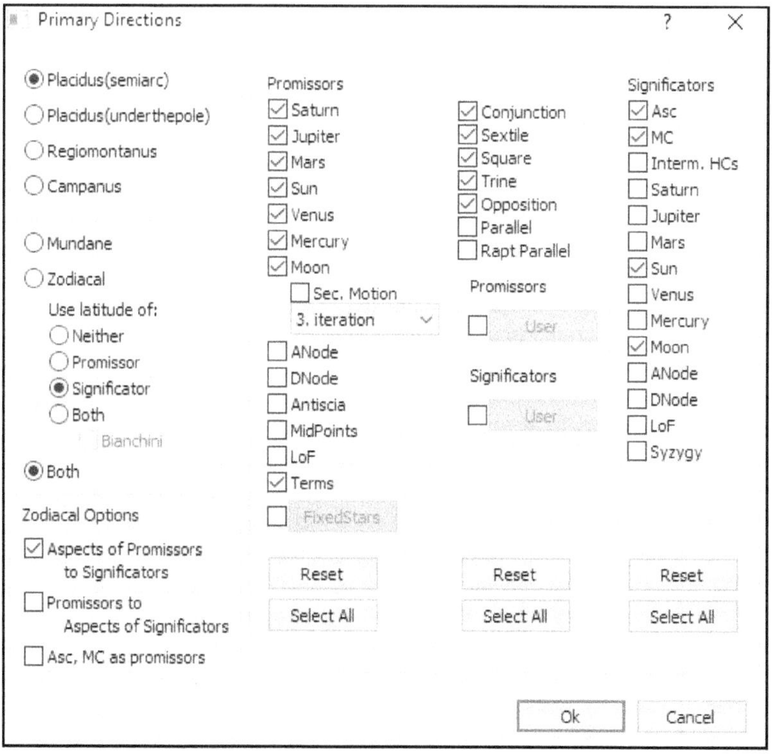

Figure 70. Settings for directions in direct motion.

which I find very effective. This will produce a list of directions that also include other mundane aspects (sextiles, squares and trines marked with an M), which I simply ignore – not an ideal solution, but workable. For zodiacal aspects, I have selected *Use latitude of significator*, ensuring that the actual body of the Moon (or of any non-luminary planet chosen as significator) is used, but no latitude assigned to aspect angles.

In the bottom left-hand corner, I have ticked only *Aspects of promissors to significators*, as we are now dealing with significators in the traditional sense and aspects in themselves cannot signify a matter. In the final, largest box, I have selected the five classical aspects; the angles and luminaries as significators; and the seven classical planets and the terms as 'promissors' (although, strictly speaking, the terms are not promissors but divisions).

Other relevant settings, not shown in this dialogue box, include the equation of time or 'key' and the choice of direct and/or converse directions. The latter refer to direct and converse in the modern sense,

					Placidus (semiarc)
M/Z	Prom	D/C	Sig	Arc	Date
Z	△ ♄	D →	Asc	0.799	1968.11.20
Z	♈ ♀	D →	MC	0.834	1968.12.02
Z	♓ ♀	D →	☽	1.722	1969.10.23
Z	✶ ☿	D →	MC	1.813	1969.11.25
Z	♑ ♄	D →	☉	3.814	1971.11.26
Z	△ ♃	D →	MC	4.573	1972.08.29
M	☉	D →	Dsc	5.65	1973.09.26
Z	☍ ☉	D →	Asc	5.651	1973.09.27
M	♄	D →	✶ ☉	5.666	1973.10.02
Z	☋ ♃	D →	Asc	5.84	1973.12.05

Figure 71. Partial list of directions in direct motion.

that is, with or against the primary motion, or forwards or backwards in time. Only directions *with* the primary motion were used before the nineteenth century, so I select only 'direct' directions. (True converse directions, also calculated *with* the primary motion, will be addressed in a moment.) Regarding the equation of time, I use the so-called key of Ptolemy or 1° per year. The second most common key used before the time of Placidus was the key of Naibod (0°59′08″ per year).

Most software will display calculated directions in tables like the one from Morinus in figure 71. The columns *M/Z* and *D/C* show the type of aspect involved (mundane or zodiacal) and the type of motion (only 'direct' directions in the modern sense, that is, *with* the diurnal motion, have been selected). The columns *Prom* and *Sig* show the moving and fixed elements of the direction, respectively ('promissor' and 'significator' in the modern sense).

To get the traditional designations for directions in direct motion, we need to read from right to left: for instance, the direction with an arc of 4.573 degrees (perfecting at the age of 4.573 years by the key of Ptolemy) would be called *MC to the trine of Jupiter* [*by direct motion*]. The last but one direction shown is a mundane (Placidean) sextile, and thus an example of the sort of aspect that I would mentally discard while going through the list. A significator entering a given set of terms is marked by the glyphs for the ruler of the terms and the sign in which they fall: thus, the ascendant entering the terms of Jupiter in Cancer has an arc of 5.84 degrees/years.

For converse directions in the traditional sense, we need to make the significators and promissors swap places. (This is because Morinus, like most software, uses these designations in the modern sense of 'fixed point' and 'moving point', respectively.) I thus select the luminaries and angles as 'promissors' and the seven planets as 'significators'. I also make sure to use the latitude of the 'promissors' and to direct them to the aspects of the 'significators', as shown in figure 72.

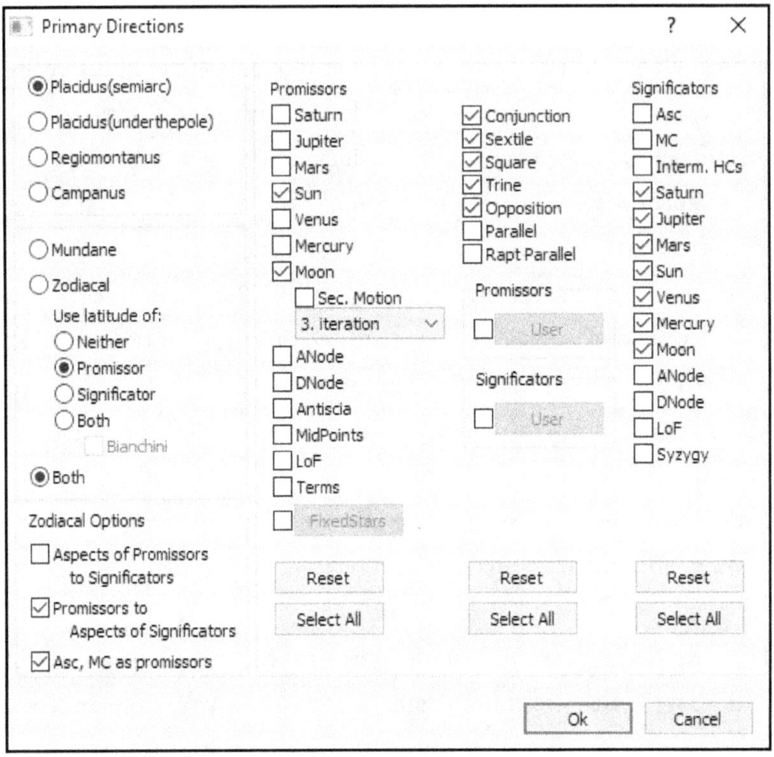

Figure 72. Settings for directions in converse motion.

This gives a list of directions like that in figure 73. Because the significators in the traditional sense are now the points being moved with the primary motion ('promissors' in the modern sense), we derive their traditional designations by reading left to right: *Moon to the body of Mars with latitude by converse motion* has an arc of 3.306 degrees; *Sun to the sextile of Saturn by converse motion* has one of 4.842 degrees; etc. There are fewer directions in this list because the terms are not included. As before, I would consider mundane (M) conjunctions and oppositions, which are identical with the corresponding zodiacal directions with latitude, but ignore mundane sextiles, squares and trines.

					Placidus(semiarc)
M/Z	Prom	D/C	Sig	Arc	Date
M	☽	D →	♂	3.306	1971.05.24
Z	☽	D →	♂	3.389	1971.06.23
Z	☉	D →	✶ ♄	4.842	1972.12.05
M	☉	D →	✶ ☽	11.358	1979.06.12
Z	☽	D →	✶ ♀	14.854	1982.12.10
M	☉	D →	✶ ♂	15.314	1983.05.27
Z	MC	D →	✶ ☉	15.957	1984.01.17
Z	Asc	D →	△ ☽	19.264	1987.05.09
Z	☽	D →	☍ ♃	19.838	1987.12.04
M	☽	D →	☍ ♃	19.91	1987.12.31

Figure 73. Partial list of directions in traditional converse motion (but still marked D for 'direct' by the software)

Appendix IV
Example chart data

All times are given in 24-hour format.

A. Male, 6 January, 1937, 19:14 CET, 56N03, 12E42

B. Female, 16 October, 1939, 23:40 CET, 56N03, 12E42

C. Female, 10 October, 1954, 07:30 CET, 53N12, 05E46

D. Male, 2 July, 1955, 14:35 CET, 60N40, 17E10

E. Male, 31 December, 1958, 12:40 CET, 56N03, 12E42

F. Male, 26 February, 1963, 06:20 CET, 55N42, 12E36

G. Male, 29 May, 1969, 16:21 CET, 55N35, 13E00

H. Female, 10 April, 1970, 00:30 CET, 63N50, 20E15

I. Male, 18 December, 1973, 10:05 EET, 60N27, 22E17

J. Male, 8 October, 1981, 14:21 CET, 55N41, 13E11

K. Male, 6 November, 1984, 10:46 GMT, 56N24, 03W28

L. Male, 31 August, 1985, 09:05 MDT, 53N17, 110W00

Presley, Lisa Marie: 1 February, 1968, 17:01 CST, Memphis, Tennessee: 35N09, 90W03

Glossary

Loanwords are of Latin origin unless otherwise specified. Words in **bold** type are technical terms with entries of their own.

anaereta	(Latinized form of the Greek *anairetēs* 'destroyer') **promissor** of the **hyleg** cutting life short
angle	**houses** 1 and 7, defined by the rising and setting points of the **ecliptic**, and 10 and 4, defined by its **culminating** and **anti-culminating** (or, alternatively, highest and lowest) points at a given time
annual horoscope	see **revolution**
anti-culmination	lowest point, intersecting the **meridian** below the **horizon**, in the apparent daily or **primary motion** of a planet or other point
application	**aspect** in the process of perfecting by the swifter planet approaching its ideal angular distance from the slower planet
Arabic part	see **lot**
ascendant	rising point of the **ecliptic**, marking its intersection with the **horizon** east of the **meridian**; sometimes used of the entire eastern half of the **horizon**, the rising **sign**, or the first **house**
ascensional difference	difference between the **right** and **oblique ascensions** of a planet or other point
aspect	angle of distance in **longitude** between zodiacal **signs** or degrees, conceived of as a 'glance' by means of which a planet exerts its influence on another planet, point or sign
asterism	see *nakṣatra*

athazir	(Latinized form of the Arabic *at-tasyīr* 'sending out') see **direction**
ayanāṃśa	(Sanskrit) 'degree of motion', value of **precession** for any given date
benefic	'well-doer', a planet primarily signifying favourable or pleasant experiences; particularly used of Venus and Jupiter
besiegement	a planet or other point being placed between two **malefics** (or, sometimes, their **aspect** points); in a secondary sense, similar placement between **benefics**
bounds	see **terms**
burj al-intihā'	(Arabic) 'sign of completion': see **profection**
burj al-muntahā	(Arabic) 'sign of the end': see **profection**
cadent	'falling' from an **angle: houses** 3, 6, 9 and 12
celestial sphere	imaginary sphere of unlimited extension within which all heavenly bodies are observed, having the place of observation for its centre
chronocrator	(Latinized form of the Greek *chronokratōr* 'ruler of time') planet ruling a given period of time, sometimes translated 'time lord'; primarily used of the **divisor**, the **promissor**, and the **ruler of the year**
collection of light	configuration where two planets not in an **applying aspect** are connected by both applying to a third planet
confines	see **terms**
conjunction	(of two or more planets or points) occupation of the same zodiacal **sign**, particularly within a specified distance or **orb**, complete at a **longitudinal** distance of 0°; sometimes included among the **aspects**
culminating time	time required for a given zodiacal **sign** to pass across the **meridian**; its **right ascension** expressed in time

culmination	highest point above the **horizon**, intersecting the **meridian**, in the apparent daily or **primary motion** of a planet or other point
cusp	defining and most effective point of a **house**, often considered its starting point (but in Indian astrology rather its centre)
daśā	(Sanskrit) 1. in pre-Islamic Indian astrology: period of life ruled and determined by a given planet and/or zodiacal **sign**, divided into subperiods, subsubperiods, etc.; 2. in **Tājika**: similar periods typically subdividing a discrete year, month, or day of life
debility	condition under which a planet is considered weak and therefore generally signifying less favourable outcomes
decan	(from Greek *dekanos*) division of a zodiacal **sign** into three equal parts of 10°, also known as 'face'; ultimately of Egyptian origin
descendant	setting point of the **ecliptic**, marking its intersection with the **horizon** west of the **meridian**; sometimes used of the entire western half of the horizon, the setting sign, or the seventh **house**
dexter	(in measuring the shortest distance between two planets or other points in the **zodiac**) 'to the right': occupying the earlier position, rising first
dignity	condition under which a planet is considered strong and therefore generally signifying more favourable outcomes
direct	(of the five non-**luminary** planets) moving forwards through the **zodiac** by **secondary motion**, against the **primary motion**
direction	(translation via Arabic *tasyīr* of Greek *aphesis* 'sending out') predictive technique based on

	the apparent daily or **primary motion** of the **celestial sphere** calculated in **oblique, right,** or **mixed ascensions**
distribution	see **division**; sometimes also used in the sense of **direction**
distributor	see **divisor**
diurnal	1. 'of the day', when the Sun is above the **horizon**: see **sect**; 2. relating to the hemisphere above the horizon
division	**terms** currently occupied by a **directed significator**
divisor	planet ruling the **division**
dodecatemory	(from Greek *dōdekatēmorion*) division of a zodiacal **sign** into twelve equal parts of 2°30', each part identified with a sign in a 'microzodiac' scheme; ultimately of Mesopotamian origin
domicile	zodiacal **sign** considered to be owned or ruled by a given planet
dvādaśāṃśa	(Sanskrit) 'twelfth-part': see **dodecatemory**
ecliptic	**great circle** described by the apparent motion of the Sun against the background of the fixed stars over the course of a year, inclined to the **equator** at a slowly shifting angle; cf. **obliquity**
equator	1. terrestrial equator: imaginary circle perpendicular to the earth's axis of rotation and dividing the earth into a northern and a southern hemisphere; 2. celestial equator: **great circle** in the same plane as the terrestrial equator
equinox	1. date on which day and night are of equal length; 2. (equinoctial point) intersection of the **ecliptic** with the celestial **equator** in northward direction (vernal equinox, 0° Aries in the **tropical zodiac**) or in southward

	direction (autumnal equinox, 0° Libra in the tropical zodiac)
exaltation	zodiacal **sign** (or a particular degree thereof) in which a planet is considered uniquely powerful
fardār	(Persian via Arabic, also *firdār*, of uncertain derivation; Latinized as *firdaria*, with variants) planetary periods of fixed lengths, probably of Persian origin
figure	horoscopic chart
geocentric	having (the centre of) the earth for its centre
great circle	circle within and concentric with the **celestial sphere**
ḥadd, ḥudūd	(Arabic) see **terms**
haddā	(also *hadda*, Sanskritized form of Arabic *ḥadd*) see **terms**
heliacal	relating to the Sun; for a planet to rise or set heliacally means to become visible for the first time after, or be visible for the last time before, its exact **conjunction** with the Sun
horizon	**great circle** forming the plane of observation within the **celestial sphere**, centred either around a place on the surface of the earth (topocentric horizon) or around the centre of the earth (geocentric horizon)
house	twelfth-part of the sky surrounding the place of observation, assigned particular spheres of influence on human affairs; identical in the simplest form with a zodiacal **sign**, but different methods of division exist based on the intersections of various **great circles** (including the **ecliptic, horizon, meridian, equator**, and **prime vertical**) or of **primary motion**
hyleg	(Latinized form, with many variants, via Arabic *hīlāj* from Persian *hīlāg*, translating the Greek *aphetēs* 'releaser') planet or point 'sent out' by

	direction, particularly to determine the length of life; cf. **significator**
IC, *imum caeli*	(Latin) the lower **midheaven**
ingress	entry of a planet into a zodiacal **sign** or a particular part thereof
inthihā	(also *inthā, anthihā, anthā*, Sanskritized form of Arabic *intihāʾ* 'completion') see **profection**
jārbakhtār	(Persian via Arabic, translating the Greek *chronokratōr* 'ruler of the time'; also, less correctly, *jānbakhtār*; Latinized as *algebuthar* with variants) see **divisor**
Ketu	see **nodes**
kisimā	(also *kisima*, Sanskritized form of the Arabic *qisma* 'division, allotment') see **division**
latitude	1. terrestrial latitude: angular distance of a place of observation north or south of the terrestrial **equator**; 2. celestial latitude: angular distance of a planet or point north or south of the **ecliptic**
longitude	1. terrestrial longitude: angular distance east or west of the **meridian** of any given location on earth; 2. celestial longitude: angular distance of a (projected) planet or point along the ecliptic, measured from 0° Aries or 0° of any **sign** in the **sidereal** or **tropical zodiac**
lord of the year	see **ruler of the year**
lot	(translation of the Greek *klēros*) imaginary point on the **ecliptic**, bearing some particular signification and derived by measuring the ecliptical distance between two points (typically planets) and projecting it from a third point (typically the **ascendant**)
luminary	the Sun or Moon
lunation	see **syzygy**
malefic	'evil-doer', a planet primarily signifying un-

	favourable or distressing experiences; particularly used of Mars and Saturn
MC, *medium caeli*	(Latin) the upper **midheaven**
meridian	**great circle** passing through the **zenith**, **nadir**, and north and south points of the **horizon** at the place of observation; also used of the same circle projected on to the surface of the earth
meridian distance	distance of a planet or point from the **meridian**, measured in degrees of **right ascension** along a circle parallel to the celestial **equator**
midheaven	intersection of the **ecliptic** with the **meridian** above the **horizon** (**culminating** point, upper midheaven) or below the horizon (**anti-culminating** point, lower midheaven)
mixed ascension	intermediate value of **right** and **oblique ascensions** used for defining the position of a planet or point within its apparent daily or **primary motion**
mudda	(Arabic) 'period': a modified version of pre-Islamic Indian *daśās* used in **Tājika**
munthahā	(also *munthā*, Sanskritized form of Arabic *muntahā* 'completed') see **profection**
nadir	point on the **celestial sphere** directly below the place of observation
nakṣatra	originally, 27 or 28 unequal asterisms in the apparent path of the Moon, corresponding to its sidereal cycle of 27.3 days; normalized in pre-Islamic Indian astrology as a division of the ecliptic into 27 equal parts of 13°20'
navāṃśa	(Sanskrit) 'ninth-part': probably indigenous Indian division of a zodiacal sign into equal parts of 3°20', each part identified with a sign in a 'micro-zodiac' scheme and identical with a quarter (*pāda*) of a *nakṣatra*
nocturnal	1. 'of the night', when the Sun is below the

	horizon: see **sect**; 2. relating to the hemisphere below the horizon
nodes, lunar	the diametrically opposed points at which the apparent path of the Moon intersects the **ecliptic**; known in Indian astrology as Rāhu and Ketu, in Arabic and European astrology as the Head and Tail of the Dragon (Latin: *Caput/Cauda Draconis*).
oblique ascension	point on the celestial **equator** rising simultaneously with a planet or point at the **horizon** of the place of observation
obliquity	(of the ecliptic) angle of inclination relative to the **equator**, caused by the tilt of the earth's rotational axis relative to the plane of its orbit around the Sun; currently around 23°26'30"
occidental	(of planets) 'western': rising and setting after the Sun and therefore visible in the western part of the sky following sunset
opposition	**aspect** angle of 180° separation or, more generally, occupation of opposite zodiacal **signs**
orb	sphere of light or astrological influence assigned to a planet in the context of its **aspects** and **conjunctions**, defined as a margin of ecliptical **longitude**
oriental	(of planets) 'eastern': rising and setting before the Sun and therefore visible in the eastern part of the sky prior to sunrise
parallax	difference in apparent position of a heavenly body (most notably, the Moon) when viewed from different vantage points; cf. **geocentric**, **topocentric**
partile	(of conjunctions and aspects) occurring within one degree; cf. synodic
pātyāyinī	(Sanskrit) 'going by subtraction': the main *daśā*

	system used for subdividing a discrete year (or, secondarily, month or day) of life in **Tājika**
pivot	see **angle**
precession	cyclical change in the direction of the earth's polar axis, resulting in a regression of the **equinoxes** through the constellations and the **sidereal zodiac**, each complete cycle of 360° lasting approximately 25,800 years
primary direction	see **direction**
primary motion	apparent daily motion of the **celestial sphere**, and hence of the **zodiac** and all planets, around the place of observation, caused by the rotation of the earth around its axis
prime vertical	**great circle** passing through the **zenith**, **nadir**, and east and west points of the **horizon** at the place of observation
profection	(corruption of Latin *perfectio*, translated via the Arabic *intihāʾ/muntahā* and ultimately derived from the Greek *sunteleō* 'to complete') symbolic motion of one zodiacal **sign** or 30° of ecliptical **longitude** per year, subdivided into faster-moving monthly and daily profections
promissor	active element of a **direction**, determining the nature of the event; generally the body or **aspect** of a planet or a fixed star
prorogation	see **direction**
prorogator	see **significator** and, in a narrower sense, **hyleg**
qāsim	(Arabic) see **divisor**
qisma	(Arabic) see **division**
quadrant	quarter of the **celestial sphere** delimited by the **horizon** and **meridian**
Rāhu	see **nodes**
rejoicing	condition considered congenial to each planet, including occupation of a particular zodiacal

retrograde	sign, a particular **house**, daytime or nighttime, and a particular **quadrant** of the **celestial sphere** (of the non-luminary planets) apparently moving backwards through the **zodiac** by **secondary motion**, in the same direction as the **primary motion**
return of light	condition, e.g. being **retrograde**, under which a planet is considered unable to manage the topics signified by another planet **applying** to it
revolution	return of the Sun to the exact ecliptical **longitude** held at birth, marking a new annual cycle of life for which a new figure is cast; also used secondarily of monthly and daily cycles
right ascension	location of a (projected) planet or point along the celestial **equator**, measured from the vernal **equinox**
rising time	time required for a given zodiacal **sign** to rise over the **horizon** at a given place of observation; its **oblique ascension** expressed in time
ruler	planet having dignity (generally by **domicile**) in a particular part of a figure
ruler of the year	planet considered a/the major **chronocrator** for a particular year, generally by ruling the **domicile** of the annual **profection** of the **ascendant**, although the Tājika definition is more complex
sahama	(Sanskritized form of Arabic *sahm*, translating the Greek *klēros*) see **lot**
secondary motion	apparent motion of a planet along the **zodiac**, caused by the orbits of the planet and the earth around the Sun and occurring chiefly in the opposite direction of the **primary motion**; cf. **direct, retrograde**
sect	(translating the Greek *hairesis*) division of planets and, occasionally, other points into two

	groups defined as **diurnal** or solar (the Sun, Jupiter and Saturn) and **nocturnal** or lunar (the Moon, Venus and Mars), respectively (Mercury being considered neutral or ambivalent)
semi-arc	path of a planet or point from **horizon** to **meridian** or vice versa, forming part of a circle parallel to the celestial **equator**; cf. **quadrant**
separation	**aspect** in the process of dissolving by the swifter planet moving away from its ideal angular distance from the slower planet
sextile **aspect**	angle of 60° separation or, more generally, occupation of **signs** forming one side of a hexagon within the **zodiac**
sidereal	defined by one or more fixed stars, relative to which the **equinoxes** regress
sign, zodiacal	equal division of the **zodiac** into twelve parts of 30°, the starting point of which is defined either **sidereally** or **tropically**
significator	1. in a general sense, a planet or other point in a **figure** signifying a topic; 2. in a **direction**, the passive element, determining the area of life affected: typically an **angle, luminary** or **lot**, but sometimes a non-luminary planet
sinister	(in measuring the shortest distance between two planets or other points in the zodiac) 'to the left': occupying the later position, rising last
solar return	see **revolution**
square	**aspect** angle of 90° separation or, more generally, occupation of **signs** forming one side of a square within the **zodiac**
stake	see **angle**
station	(of the non-luminary planets) apparently ceasing its **secondary motion** prior to changing course from **direct** to **retrograde** or vice versa

succedent	'following' an angle: houses 2, 5, 8 and 11
superior	(of aspects) cast by a planet in **dexter** position
synodic	1. referring to a **conjunction** in a single degree, particularly of any planet with the Sun; 2. referring to the entire cycle of a planet's motion relative to the Sun, such as that of the Moon from one New (or Full) Moon to the next
syzygy	**conjunction** or **opposition** of the Sun and Moon (New Moon and Full Moon, respectively)
Tājika	(Sanskritized form of the Persian *tāzīg*, ultimately from the Arabic tribal name Ṭayyi') Indian form of Perso-Arabic astrology developed in the late medieval and early modern periods
tasyīr	(Arabic) 'sending out': see **direction**
terms	(from Latin *termini*, translating the Greek *horia*) division of a zodiacal **sign** into five unequal parts, each ruled by one of the five non-luminary planets; ultimately of Mesopotamian origin
time lord	see **chronocrator**
topocentric	having the place of observation (on the surface of the earth) for its centre
transit	real-time movements of planets through the **zodiac**, particularly as superimposed on a **figure** such as that of a nativity
translation of light	configuration where two planets not in an **applying aspect** are connected by a third planet separating from one and applying to the other
triṃśāṃśa	(Sanskrit) 1. pre-Islamic Indian version of the **terms**; 2. occasionally used in **Tājika** as a synonym of *haddā* (Graeco-Arabic terms)
trine	**aspect** angle of 120° separation or, more generally, occupation of **signs** forming one side of an equilateral triangle within the **zodiac**

triplicity	group of three zodiacal **signs** forming an equilateral triangle and ruled jointly by three planets: one primary, one secondary, and one participating
tropical	defined by the **equinoxes**, relative to which the fixed stars progress
varṣaphala	(Sanskrit) 'results of the year': see **revolution**
yoga	(Sanskrit) 'combination, arrangement': in **Tājika**, 16 categories of planetary interrelations resting chiefly on **aspect** configurations and zodiacal **dignities** or **debilities**
zenith	point on the **celestial sphere** directly above the place of observation
zodiac	belt extending some 9° of latitude north and south of the **ecliptic**, divided equally into twelve **signs**, within which the planets are seen to move

Bibliography

Text editions and works in classical languages

Abenragel	ʿAlī ibn Abī r-Rijāl. *Albohazen Haly filii Abenragel libri de iudiciis astrorum*. Basilea [Basel]: Henrichus Petrus, 1551.
Albubather	Abū Bakr al-Ḥasan ibn al-Khaṣīb. *Albubather et Centiloquium Divi Hermetis*. Venetiis [Venice]: Io. Baptista Sessa, 1501.
Al-Qabīṣī	Charles Burnett, Keiji Yamamoto and Michio Yano, edd. and transl. *Al-Qabīṣī (Alcabitius): The Introduction to Astrology. Editions of the Arabic and Latin texts and an English translation*. London: The Warburg Institute, 2004.
Anon. *Quad.*	*In Claudii Ptolemaei Quadripartitum enarrator ignoti nominis, quem tamen Proclum suisse quidam existimant*. Basileæ [Basel], 1559.
Astr. Gall.	Jean-Baptiste Morin. *Astrologia Gallica principiis & rationibus propriis stabilita, atque in XXVI. libros distributa*. Hagae-Comitis [The Hague]: Adrianus Vlacq, 1661.
Bṛhajjātaka	Swami Vijnanananda [Hari Prasanna Chatterjee], ed. and transl. *The Bṛihajjâtakam of Varâha Mihira*. 2nd ed. New Delhi: Oriental Books Reprint Corporation, 1979.
Carm. astr.	David Pingree, ed. and transl. *Dorothei Sidonii Carmen astrologicum*. Leipzig: Teubner, 1976.
CCAG	Franz Cumont et al., edd. *Catalogus codicum astrologorum graecorum*. Bruxelles, 1898–1936.

Firm. Mat.	Wilhelm Kroll, Franz Skutsch and Konrat Ziegler, edd. *Iulii Firmici Materni Matheseos libri VIII*. Leipzig: Teubner, 1897–1913.
Hāyanaratna	Martin Gansten, ed. and transl. *The Jewel of Annual Astrology: A Parallel Sanskrit-English Critical Edition of Balabhadra's Hāyanaratna*. Leiden and Boston: Brill, 2020. Available online at: https://doi.org/10.1163/9789004433717
Junctinus	Francesco Giuntini. *Speculum Astrologiae*. Lugduni [Lyons]: Q. Phil. Tinghi, 1581.
Karmaprakāśa	Śrīdhara Jaṭāśaṅkara Śarman, ed. *Saṭīkaṃ sodāharaṇaṃ Manuṣyajātakam*. Mumbai [Bombay], 1886–1887.
Kūshyār	Michio Yano, ed. and transl. *Kūšyār Ibn Labbān's Introduction to Astrology [Al-madkhal fī sināʿat aḥkām an-nujūm]*. Tokyo: Institute for the Study of Languages and Cultures of Asia and Africa, 1997.
Lib. Arist.	Charles Burnett and David Pingree, edd. *The Liber Aristotilis of Hugo of Santalla*. London: Warburg Institute, 1997.
Opusculum	Johann Schöner. *Opusculum astrologicum*. Norimbergæ (Nuremberg): Iohan. Petreius, 1539.
Paul. Al.	Emilie Boer, ed. *Παύλου Ἀλεξανδρέως Εἰσαγωγικά = Pauli Alexandrini Elementa Apotelesmatica*. Leipzig: Teubner, 1958.
Ptol. *Tetr.*	Wolfgang Hübner, ed. *Claudii Ptolemaei opera quae exstant omnia* 3.1: *Ἀποτελεσματικά*. Leipzig: Teubner, 1998.
Sefer ha-Moladot	Shlomo Sela, ed. and transl. *Abraham Ibn Ezra on Nativities and Continuous Horoscopy: A*

	Parallel Hebrew-English Critical Edition of the Book of Nativities and the Book of Revolution. Leiden and Boston: Brill, 2014.
Tājikabhūṣaṇa	Sītārāma Śāstrin, ed. and transl. (Hindi). *Tājikabhūṣaṇa Vidvadvaraśrīgaṇeśadaivajña-viracita.* Bambaī [Mumbai]: Khemarāja Śrīkṛṣṇadāsa, 2005.
Tājikasāra	Raghuvaṃśa Śarma Śāstrin, ed. *Hariharabhaṭṭa-viracitam Tājikasāram Harṣaganiviracitayā Kārikākhyayā vyākhyayā samalaṅkṛtam.* Mumbayyāṃ [Mumbai]: Bhagīrathātmaja Hariprasāda, 1898–1899.
Vett. Val.	David Pingree, ed. *Vettii Valentis Antiocheni Anthologiarum libri novem.* Leipzig: Teubner, 1986.

Works and translations in modern languages

Baldwin, Richard S.
    1974   *The Morinus System of Horoscope Interpretation.* Washington, DC: American Federation of Astrologers.

Bezza, Giuseppe
    1996   'La profezione: Come si calcola, come si interpreta'. *Linguaggio Astrale* 104, 5–24. [An English translation is available online at: http://www.cieloeterra.it/eng/eng.articoli.profezione/profezione.html]

Brennan, Chris
    2017   *Hellenistic Astrology: The Study of Fate and Fortune.* Denver, CO: Amor Fati Publications.

Burnett, Charles and Ahmed al-Hamdi
    1991/92   'Zādānfarrūkh al-Andarzaghar on Anniversary

Horoscopes'. *Zeitschrift für Geschichte der Arabisch-Islamischen Wissenschaften* 7, edd. Fuat Sezgin et al., 294–499. Frankfurt am Main: Institut für Geschichte der Arabisch-Islamischen Wissenschaften.

Burnett, Charles and David Pingree
    1997   *The Liber Aristotilis of Hugo of Santalla*. London: Warburg Institute.

Burnett, Charles and Keiji Yamamoto
    2019   *The Great Introduction to Astrology by Abū Maʿšar*. 2 vols. Leiden and Boston: Brill.

Burnett, Charles, Keiji Yamamoto and Michio Yano
    2004   *Al-Qabīṣī (Alcabitius): The Introduction to Astrology. Editions of the Arabic and Latin texts and an English translation*. London: The Warburg Institute.

Dykes, Benjamin N.
    2009   *Persian Nativities Volume I: Māshāʾallāh & Abū ʾAli*. Minneapolis, MN: Cazimi Press.
    2010   *Persian Nativities Volume II: ʿUmar al-Tabarī & Abū Bakr*. Minneapolis, MN: Cazimi Press.
    2017   *Dorotheus of Sidon: Carmen Astrologicum: The ʿUmar al-Tabarī Translation*. Minneapolis, MN: Cazimi Press.
    2019a   *The Astrology of Sahl b. Bishr Volume I: Principles, Elections, Questions, Nativities*. Minneapolis, MN: Cazimi Press.
    2019b   *Persian Nativities IV: On the Revolutions of the Years of Nativities by Abū Maʾshar*. Minneapolis, MN: Cazimi Press.

Gansten, Martin
    2009   *Primary Directions: Astrology's Old Master*

	Technique. Bournemouth: The Wessex Astrologer.
2010	'Reshaping Karma: An Indic Metaphysical Paradigm in Traditional and Modern Astrology'. *Cosmologies*, ed. Nicholas Campion, 52–68. Lampeter: Sophia Centre Press.
2018	'Origins of the Tājika System of Astrological Aspects and Dignities.' *History of Science in South Asia* 6, 162–199. Available online at: https://doi.org/10.18732/hssa.v6i0.34
2019	'Samarasiṃha and the Early Transmission of Tājika Astrology'. *Journal of South Asian Intellectual History* 1.1, 79–132. Available online at: https://doi.org/10.1163/25425552-12340005
2020	*The Jewel of Annual Astrology: A Parallel Sanskrit-English Critical Edition of Balabhadra's Hāyanaratna*. Leiden and Boston: Brill. Available online at: https://doi.org/10.1163/9789004433717

Gansten, Martin and Ola Wikander
  2011   'Sahl and the Tājika Yogas: Indian Transformations of Arabic astrology'. *Annals of Science* 68.4, 531–546.

Gramaglia, Eduardo J. and Benjamin N. Dykes
  2017   *Astrological Works of Theophilus of Edessa*. Minneapolis, MN: Cazimi Press.

Hand, Robert
  1994   *Opusculum Astrologicum*. Berkeley Springs, WV: Golden Hind Press.

Holden, James H.
  1994   *Astrologia Gallica Book Twenty-Two: Directions*. Tempe, AZ: American Federation of Astrologers.

2002 *Astrologia Gallica Book Twenty-Three: Revolutions*. Tempe, AZ: American Federation of Astrologers.
 2009 *Rhetorius the Egyptian: Astrological Compendium Containing his Explamation and Narration of the Whole Art of Astrology*. Tempe, AZ: American Federation of Astrologers.
 2011 *Julius Firmicus Maternus: Mathesis*. Tempe, AZ: American Federation of Astrologers.
 2012 *Paul of Alexandria: Introduction to Astrology*. Tempe, AZ: American Federation of Astrologers.

Jones, Alexander and John M. Steele
 2011 'A New Discovery of a Component of Greek Astrology in Babylonian Tablets: The "Terms"'. *ISAW Papers* 1. Available online at: http://doi.org/2333.1/k98sf96r

Lilly, William
 1647 *Christian Astrology*. London: Printed by Tho. Brudenell for John Partridge and Humph. Blunden.

Pingree, David
 1973 'Astrology'. *Dictionary of the History of Ideas: Studies of Selected Pivotal Ideas* 1, 118–126. New York: Charles Scribner's Sons.
 1989 'Classical and Byzantine Astrology in Sassanian Persia'. *Dumbarton Oaks Papers* 43, 227–239.

Riley, Mark
 2010 *Vettius Valens: Anthologies*. Published online: https://www.csus.edu/indiv/r/rileymt/Vettius%20Valens%20entire.pdf

Robbins, Frank Egleston
 1940 *Ptolemy: Tetrabiblos*. Cambridge, MA: Harvard University Press.

Robson, Vivian Erwood
    1923   *The Fixed Stars and Constellations in Astrology.* London: Cecil Palmer.

Sela, Shlomo
    2014   *Abraham Ibn Ezra on Nativities and Continuous Horoscopy: A Parallel Hebrew-English Critical Edition of the Book of Nativities and the Book of Revolution.* Leiden and Boston: Brill.

Vijnanananda, Swami [= Hari Prasanna Chatterjee]
    1979   *The Bṛihajjâtakam of Varâha Mihira.* 2nd ed. New Delhi: Oriental Books Reprint Corporation.

Yano, Michio
    1997   *Kūšyār Ibn Labbān's Introduction to Astrology.* Tokyo: Institute for the Study of Languages and Cultures of Asia and Africa.

Index

For frequently occurring terms, only references of general importance have been included; some very frequent terms have been entirely excluded.

Abenragel, *see* ar-Rijāl
Abraham ibn Ezra   10, 48–49
   quoted   67
Abū Bakr al-Ḥasan ibn Khaṣīb   38
Abū Maʿshar al-Balkhī   2–3, 7, 10, 30, 47, 49, 54–56, 61, 84, 117, 139, 161, 163, 179–180, 182–183, 184–185, 186
   quoted   29, 117, 136, 182
Albubather, *see* Abū Bakr
Alcabitius houses   16, 37
Alexander the Great   9
Alexandria   14
algebuthar   32
   see also divisor
anaereta   139, 162
al-Andarzaghar, Zādānfarrūkh   47–49, 55, 139, 205
   quoted   28–29
angles, angular houses   20, 24, 31, 35, 39, 53, 54, 57, 69, 116, 180, 208, 209
annual constant   47–48
antigenesis, *see* recasting of the nativity

aphesis   4, 24
Apotelesmatics of Ptolemy   23, 42
   see also Tetrabiblos
Arabic language   v, 2, 4, 8, 9, 10, 14, 20, 23, 25, 28, 31–32, 34, 37, 38, 39, 59, 62, 84–85, 190, 191
'Arabic part'   19
   see also lot; *sahm, sahama*
'aspect-point conjunction'   70, 113
aspects   11, 19, 20–21, 26–31, 40, 41, 43–44, 53, 94, 117, 118, 141, 162, 163, 179, 180, 188, 192, 207–209
   applying and separating   21, 56–57, 59, 162, 192
   configurations   51, 56–58, 60, 61, 67, 83
   dexter and sinister   21
   Indian   20
   latitude of, in directions   68–70, 88, 207–209
   minor   21
   mundane versus zodiacal   68–69, 207–210

partile   21, 56, 192
   superior   21
asterism (*nakṣatra*)   9, 10, 50, 189, 191–192
astrolabe   v
Astrologia Gallica   183
athazir   25
   see also *tasyīr*
ayanāṃśa, see precession

Babylonia, see Mesopotamia
Balabhadra Daivajña   190
Balbillus, Tiberius Claudius   133
al-Battānī, Muḥammad ibn Jābir   48
besiegement   94, 141
Bezza, Giuseppe   39
biodotēr   32
Bonatti, Guido   10
Book of Aristotle   47
bounds   20, 206
   see also terms
Brennan, Chris   87
burj al-intihā', burj al-muntahā   39
   see also profection
Burnett, Charles   47
Byzantium   9–10, 51, 205

cadent houses   18, 53, 54, 57
Campanus houses   207
Carmen astrologicum, quoted   46
Castor   124

celestial sphere   33, 201
Chaucer, Geoffrey   v
Chinese astrology   11–12
Christians   10
chronocrator   32, 38, 40, 41, 42, 43–44, 46, 53, 55–56, 58, 60–61, 84, 86, 89, 94, 95, 139, 141, 142, 160, 161, 162, 166, 172, 179, 186, 187, 193
circumambulation   42
collection of light   56
colonialism   8–9
committing strength, disposition and nature   57
confines   20, 206
   see also terms
Constantinople   9
'continuous astrology'   1
converse motion, see directions
co-rising   68–69, 70, 74, 124
culminating times   33–34, 199
   see also right ascension

daśā   24, 38, 84, 189–192
debility   19, 57, 58, 163, 166, 193
decan   19
dignity   19–20, 53, 56–57, 61, 96, 98, 160, 163, 166, 193
directions (primary)
   and house systems   36–37
   calculating   v, 32–35, 67–71, 197–204
   conflicting indications of   25, 117–118

converse and direct   35–36, 67–68, 69, 137–138, 197, 208–211
 duration of   30–31, 146
 early methods of   27
 equation of time ('keys') in   70
 from the revolution figure   179, 182–183
 in Indian astrology   37–38
 latitude in   68–70
 method, summary of   24–30
 mundane   69, 207–210
 position-circle ('Regiomontanus') method   34–35, 36–37, 197, 206–207
 prenatal   36, 197
 relation to other techniques   2, 41–42, 43–44, 53–55, 58–61, 71–72, 86–87, 102, 141, 161, 192–193
 semi-arc ('Placidus') method   34, 36–37, 201–202, 206–207
 software settings for,   205–211
 terminology   4, 23–24, 31–32, 67
 time of results   28
 'under the pole'   35, 138
 zodiacal   68–70
direct motion, see directions
distribution, distributor   32
 see also division, divisor
division, divisor   4, 28–32, 38, 43, 53, 56, 60, 61, 67, 72, 76, 83, 84, 86–87, 117, 119, 136, 192, 208
dodecatemory   20, 184
Dorotheus of Sidon   20, 23, 27, 40, 42, 60, 133, 205, 206
 quoted   46
dvādaśāṃśa, see dodecatemory
Dykes, Benjamin   2, 31–32, 47, 179, 183

Egypt   7, 18, 20
encountering star (planet)   31, 42, 118, 179
 see also promissor
equal houses   16–17, 37
equation of time   70, 208–209
equinox   13–14, 48, 50
exaltation   19, 56, 96

face, see decan
fall   18, 19, 96
fardār, firdār ('firdaria')   24, 38, 84
Firmicus Maternus, Julius   16, 17
 quoted   17
fixed stars   13, 15, 48, 50, 77, 124, 138, 146, 206
fixing (*pēxis*)   42

geocentric position   71, 206
Giuntini, Francesco, quoted   49
globalization   9
greater condition   178–183, 185, 190, 193
Greek language   v, 2, 4, 8, 9,

10, 11, 19–20, 23, 24, 32, 39, 42, 46, 47, 62, 184, 185

ḥadd, ḥadda/ḥaddā   20, 37, 190
  see also terms
Hāyanaratna   190, 192
Hellenistic period   8, 9, 11, 14–15, 16, 37, 44, 70, 84, 189, 205
hīlāj   25
  see also hyleg
Holden, James   17
horizon   18, 33–34, 68–69, 71, 88, 137
  artificial, *see* position circle
horoscopic astrology   v, 2, 7, 9–12, 14
house division, systems of   15, 16–18, 36–37
hyleg   25, 37, 85, 133

India, Indian astrology   v, 1, 3, 7–11, 12, 13, 14, 15, 16, 17, 19–20, 23, 24, 37–38, 48–51, 55, 84, 85, 139, 186, 189–192, 195, 196, 205
inthihā, inthā   39, 50
  see also burj al-intihāʾ; *munthahā*
Islam   9, 23

jārbakhtār, jānbakhtār   32
  see also divisor
al-Jayyānī, Muḥammad ibn Muʿādh   34
Jews   10, 48
Junctinus, *see* Giuntini

jyotiṣa, jyotiḥśāstra   8

karma   10
Karmaprakāśā, quoted   37
key, *see* equation of time
kisimā   38
  see also qisma; division
Kotyk, Jeffrey   12
Kūshyār ibn Labbān   180, 185
  quoted   185

Late Antiquity   15, 23, 70, 206
Latin Europe   9, 10, 12, 23
Latin language   4, 9, 10, 11, 19, 31, 39, 42, 47, 69, 178
Leo, Alan   12, 35
lesser condition   164, 178–182, 185, 190, 193
lord of the year, *see* ruler of the year
lots   19, 39, 206
  Lot of Children   134
  Lot of Fortune   25, 31, 124, 206
  Lot of the Daimon (Spirit)   147
  Lot of the Father   94

Mahendrasūri   v
maiora esse, *see* greater condition
Mak, Bill   12
Manuṣyajātaka, *see* Karmaprakāśā
Māshāʾallāh ibn Atharī   14, 47, 49
  cited   86–87

Mayan astrology   11
medieval period   2, 3, 9, 10, 12, 16, 23, 27, 28, 31, 40, 41, 49, 51, 52, 70, 84, 96, 178, 185, 189, 197, 200, 202, 205, 206
meridian   16, 34, 201–202
Mesopotamia (Babylonia)   7, 13, 185
Middle Ages, *see* medieval period
'mighty days'   183
   see also greater condition
minora esse, *see* lesser condition
mixed ascension   34, 38, 183, 202–204
   see also semi-arc
moirai   20
   see also terms
month, different varieties   184–185
Morin de Villefranche, Jean-Baptiste   52, 70, 98, 115, 183
mudda-daśā   190–192
Mughals   11
Müller, Johann   34
   see also Regiomontanus
munthahā, munthā   39, 85
   see also burj al-intihā'
Muslims   9, 10, 50

Naibod, Valentin   70, 209
nakṣatra, *see* asterism
navāṃśa (ninth-part)   10, 20
nisarga-daśā, *naisargika-daśā*   190
nodes, lunar (Rāhu and Ketu)   19, 191–192, 206
North Scale (Northern Claw)   77

oblique ascension   33–34, 38, 183, 200, 204
orbs of aspect   15, 18, 21, 192
Orion   16

Pancharius   16
paradosis   39
   see also profection
parallax   15, 71, 206
paranatellonta, *see* co-rising
pātyāyinī daśā   190
Paul of Alexandria   184
peripatos, *see* circumambulation
perturbation   47–48
pēxis, *see* fixing
Pingree, David   1, 7, 8, 47
pivot   20
   see also angle
Placido de Titi (Placidus)   35, 67, 68, 69
Placidus houses and directions   35, 37, 68, 69, 138, 206–207, 209
Porphyry houses   16
position circle   34–35, 37, 69, 138, 197, 206–207
precession   15, 48–51, 204, 205
Presley, Lisa Marie   87–88, 90, 201–204
primary directions, *see* directions
primary motion   35–36, 68, 70, 197, 202, 209–210

profections 2, 23, 24, 31, 43
  annual 38–40, 44, 46, 50, 53, 58, 60, 70, 84–88, 90
  continuous or discrete 86, 178–180
  daily 41
  directions, relation to 31, 43, 86–88, 95, 100
  etymology 39
  houses from 54, 163
  monthly 41, 44
  planets ruling and occupying 84–85, 96
  transits, relation to 41–42
  see also greater condition; lesser condition
progressed horoscope 35
promissor (promittor) 29–31, 34, 36, 38, 42, 43, 53, 60, 67, 68–70, 72, 78, 84, 86, 87, 88, 118, 139, 197–204
Ptolemy, Claudius 14, 16, 18, 23–28, 30, 31, 33–35, 37, 38–39, 41–44, 48, 49, 51, 70, 75, 84, 87, 96, 112, 133, 184–186, 189, 193, 197, 200, 205, 206–207, 209
  quoted 25, 39, 118, 186

al-Qabīṣī, ʿAbd al-ʿAzīz 37
qāsim 28, 31–32
  see also divisor
qisma 4, 28, 31, 38
  see also division
quadrant houses 16, 18

radix 42
Rāhu and Ketu, *see* nodes
Raṅganātha 51
recasting of the nativity 40, 46
reception/non-reception 56–57
Regiomontanus houses and directions 34–35, 37, 207
Renaissance 1, 23, 30, 146, 183, 185
repetition, as interpretative principle 40, 58–61, 163, 193
return of light 57
revolution
  annual, definition and origin of 46–48
  ascendant of 54–56, 139
  daily and monthly 41, 44, 183–186
  interpreting 52–54, *see also* repetition
  location used for 52
  precessed 51–52
  primary directions in, *see* directions
  sidereal versus tropical 48–51
Rhetorius 16
right ascension 33, 197–199
ar-Rijāl, ʿAlī ibn Abī, quoted 25–26, 161
rising times 14, 33, 71, 200
  see also oblique ascension
Romaka 51
ruler of the year 39, 50–51, 53,

56, 60, 84–85, 86–87, 90, 95, 96, 104

Sahl ibn Bishr   3, 14, 57, 205
    quoted   86–87
sahm, sahama   19
    see also lots
sālkhudā   84
    see also ruler of the year
Samarasiṃha   37–38
Sanskrit language   v, 2, 3, 4, 8, 9, 10, 11, 15, 20, 38, 39, 47, 51, 57, 62, 185, 189–192
Sāyanābdaphalodgama   51
Scheat   138
Schöner, Johann   30
    quoted   146
secondary directions/progressions   35
secondary motion   33, 35, 71
sect   41, 83, 85, 127
semi-arc   34–35, 37, 68, 197, 200–202
seven ages of man   23–24
sidereal solar year   48–52, 55, 183
sidereal zodiac   13–15, 18, 27, 50–52, 76, 87, 129, 204, 205
    Sassanian   22
significator   24–28, 31–36, 39–44, 46, 53–54, 56, 61, 67–69, 72, 87, 115–116, 118–119, 141, 161, 162, 172, 192–193, 197–204
    defined   31, 36

of life, *see* hyleg
'small days'   183
    see also lesser condition
solar return, term   47, 52, 102
    see also revolution
solar year, *see* sidereal solar year; tropical solar year
South Scale (Southern Claw)   146
Speculum Astrologiae, quoted   49–50
Śrīpati   16
stake   20
    see also angle
stations, planetary   163, 166–172
Stephanus the Philosopher   42, 44
succedent houses   54, 57
Syria   10, 48

Tājika astrology   3, 10–11, 19–20, 23, 37–39, 47, 48, 50, 54, 55, 56–57, 84–85, 139, 186, 189–192, 195, 196, 205, 206
Tājikabhūṣaṇa, referenced   62
Tājikasāra, referenced   62
Tājikayogasudhānidhi, quoted   50
tasyīr, tasīra   25, 38, 190
terms of the planets
    alternative designations   20
    different versions of   19–20
    directions through   26–31, 37–38, 42, 43, 53, 55, 60, 61, 67, 76, 115–116, 161, 192–193, 204, 205, 206, 208, 209

in Indian astrology 20, 37–38, 195
in profections 179–180
origin 13
see also division
Tetrabiblos 23, 42, 185
quoted 25, 39, 118, 186
Theosophists 11, 12
time lord, *see* chronocrator
topocentric position, *see* parallax
transits 2, 23, 24, 33, 35, 40, 41–42, 43, 44, 96
of chronocrators 41–42, 87
stationing 163, 166–172
through the divisions 42, 77
through the sign of profection 39, 40, 84–85
to natal positions 40, 45, 172
within a year of life 161, 162–164, 172, 179, 186, 193
translation of light 56
trepidation 15
triṃśāṃśa 20
see also terms
triplicity 19–20, 85, 196
trirāśi, see triplicity
tropical solar year 48–52, 55, 183
tropical zodiac 14–15, 18, 27, 49–52, 198, 204, 205
twelfth-part, *see* dodecatemory

'Umar ibn al-Farrukhān aṭ-Ṭabarī 86, 164, 178–180, 182, 190

Valens, Vettius 16, 27, 39–40, 84, 133, 144, 205
quoted 14, 46–47
Varāhamihira 190
varṣaphala 10, 192
varṣeśvara, see ruler of the year
Vedic, term 8–9, 11, 13, 14
vimśottarī daśā 190–191
void of course 57

western astrology 7–12, 13, 15, 21, 35
whole-sign houses 16–18

Yādavasūri 50
Yaḥyā ibn Abī Manṣūr 48–49
yantrarāja, see astrolabe
year, *see* sidereal solar year; tropical solar year
yoga, in Tājika astrology 56–57